THIRD EDIT

M000290666

Organized Crime in America

Jay S. Albanese

Niagara University

anderson publishing co.
p.o. box 1576
cincinnati, oh 45201-1576
(513) 421-4142

Organized Crime in America, Third Edition

Copyright © 1996 by Anderson Publishing Co./Cincinnati, OH

All rights reserved. No part of this book may be reproduced in any form or by any electronic or mechanical means including information storage and retrieval systems without permission in writing from the publisher.

ISBN 0-87084-028-2
Library of Congress Catalog Number 96-76762

 The text of this book is printed on recycled paper.

Gail Eccleston *Editor*   *Managing Editor* Kelly Grondin

Cover design by Edward Smith Design, Inc./Cover photograph courtesy of Dr. Jay S. Albanese

To

Those who understand why you never hear

anyone referred to as a "former"

organized crime figure

Introduction

Organized crime remains one of the most fascinating manifestations of criminal behavior, yet it remains one of the least understood. Since the first edition of this book, there has been a Presidential Commission on Organized Crime, many important convictions of major racketeers, massive attention given to the importation and use of narcotics in North America, and closer scrutiny to the entrepreneurial aspects of organized crime. This book reports on these, and other, significant developments in organized crime in recent years.

This new edition attempts to convey in a concise manner the nature, history, and theories of organized crime, together with the criminal justice response. This includes an evaluation of the investigation, prosecution, defense, and sentencing of organized criminals to date. In addition, a review of alternative futures in the prevention of organized crime is conducted. This book is designed, therefore, to provide a synthesis of important developments in the understanding, prevention, and criminal justice response to organized crime.

This book is the only existing book on organized crime that devotes more than one-third of its contents to the *criminal justice response* to organized crime, making it ideal for use in criminal justice courses. Another entire chapter is devoted to law, and still another to the two Presidential investigations of organized crime in the last 30 years.

The careful reader of this book will come away with a clear understanding of the definition of organized crime, how it is categorized under law (as a number of distinct crimes), the individual causes of organized crime, models to explain its persistence, the history of the Mafia, Presidential investigations, nontraditional groups, and investigation, prosecution, defense, and sentencing of organized crime suspects, defendants, and offenders. A final chapter addresses the significant issues that will influence the future of organized crime and the criminal justice response. Rather than merely summarizing the existing literature in encyclopedic fashion, this book *organizes* information in a meaningful way. This will empower the student to separate the fact from fiction of organized crime. The incorporation of critical thinking exercises throughout the book will reinforce the student's ability to apply the important principles of organized crime in new fact situations, and to anticipate portentous issues in the future.

Acknowledgments

My own intellectual history in this area has contributed greatly to the composition of this book. First, several people at Rutgers served to initiate and stimulate my interest in organized crime. Richard Sparks got me interested in the subject during a graduate course, when he declared, "organized crime is more than a bunch of uncouth Italians." Dwight Smith provided insights in both conversation and through his publications. The School of Criminal Justice at Rutgers, and the resources of the National Council on Crime and Delinquency library there, continue to provide opportunities for me as an alumnus to develop professional, personal, and social relationships, some of which were first established years ago as a graduate student. Many life-long friends were made from among the faculty and students there. Phyllis Schultze of the NCCD library helped me locate many elusive sources in the course of preparing this edition. Her pleasant disposition made research and writing a much more enjoyable task. In a similar vein, Leslie King continues to disagree with some of my conclusions, but remains willing to discuss them.

Bill Simon, Kelly Grondin, and Michael and Susan Braswell of Anderson Publishing Co. encouraged the completion of this third edition, and they deserve thanks for seeing it through. Gail Eccleston was a thorough, but understanding, editor. Also, the many instructors who thought the book's organization and contents were worthy of classroom adoption have my appreciation for making previous editions a success. I believe this third edition is a much better book. An earlier version of Chapter 4 appeared in the *Handbook on Organized Crime in the United States* published by Greenwood Press. It is reproduced here with permission of the publisher.

Finally, it is important to thank a number of my friends and former students at Niagara University. In my years at Niagara, I have made many friends among colleagues, students, and alumni. Hopefully, we have influenced one another in a positive way. Although we sometimes disagreed on the path toward knowledge and experience, the premise of our pursuit never varied: at no time did we forget to have fun along the way.

Contents

Chapter 1

What is Organized Crime?

If you do big things they print only your face, and if you do little things, they print only your thumbs.
—Arthur "Bugs" Baer

The Fascination with Organized Crime

Organized crime is perhaps the most interesting form of criminal behavior. Public fascination with the "Mafia," the "Mob," the "Syndicate," and other suggestive descriptions has remained strong for more than a century. *The Godfather*, a novel, was originally published in 1969 and is the most popular book about crime ever published. It is also the best-selling novel in history.[1] More than 13 million copies have been sold. A subsequent movie version was released in 1972 that grossed $166 million, making it one of the most successful movies ever made.[2]

This peculiar fascination with organized crime has often made it difficult to separate the fact from the fiction, however, and it has discouraged many criminologists from seriously studying the problem. Furthermore, its complexity, mystique, and apparent success have made reliable information difficult to come by. It has only been during the last three decades that serious efforts to study organized crime objectively have flourished. Nearly 30 years ago, for example, the President's Crime Commission established a task force to investigate organized crime specifically. Their conclusions about the state of knowledge at that time were quite candid.

> Our knowledge of the structure which makes "organized crime" organized is somewhat comparable to the knowledge of Standard Oil which could be gleaned from interviews with gasoline station attendants. Detailed knowledge of the formal and informal structure of the confederation of Sicilian-Italian "families" in the United States would represent one of the greatest crimi-

1

nological advances ever made, even if it were universally recognized that this knowledge was not synonymous with knowledge about all organized crime in America.[3]

Those investigators who have attempted to analyze the structure and functioning of particular organized criminal groups have pointed to the need for additional case studies that would help to confirm or deny their findings.[4] As Annelise Anderson has maintained, there is a need for information, "not about law enforcement, but about organized criminal activity itself, by which the government's new legislation and its expanding level of effort can be evaluated."[5] Even the U.S. General Accounting Office, the investigative arm of Congress, concluded that the absence of a consensus in the Justice Department about the fundamental definition of organized crime has hampered the potential success of crime control programs designed to combat it.[6] The President's Commission on Organized Crime, appointed by Ronald Reagan, also did not offer any clear definition of organized crime. Rather, it described a series of characteristics of "criminal groups," "protectors," and "specialist support" necessary for organized crime.[7]

This apparent confusion over what constitutes organized crime is puzzling, given the long history of interest in the subject. Key words like "mafia," "mob," "syndicate," "gang," and "outfit" are often used to characterize it, but the precise meaning of these terms is often lost in discussions of the "appearances" and "earmarks" of organized crime.

A Definition Beyond "I Know It When I See It"

U.S. Supreme Court Justice Potter Stewart once said he did not know precisely what it is, but "I know it when I see it."[8] He was talking about obscenity, but he may as well have been speaking of organized crime. Synthesizing all that has been written about organized crime, especially during the last 30 years, it is possible to arrive at a consensus definition.

There appear to be as many descriptions of organized crime as there are authors. An analysis by Frank Hagan attempted to elicit common elements of the various descriptions of organized crime. After discovering that many books failed to provide explicit definitions of organized crime, he found that definitions had been offered by 13 different authors in books and government reports about organized crime written during the previous 15 years.[9] I have updated Hagan's analysis with several authors who have attempted to define organized crime more recently.[10]

The good news is that there is an emerging consensus about what actually constitutes organized crime. The bad news is that 11 different aspects of organized crime have been included in the definitions by the various authors, but few were mentioned often. Table 1.1 summarizes these 11 attributes and how many authors have included them in their definition.

As Table 1.1 indicates, there is great consensus in the literature that organized crime functions as a continuing enterprise that rationally works to make a profit through illicit activities, and that it insures its existence through the use of threats or force and through corruption of public officials to maintain a degree of immunity from law enforcement. There also appears to be some consensus that organized crime tends to be restricted to those illegal goods and services that are in great public demand through monopoly control of an illicit market.

Table 1.1
Definitions of Organized Crime in the Literature

Characteristics	Number of Authors
Organized Hierarchy Continuing	15
Rational Profit through Crime	12
Use of Force or Threat	11
Corruption to Maintain Immunity	11
Public Demand for Services	6
Monopoly over Particular Market	5
Restricted Membership	3
Non-Ideological	3
Specialization	3
Code of Secrecy	3
Extensive Planning	2

There is considerably less consensus, as Table 1.1 illustrates, that organized crime has exclusive membership, has ideological or political reasons behind its activities, requires specialization in planning or carrying out specific activities, or operates under a code of secrecy. As a result, it appears that a definition of organized crime, based on a consensus of writers over the course of the last three decades, would read as follows:

> Organized crime is a continuing criminal enterprise that rationally works to profit from illicit activities that are often in great public demand. Its continuing existence is maintained through the use of force, threats, monopoly control, and/or the corruption of public officials.

There are, of course, some confounding factors to be addressed. That is, how does an otherwise legitimate corporation that collects toxic waste, but dumps some of it illegally, fit into this definition? Is a motorcycle gang, that sells drugs as a side-line, part of organized crime? What about a licensed massage parlor that also offers sex for money to some customers? As a large number of investigators have recognized, perhaps organized crime does not exist as an ideal type, but rather as a "degree" of criminal activity or as a point on the "spectrum of legitimacy."[11] That is to say, isn't the primary difference between loansharking and a legitimate loan the interest rate charged? Is not the real difference between criminal and non-criminal distribution of narcotics whether or not the distributor is licensed (i.e., doctor or pharmacist), or unlicensed, by the state? The point to keep in mind is that organized crime is actually a type of a larger category of behavior that may be called "organizational" or "white-collar" crime.

It is apparent that crimes by corporations during the course of business, or crimes by politicians or government agencies can also be considered part of "organized" crime. For example, official misconduct by a government official, obstruction of justice as in the Iran-Contra and Watergate scandals, and commercial bribery, are all types of organized criminal behavior. Inasmuch as they fulfill the requirements of the definition above in some cases, they constitute a part of what is known as organized crime. As the National Advisory Committee on Criminal Justice Standards and Goals has recognized, there are more similarities than differences between organized and the so-called "white-collar" crimes.

> Accordingly, the perpetrators of organized crime may include corrupt business executives, members of the professions, public officials, or members of any other occupational group, in addition to the conventional racketeer element.[12]

There also exist some important differences between organized and organizational or "white-collar" crime. Perhaps the most significant distinction is the fact that organizational crimes generally occur during the course of otherwise legitimate business or governmental affairs. Organizational crime, therefore, most often occurs as a *deviation from legitimate business activity*. On the other hand, organized crime, as defined earlier, takes places through a *continuing criminal enterprise* that exists to profit *primarily* from crime.

It is important to keep in mind the fact that organized crime is not restricted to the activities of criminal syndicates. As Pontell and Calavita concluded in their study of the savings and loan scandal of the 1980s, if we reserve the term "organized crime" for continuing conspiracies that include the corruption of government officials, "then much of the savings and loan scandal involved organized crime."[13] In interviews with the Federal Bureau of Investigation, Secret Service, and regulatory agencies, they found a "recurring theme" of conspiracies between savings and loan officials ("insiders") and accountants, lawyers, and real estate developers ("outsiders"). Comparing these kinds of corrupt relationships with more traditional organized crime techniques of no-show jobs at construction sites, or payoffs for "protection," reveal they are more similar than different. Examples like this illustrate that there is, in fact, much crime that is committed by corporations, politicians, and government agencies that is as serious and harmful as the crimes of criminal enterprises.[14] This book will focus on the activities of continuing criminal enterprises, however, in an effort to separate the myth from the reality of organized crime. This criminal activity has been shrouded in a cloak of folklore, politics, and Hollywood productions that have done little to make the causes and effects of organized crime more apparent to the public, to policymakers, and to the criminal justice system.

A Typology of Organized Crime Activity

For all the mystique that permeates discussions of organized crime, there has been relatively little attention given to establishing the precise behaviors we are talking about. That is to say, what types of illegal acts are we referring to when we speak of organized crime?

When one examines the descriptions and definitions of organized crime in various criminal codes and case studies, three categories of illicit behavior emerge. These categories reflect the precise crimes that are implied when one speaks of "organized crime activity." The three categories include: provision of illicit services, provision of illicit goods, and the infiltration of legitimate business. Within each of these categories are more specific crimes that often draw the attention of the criminal justice system.

The *provision of illicit services* involves an attempt to satisfy the public demand for money, sex, and gambling that legitimate society does not fulfill. The specific crimes involved include: loansharking, prostitution, and gambling. Loansharking is the lending of money to individuals at an interest rate in excess of that permitted by law. Organized prostitution offers sex for pay on a systematic basis. Numbers gambling, for example, is a lottery that operates without approval of the state. Each of these crimes occurs as a continuing enterprise due to the failure of a sizable portion of the public to obtain money, sex, or gambling in a legitimate way, such as through bank loans, marriage, or state lotteries.

The *provision of illicit goods* is a category of organized crimes that offers particular products that a segment of the public desires, but cannot obtain through legitimate channels. The sale and distribution of drugs and the fencing and distribution of stolen property are examples of specific crimes in this category. There is a great demand for drugs in North America, such as marijuana, cocaine, valium, and heroin, that are either illegal or are distributed under very strict regulations imposed by the government. Needless to say, these regulations do not diminish the demand for these drugs and, as a result, some people attempt to obtain them illegally. In a similar way, a significant portion of society desires to buy products at the lowest price possible, regardless of where the seller originally obtained them. Due to this demand, organized criminals have arisen who "fence" stolen merchandise by buying stolen property and then selling it to customers who do not care from where it came.

The third category of organized crime is the *infiltration of legitimate business*. Labor racketeering and the takeover of waste disposal companies are two examples of infiltration of legitimate business. Labor racketeering involves the use of force or threats to obtain money for insuring jobs or labor peace. This often entails the threat to employers or employees that if money is not paid, there will be no job, or that violence, strikes, and/or vandalism will occur at the company. In a similar way, waste disposal companies in some areas have been taken over through the use of coercion to intimidate legitimate owners to sell the business or to have it operated by an outsider by means of intimidation.

Table 1.2 illustrates this three-part typology of organized crime.

Table 1.2
A Typology of Organized Crime

Type of Activity	Nature of Activity	Harm
Provision of Illicit Goods and Services	Gambling, lending, sex, narcotics, stolen property.	• Consensual activities • No inherent violence • Economic harm
Infiltration of Legitimate Business	Coercive use of legal businesses for purposes of exploitation.	• Nonconsensual activities • Threats, violence, extortion • Economic harm

The provision of illicit goods and services is distinguished most clearly from the infiltration of legitimate business in its *consensual* nature and *lack of inherent violence*. Organized crime figures who offer illegal betting, loansharking, or drugs rely on the existing demand among the public to make money. They also rely heavily on return business, so they want the illicit transaction to go well to insure future bets, loans, and other illicit sales. It is very unusual for criminal syndicates to *solicit* business in this fashion. Instead, those interested in illicit goods and services seek out the illicit opportunities. Violence plays no inherent role in the activities themselves, although bad debts cannot be collected through the courts, as they can for loans and sales in the legitimate market. Therefore, violence or threats occur when one party to the transaction feels cheated or shortchanged, and there is no legal alternative for resolving the dispute. Violence can also occur in an attempt to control or monopolize and illicit market. If a group wishes to corner the market on illicit gambling in a particular area, it may threaten or intimidate its illicit competitors. Once again, these threats are used as an enforcement mechanism, rather than as an intrinsic part of the provision of illicit goods and services themselves.

The infiltration of legitimate business is more *predatory* than the provision of illicit goods and services. Here, organized crime groups attempt to *create* a demand for their services, rather than exploit an existing market as in the case of illicit goods and services. Demands for "protection" money or no-show jobs to avoid property damage, work stoppages, or violence are examples of the predatory nature of the infiltration of legitimate business. In legal terms, organized crime uses coercion or extortion in the infiltration of legitimate business that involve implied or explicit threats to obtain a criminal objective. Coercion and extortion are not necessary to provide illicit goods or services because the demand already exists among the public.

A Typology of Organized Criminals: Ethnicity, Organization, Gender

Some typologies of organized crime attempt to classify its forms by looking at *who* is involved in the activity, rather than by looking at the *activity itself*. For example, it is common to see discussions of traditional "street" crimes that include breakdowns by sex or race, or other demographic descriptors. Such categorizations are less common in the case of organized crime, especially because estimates of its true extent involve so much guesswork (see next section). Organized crime typologies focus more often on ethnicity and the nature of the structure of organized crime groups. These will be considered here, as will a brief discussion of gender.

Ethnicity of Organized Criminals

Ethnicity is perhaps the most common of all categorizations of organized crime, although it might be the most misleading. This is true for several important reasons:

- Organized crime is committed by a wide variety of ethnic groups, making ethnicity a poor indicator of organized crime activity,

- There is evidence that organized crime activities are often not carried out *within* the boundaries of a specific ethnic group, making it inter-ethnic,

- Other variables, such as local market conditions and criminal opportunities, may be much better indicators of organized crime than is ethnicity.

There is a growing body of evidence that organized crime is not limited to the activities of a single, or even a few, ethnic groups. The President's Commission on Organized Crime described "organized crime today" as 11 different groups that included:

- La Cosa Nostra (Italian)
- Outlaw Motorcycle Gangs
- Prison Gangs
- Triads and Tongs (Chinese)
- Vietnamese Gangs
- Yakuza (Japanese)
- Marielitos (Cuban)
- Colombian Cocaine Rings
- Irish Organized Crime
- Russian Organized Crime
- Canadian Organized Crime

This curious mixture includes groups defined in terms of ethnic or national origin, those defined by the nature of their activity (i.e., cocaine rings), those defined by their geographic origin (i.e., prison gangs), and those defined by their means of transportation (i.e., motorcycle gangs).[15] Such a haphazard approach to defining and describing organized crime does little to help make sense of its causes, current events, or how policies against organized crime should be directed.

There is even evidence, as both the President's Commission and independent researchers have pointed out, that these groups and others (such as Jewish gangs) have worked with each other in the past and continue to do so in the present.[16] As a consequence, ethnicity is not a very powerful explanation for the existence of organized crime, due to the large number of ethnic groups involved, their interaction with each other in criminal undertakings, and the fact that ethnicity is probably no more a causal factor than are motorcycles. Biographical attributes, like methods of transportation, may help to *describe* a particular person or group, but they do little to *explain* that person's or group's behavior (especially when compared to other members of that ethnic group who do not engage in organize crime activity).

A look at several investigations of ethnically based organized crime reveals why it is a weak descriptor. In addition to the fact that no single or multiple ethnic combination accounts for organized crime, ethnicity also has been found to be secondary to local criminal opportunities in explaining organized crime. A study of the early twentieth-century illicit cocaine trade in New York by historian Alan Block found major players with Jewish backgrounds but also "notable is the evidence of interethnic cooperation" among New York's criminals.[17] He found evidence of Italians, Greeks, Irish, and Black involvement, people who did not always work within their own ethnic group. Instead, he found these criminals to be "in reality criminal justice entrepreneurs" whose criminal careers were not within a particular organization but were involved in a "web of small but efficient organizations."[18]

A more recent ethnography of the underground drug market by Patricia Adler in "Southwest County" found the market to be "largely competitive," rather than "visibly structured." She found participants "entered the market, transacted their deals, [and] shifted from one type of activity to another," responding to the demands of the market, rather than through ethnic structures or concerns.[19]

Similarly, a study of illegal gambling and loansharking by Peter Reuter in New York found economic considerations dictated entry and exit from the illicit marketplace. He found the criminal enterprises he studied in three areas "not monopolies in the classic sense or subject to control by some external organization."[20] Like the other investigations of organized crime groups, Reuter found that local market forces shaped the criminal behavior more so than ethnic ties or other characteristics of the criminal groups.

Organization of Crime Groups

There is a growing body of evidence indicating that organized crime groups evolve around specific illicit activities, rather than the opposite. Desirable illicit activities, made desirable due to public demand, the local market, or other opportunity factors, appear to dictate how and what type of criminal group will emerge to exploit the opportunity. Less often, a group will attempt to "manufacture" a criminal opportunity through intimidation or extortion. This is probably due to human nature: it is easier, and it takes less energy, to exploit an existing market for illegal gambling, drugs, or stolen property, than it does to "move in" on a pre-existing legal or illegal business for illicit purposes.

Consider the classic ethnographic study by Francis and Elizabeth Reuss-Ianni, where he became a participant-observer of an organized crime group for two years, and made observations of two other criminal groups. He found these groups to "have no structure apart from their functioning; nor do they have structure independent of their current 'personnel'."[21] Joseph Albini's pioneering study of criminal groups in the United States and Italy drew a similar conclusion. Rather than belonging to an organization, those involved in organized crime engaged in relationships "predicated by the particular activity engaged in at any given time." The criminal "syndicate" is, in fact, "a system of loosely structured relationships functioning primarily because each participant is interested in furthering his own welfare."[22]

These studies suggest that the structure of organized crime groups derive from the activities they are engaged in, rather than by pre-existing ethnic ties. Criminal-turned-informer Joseph Valachi testified before the U.S. Senate about his experience with a New York Italian-American crime group. He stated the function of the "family" or group was mutual protection, otherwise, "everybody operates by himself."[23] Therefore, significant attention must be given to how specific illegal activities generate particular types of criminal organizations. This is will discussed further in Chapter 4.

Gender and Organized Crime

Historically, gender has played little role in the study of organized crime. Organized crime has been seen as masculine behavior with women involved only for purposes of exploitation (as in the case of prostitution) or as silent supporters of their husbands' or loved ones' questionable activities. In recent years, however, closer attention has been paid to the role of women in organized crime with some surprising results.

In an analysis of biographies, autobiographies, and case studies, James Calder attempted to understand more systematically the lives of "mafia women."[24] These women were wives, daughters, mothers, nieces, and sisters of mafia figures. He found these women were not the receding, ignorant companions, as they often have been portrayed in fiction. Instead, he found considerable evidence that these women "have significant insight to, and awareness of criminal affiliations" of their male counterparts. These women often are not contented or happy with their lives or position. They frequently feel cheated or manipulated by their men.[25] Finally, he found that these women sometimes rebel against their lifestyle, usually by way of arguments, separations, divorces, and occasional violence.

On the other hand, there exist women involved in organized crime in their own right without dependent connections to men. An example is Arlyne Brickman, who was mistress to a number of prominent organized crime figures, including Bugsy Siegel and Joe Columbo.[26] As her biographer observed:

> Arlyne seems to feel no loyalty to anyone, an observation that, at times, caused me to suspect she might be a sociopath, cruising through life a shark, simulating human emotion whenever it suited her purposes. A closer look at her history, however, led me to conclude that Arlyne does feel loyalty, however fleeting, to whomever happens to be stroking her ego.[27]

This characterization of a self-centered, emotionless person that has the appearance of a sociopath is a description that usually has characterized male organized crime figures, not females. In her role as mistress, Arlyne Brickman delivered messages between criminal figures, operated in the illegal gambling and drug markets, and eventually became a government informant when her daughter's life was threatened.[28] In many ways, her activities parallel those of male organized crime figures.

In an ethnographic study of three female gangs in the New York City area, Anne Campbell spent six months with each gang. The gangs were mixed racially, ethnically, and in terms of their reason for organizing. The three female gangs included a street gang, a biker gang, and a religious-cultural (Islamic) gang. As Campbell found in both her historical and empirical research,

> Girls have been part of gang life for over a hundred years, from social clubs through years of prohibition and corruption to the "bopping" gangs of the 1950s and through the civil disorders of the 1970s . . . [G]irls appear increasingly as sisters in the gang instead of molls.[29]

This growing awareness of the role of women as something more than mistresses to organized crime figures and gang members will be an interesting trend to watch in the future. Campbell found that girls still "exist as an annex to the male gang," however, and the "possibilities open to them is dictated and controlled by the boys."[30] Whether the emergence of women as independent players in organized crime becomes more common, as demonstrated in the case of Arlyne Brickman, will depend to some extent on our willingness to examine their lives more closely, and as something more than mistresses to the mob.

How Much Organized Crime is There?

The true extent of organized crime is unknown. Characteristic organized crimes, such as conspiracy, racketeering, and extortion are not counted in any systematic way. Other offenses are known only when they result in arrests by police. The problem in relying on police arrests as a measure of criminal activity are apparent: much crime is undetected, some that is detected is not report to police, and arrest rates go up or down depending on police activity and not necessarily criminal activity. Keeping these reservations in mind, the Federal Bureau of Investigation tabulates arrests made by police nationwide for several offenses characteristic of organized crime. Trends in these arrests over the last 30 years are presented in Table 1.3.

As Table 1.3 illustrates, arrests for three of the four offenses have increased markedly over the last three decades, whereas arrests for gambling have dropped dramatically. These increases and decreases can be attributed to two primary factors:

- Change in public and law enforcement priorities, and

- Change in population base and numbers of police in the United States.

Table 1.3
Arrests for Crimes Related to Organized Crime

Offense	1960	1970	1980	1990	30-Year Change
Drug Abuse Violations	31,613	265,734	351,955	785,536	25 times higher
Gambling	121,611	75,325	37,805	13,357	9 times lower
Prostitution and Commercialized Vice	29,060	45,803	67,920	80,888	3 times higher
Stolen Property (buy, receive, possess)	10,125	46,427	76,429	119,102	12 times higher

Both the population of the United States and the number of sworn police officers have grown dramatically during the last three decades. Therefore, one would expect a "natural" increase in the numbers of arrests simply because there are more potential offenders and victims in the population, as well as more police looking for them. In a similar way, the public mood has shifted during the last three decades, especially with regard to gambling and drugs. Gambling has been legalized in many forms in a majority of the United States during the last 30 years, due to a shift in the public perception from gambling as a "vice" to gambling as a "form of recreation."[31] Conversely, growing public concern about drugs developed over the same period. The huge increases in drug arrests (25 times higher in 1990 than in 1960) are matched only by the huge decline in gambling arrests (9 times lower over the same period). These changes clearly indicate shifting public, and hence law enforcement, priorities regarding the seriousness of these forms of criminal behavior.

It is possible that the incidence of these offenses has changed over the years, but arrest statistics do not permit us to know for sure. The fact that prostitution and commercialized vice arrests have nearly tripled in 30 years, and arrests for stolen property have increased nearly 12 times above the 1960 level suggests that more police, greater enforcement priority, and more actual cases have combined to produce these large increases in arrests.

It is important to keep in mind that not all gambling, drug, prostitution, or stolen property arrests have anything to do with organized crime. It is likely that a large number of these arrests were of individuals possessing illicit goods, or engaging in illicit services, absent organized crime connections. There has been no way yet devised to separate the organized crime versus non-organized cases for these offenses, but it would not be difficult to do so. Once the concern about organized crime reaches the level that concern about drugs has attained, greater effort will be devoted to knowing its true extent and trends.

The Remainder of this Book

Following this examination of the nature, definition, and typology of organized crime, the remainder of the book attempts to accomplish its objectives by answering seven specific questions:

1. What are the *precise crimes* we consider "organized crime"?

2. Why do people engage in organize crime as *career criminals*, and is it possible that what we know about various organized crime groups can be *synthesized into a meaningful explanation* of the continuing existence of these groups?

3. What is the history and current status of the *Mafia* in the United States?

4. What is the *government's view* of organized crime, and how is it changing?

5. How do non-Mafia, or *nontraditional organized crime groups*, differ from their traditional counterparts?

6. Who *investigates, prosecutes, and defends* organized crime, what tools do they use, and how successful are they?

7. What is the best way to *sentence* organized crime offenders and organizations, and what are the prospects for *long-term prevention*?

Most books on organized crime discuss it in general terms. Its general characteristics, general tendencies, and so forth. What this approach lacks is the specificity required for meaningful research and investigations in the field. The term "organized crime" appears rarely in law, referring to a generic category of behaviors. Chapter 2 clearly separates these categories into specific offenses, so students of organized crime can understand the precise definitions and limits of those offenses we collectively call "organized crime."

Why people engage in organized crime, often as career criminals, is a fascinating question. Chapter 3 will summarize what is known about the causes of organized crime, using past research and excerpts from the biographies of convicted organized crime members. Chapter 4 synthesizes this information into a three-part model of organized crime. This paradigm summarizes all the existing writing and research on the subject.

The history of the Mafia is shrouded in myth and folklore. Chapter 5 recounts the episodic history of the Mafia, the connection to Italy, and separates the myth from reality in where the Mafia came from, how it has changed, and where it is today.

The government's perception of the nature and threat posed by organized crime fundamentally influences both law, policy, and enforcement initiatives. Chapter 6 compares the two major presidential investigations of organized crime in the United States during the last 30 years. How organized crime has changed, and the government's response to it are clearly manifested in this comparison.

There is a great deal of organized crime that is not connected to the Mafia in any way. Chapter 7 provides a description of the types of activities engaged in by these nontraditional groups, and how their structure and orientation differs from Mafia-linked organized crime.

The criminal justice response to organized crime is often given short shrift in books about organized crime. Here, more than three chapters are devoted to the investigation, prosecution, defense, and sentencing issues in organized crime cases. A description of the types of criminal justice professionals who conduct these efforts, the nature and limits of the tools they use, and the outcomes of organized crime cases are all considered. Current "hot" issues, such as the controversy over "mob lawyers," the limits placed on undercover operations, entrapment, and sentencing options in organized crime cases are all considered here.

The final section of the book examines the prospects for organized crime, and its reduction, in the future. The ongoing debate over greater legalization versus greater criminalization of conduct, different strategies for fighting illegal narcotics, and better techniques for dealing with the infiltration of legitimate business are all detailed here.

References to Chapter 1

[1]   Thomas J. Ferraro, *Ethnic Passages: Literary Immigrants in Twentieth Century America* (Chicago: University of Chicago Press, 1993), p. 13.

[2]   Pace, Eric. "Crime's Lingering Allure," *The New York Times* (June 6, 1982), p. F9.

[3]   President's Commission on Law Enforcement and Administration of Justice. *Task Force Report: Organized Crime* (Washington, DC: U.S. Government Printing Office, 1967), p. 33.

[4]   Ianni, Francis A.J. and Reuss-Ianni, Elizabeth. *A Family Business: Kinship and Social Control in Organized Crime* (New York: New American Library, 1973), p. 193.

[5]   Anderson, Annelise G. *The Business of Organized Crime: A Cosa Nostra Family* (Stanford, CA: Hoover Institution Press, 1979), p. 139.

[6]   U.S. Comptroller General. *War on Organized Crime Faltering—Federal Strike Forces Not Getting the Job Done* (Washington, DC: U.S. General Accounting Office, 1977).

[7]   President's Commission on Organized Crime. *The Impact: Organized Crime Today* (Washington, DC: U.S. Government Printing Office, 1987), pp. 25-32.

[8]   *Jacobellis v. Ohio*, 84 S. Ct. 1676 (1964).

9   Hagan, Frank E. "The Organized Crime Continuum: A Further Specification of a New Conceptual Model," *Criminal Justice Review*, (Spring, 1983), vol. 8, pp. 52-57.

10 Howard Abadinsky, *Organized Crime* Fourth Edition (Chicago: Nelson-Hall, 1994); Michael Maltz, "On Defining Organized Crime," in Alexander, H. and Caiden, G., eds. *The Politics and Economics of Organized Crime* (Lexington, MA: Lexington Books, 1985).

11 Smith Dwight C. "Paragons, Pariahs, and Pirates: A Spectrum-Based Theory of Enterprise," *Crime & Delinquency* (July, 1980), vol. 26, pp. 358-386; Martin, W. Allen. "Toward Specifying a Spectrum-Based Theory of Enterprise," *Criminal Justice Review*, (Spring, 1981), vol. 6, pp. 54-57; Albanese, Jay. "What Lockheed and La Cosa Nostra Have in Common: The Effect of Ideology on Criminal Justice Policy," *Crime & Delinquency*, (April, 1982), vol. 28, pp. 211-232; Hagan, Frank E., "The Organized Crime Continuum," *Criminal Justice Review* (Spring, 1983), vol. 8, pp. 52-57; Sacco, Vincent F. "An Approach to the Study of Organized Crime," in Silverman, R.A. and Teevan, J.J. eds. *Crime in Canadian Society*, Third Edition (Toronto: Butterworth, 1986).

12 National Advisory Committee on Criminal Justice Standards and Goals. *Report of the Task Force on Organized Crime* (Washington, DC: U.S. Government Printing Office, 1976), p. 213.

13 Henry N. Pontell and Kitty Calavita, "White-Collar Crime in the Savings and Loan Scandal," *The Annals*, 525 (January, 1993), p. 39.

14 See Albanese, Jay. *White-Collar Crime in America* (Englewood Cliffs, NJ: Prentice Hall, 1995).

15 President's Commission on Organized Crime, *The Impact: Organized Crime Today* (Washington, DC: U.S. Government Printing Office, 1987), pp. 33-128.

16 Alan A. Block, "The Snowman Cometh: Coke in Progressive New York," *Criminology*, 17 (May, 1979), pp. 75-99; President' Commission on Organized Crime, pp. 64, 81, 91.

17 Alan A. Block, p. 95.

18 Ibid.

19 Patricia A. Adler, *Wheeling and Dealing: An Ethnography of an Upper-Level Drug Dealing and Smuggling Community* (New York: Columbia University Press, 1985), p. 80.

20 Peter Reuter, *Disorganized Crime: The Economics of the Visible Hand* (Cambridge, MA: MIT Press, 1983), pp. 175-176.

21 Francis A.J. Ianni with Elizabeth Reuss-Ianni, *A Family Business: Kinship and Social Control in Organized Crime* (New York: New American Library, 1973), p. 20.

22 Joseph L. Albini, *The American Mafia: Genesis of a Legend* (New York: Irvington, 1971), p. 288.

23 U.S. Senate Committee on Government Operations Permanent Subcommittee on Investigations, *Organized Crime and Illicit Traffic in Narcotics: Hearings Part I* 88th Congress, 1st session (Washington, DC: U.S. Government Printing Office, 1963), p. 111.

24 James D. Calder, "Mafia Women in Non-Fiction," in Jay Albanese, ed. *Contemporary Issues in Organized Crime* (Monsey, NY: Willow Tree Press, 1995).

[25] See, for example, Nina Castellano, wife of Paul Castellano, as portrayed by Joseph F. O'Brien and Andris Kurins, *Boss of Bosses* (New York: Simon and Schuster, 1991) and Rosalie Profaci's marriage to Bill Bonanno, as portrayed by Rosalie Bonanno with Beverly Donofrio, *Mafia Marriage: My Story* (New York: Avon, 1991).

[26] Teresa Carpenter, *Mob Girl* (New York: Zebra Books, 1993).

[27] Ibid., pp. 15-16.

[28] Ibid.

[29] Anne Campbell, *The Girls in the Gang* (New York: Basil Blackwell, 1984), p. 266.

[30] Ibid.

[31] See Jay S. Albanese, "Casino Gambling and Organized Crime: More Than Reshuffling the Deck," in Albanese, J., ed. *Contemporary Issues in Organized Crime* (Monsey, NY: Willow Tree Press, 1995).

Chapter 2

Characteristic Organized Crimes

Laws were made to prevent the strong from always having their way.
Ovid (43 B.C. - 17 A.D.)

Organized crime is often defined in sweeping terms. Comments like "mob-linked" activity, crimes that bear the "earmarks of the mafia," and other suggestive terms do not help us differentiate organized crimes from conventional crimes in an objective way. This chapter is designed to insert some clarity in classifying organized crimes, and in distinguishing them from traditional crimes.

Legal Definitions of Organized Crimes

Organized crimes can be arranged into five categories of offenses that correspond to the typology provided in Chapter 1. Conspiracy is the most characteristic organized crime because it punishes *planning* to commit a crime. This planning aspect of organized crime is what distinguishes it from most street crimes.

The provision of illicit goods or services includes conspiracy because they involve the *organized or planned* provision of illegal drugs, stolen property, gambling, loansharking, or sex. Each of these offenses will be considered separately in this chapter. A crime characteristic of the infiltration of legitimate business is extortion, which involves taking property through the use of threats of future harm. The fifth type of organized crime is racketeering which punishes ongoing criminal conspiracies. These five types of organized crimes are summarized in Table 2.1.

17

Table 2.1
Characteristic Organized Crimes

Type of Organized Crime	Nature of the Offense
Conspiracy	Prohibits the planning of a criminal act.
Illicit Goods: Drugs Stolen Property	Prohibits the possession and distribution of and these products under specific circumstances.
Illicit Services: Gambling, Loansharking, Sex	Prohibits the marketing and distribution of these services under certain circumstances.
Extortion	Prohibits taking property through the use of threats of future harm.
Racketeering	Prohibits engaging in ongoing criminal conspiracies.

This summary of characteristic organized crimes does not answer important questions. *How much participation* or planning is necessary to be liable for conspiracy? Is one liable for the *actions of others* in a conspiracy? What *type of harm* suffices for extortion? Is a landlord liable for the actions of his tenants under the law of racketeering, if his property is used to run a crackhouse? Can illegal gambling debts be collected lawfully? Does a sex-related product have to be legally obscene before it can be prohibited? These, and many other, questions arise quickly, once we start asking questions about the precise limits of the crimes characteristic of organized crime. The remainder of this chapter uses actual cases to illustrate how the criminal law draws the boundaries among organized crime, conventional crimes, and otherwise lawful behavior.

Conspiracy

Conspiracy is essential to understanding organized crime. This is because the term "organized" connotes planned criminal activity. Indeed, the difference between an individual college student who grows marijuana in his basement for his own use, and another who develops a scheme to sell that marijuana to pay tuition, is the difference between conventional and organized crime. Actual cases help to illustrate where this boundary is drawn in practice.

Do Marijuana Purchases Suffice for Liability?

Two brothers, Paul and Richard Heilbrunn, established a company "Heilbrunn and Friends," (H&F) with associates Charles Stockdale and Richard Bernstein. It was begun as a food distribution warehouse, but it was actually used to import marijuana and distribute it in central Indiana. H&F threw a party on the occasion of the Indianapolis 500 race, where Stockdale and Bernstein, through a third party, approached Michael Helish about purchasing marijuana. They approached him because they believed Helish "could move a lot for us."[1] Helish was interested. Bernstein eventually shipped 5,500 pounds of marijuana to Helish through a third party in Carmel, Indiana. Helish provided $100,000 in front money, and made weekly payments thereafter of several hundred thousand dollars each. In total, Helish paid approximately $1.5 million for the marijuana.

Helish was ultimately caught and charged with conspiring with the H&F organization to possess marijuana with intent to distribute. He was convicted at trial, fined, and sentenced to 14 years in prison.[2]

On appeal, Helish argued that, while there is ample evidence to show he purchased marijuana from the H&F organization, there is no evidence of his *participation* in their conspiracy to *distribute* drugs. In essence, he claimed to be a "buyer" and not part of the H&F distribution conspiracy.

The U.S. Court of Appeals delineated how the law distinguishes mere customers of illegal goods from members of the conspiracy that provide those goods. To prove membership in a conspiracy, the government must "present sufficient evidence to demonstrate that the defendant knew of the conspiracy and that he intended to join and associate himself with its criminal design and purpose."[3] Although it is clear that "merely purchasing drugs or other property from a conspiracy, standing alone, can never establish membership in a conspiracy," a person who buys from a conspiracy "for resale is a member of the conspiracy if he at least knows its general aims."[4] The Court makes it plain that a mere consumer of illegal goods does not automatically become part of a conspiracy. Participation is only inferred when there is evidence that he or she knew of the conspiracy and participated in it voluntarily. As the Court concluded, "Helish dealt continuously with [the H&F organization]. His purchases were not discrete transactions requiring limited contact with the conspiracy; rather they required an ongoing relationship that soured only when Helish failed to move the marijuana fast enough to satisfy Bernstein."[5] The Court of Appeals upheld Helish's conviction for conspiracy, pointing to two important aspects of conspiracy: no formal agreement is required among the co-conspirators, and participation need be only slight for liability. Although Helish did not participate in *running* the H&F organization, his ongoing purchases *furthered its illegal objectives* rendering him liable for conspiracy.

Can a Single Cocaine Transaction be Linked to a Conspiracy?

Another important part of the crime of conspiracy is how independent acts can be linked together as part of a single conspiracy. Consider the case below.

An FBI informant, Clarence Greathouse, agreed to provide Angelo Lonardo, an alleged organized crime figure, with cocaine to be sold by "people" chosen by Lonardo. Equipped with a body recorder, Greathouse met with Lonardo to arrange the sale. Greathouse demanded one-half of the money before delivery, and he asked that each of Lonardo's people purchase at least one-quarter kilogram of cocaine. Lonardo agreed.

Two weeks later, when the cocaine arrived, Lonardo wanted Greathouse to speak with "his friend" on the telephone. The "friend" was William Bourjaily, who asked questions about payment and the quality of the cocaine. Lonardo subsequently told Greathouse to park his car behind the Hilton Hotel in Cleveland, Ohio and meet him in the lobby. Greathouse followed the instructions and had four quarter-kilogram bags of cocaine in a Sheraton laundry bag in the car. Greathouse entered the Hilton, while two FBI agents remained on surveillance in the parking lot.

The FBI agents spotted William Bourjaily driving around the parking lot and examining various parked cars. Inside the hotel, Greathouse gave his car keys to Lonardo who walked to Greathouse's car. Lonardo removed the cocaine from under the seat and handed it to Bourjaily who was still in his car.

The FBI agents immediately arrested Bourjaily and Lonardo and recovered the cocaine from Bourjaily's car. Under the passenger seat they found a leather bag containing $19,000 in cash with a receipt made out to Bourjaily. They found another $2,000 in the glove compartment.[6]

Bourjaily was convicted at trial for conspiracy to distribute cocaine. He appealed, arguing the evidence was insufficient to prove his participation in a conspiracy beyond a reasonable doubt. The U.S. Court of Appeals acknowledged the government's burden of proof.

> For conviction, Bourjaily must have been shown to have agreed to participate in what he knew to be a joint venture to achieve a common goal. However, an actual agreement need not be proved. Drug distribution conspiracies are often "chain" conspiracies such that agreement can be inferred from the interdependence of the enterprise.[7]

The Court concluded that a jury could rationally conclude that Bourjaily was a willful member of a conspiracy to distribute cocaine. This was supported by the facts that "Bourjaily took the cocaine from Lonardo" in the parking lot, Lonardo referred to Bourjaily as "his friend," and the large volume of narcotics involved "creates an inference of conspiracy." Further-more, Bourjaily's contention that he did not know the substance in his car was cocaine "is meritless in light of the money found in his car, Lonardo's statements, and the phone call Greathouse had with Lonardo's 'friend'."[8]

As this case makes clear, a conspiracy is an agreement (written, oral, or tacit) between two or more persons to commit a criminal act, or to achieve by unlawful means an act not in itself criminal. If a person con-spires with his associates to sell narcotics, for example, it is possible to be convicted of both conspiracy *and* drug offenses.

How Much is Required Beyond a Criminal Agreement?

An interesting aspect of conspiracy is how it distinguishes between "thinking" about a crime, and actually going through with it. If two friends sit in a room and say, "that guy should be shot!," do we have a conspiracy? The answer is no, but if one of the two friends then drew a map diagram-ming how such a shooting could occur, would that be sufficient for liabili-ty? What if one of them went out and bought a gun? The issue, therefore, is that conspiracy punishes "planning" a criminal offense, but the law cannot punish mere thought. An actual act, or *actus reus*, must occur to be held liable for any crime, because the law punishes actions, not thoughts.

Virtually all conspiracy statutes on the state and federal level contain a phrase that a conspirator must perform "any act to effect the object of the conspiracy" in addition to planning.[9] The purpose of requiring an overt action *in addition* to the planning is to make clear the intention of carrying out the conspiracy, even if it never occurs. This distinguishes, for the pur-poses of punishment, idle talk from a true criminal design.

In a landmark case in 1994, the U.S. Supreme Court assessed the valid-ity of a conspiracy conviction in an Alaskan drug case. Lee Shabani entered into a drug distribution scheme with his girlfriend, her family, and others. Shabani brought cocaine from California to Anchorage, and his girlfriend and an associate sold the drugs, primarily to her relatives. An FBI agent purchased some of these drugs in an undercover operation, and Shabani's girlfriend agreed to cooperate with the prosecution.[10]

Shabani stood trial alone for conspiracy to distribute cocaine. He was convicted at trial and sentenced to 13 years in prison. He argued that an "overt act in furtherance of the conspiracy" is an essential element of the offense, and that the judge failed to instruct the jury of this fact. This is sig-nificant because Shabani claimed at trial that there was no direct evidence linking him to any of the drug sales. Also, all the major witnesses against him, his girlfriend and her relatives, testified pursuant to plea agreements. Shabani claimed they had invented a story to involve him and gain lenient treatment for themselves.[11]

The U.S. Court of Appeals reversed his conviction and remanded his case for a new trial, agreeing that the trial judge should have told the jury about the need to find an overt act in furtherance of the conspiracy.[12] The U.S. Supreme Court agreed to hear this case due to differences in interpretation of the federal drug conspiracy law among the circuits of the U.S. Court of Appeals.

The U.S. Supreme Court reinstated Shabani's conviction. In examining the federal drug conspiracy statute, it was found to prohibit:

> Any person who attempts or conspires to commit any offense defined in this title is punishable by imprisonment or fine or both which may not exceed the maximum punishment prescribed for the offense, the commission of which was the object of the attempt or conspiracy.[13]

The language of this statute does not specifically require an overt act in furtherance of the conspiracy. The Supreme Court noted that other federal conspiracy statutes, including the Organized Crime Control Act, *do* require an overt act for a conspiracy conviction.[14] Because Congress included the requirement of an overt act in these other federal conspiracy statutes, the U.S. Supreme Court inferred that "Congress appears to have made the choice quite deliberately" in *omitting* the act requirement from the drug conspiracy statute.[15] In responding to Shabani's appeal, the Court recognized that the law of conspiracy "does not punish mere thought; the criminal agreement itself is the actus reus."[16] It can be concluded, therefore, that the federal drug conspiracy statute does not require an overt act as a necessary element, but most other federal and state conspiracy statutes require such an act in furtherance of the conspiracy's objectives.

Can One Withdraw from a Conspiracy by Simply Walking Away?

Organized crime poses many unique problems. One of them is when leaders of conspiracies help to plan crimes, but then lower-level figures actually carry them out. The law of conspiracy aims to punish this higher-level planning by making it difficult to "wash your hands" of involvement in a criminal scheme by simply avoiding involvement in the ultimate crime itself.

In an interesting case in Chicago, William Wemette was the owner of an adult video store there. For 15 years he and his partner paid a "street tax" to members of the Chicago "Outfit," an organized crime group. Wemette paid this tax to protect his himself and his business from harm. When he was having financial problems with his business, the "street tax" collector said "if he did not pay the tax," his business would be shut down perhaps by "an accident or a fire."[17] Wemette complained to other organized crime figures, and he was told to speak with Frank Schweihs, who had a reputation for violence. Schweihs arranged for a new collector, Anthony Daddino, to begin collecting the "street tax" payments. Daddino collected $1,100 per month from Wemette until Wemette refused to deal with him any longer.

Wemette ultimately contacted the FBI, when he could no longer meet the burden of the payments, and agreed to record his conversations with Daddino and Schweihs. After several months of audio and video recordings of these conversations, both Daddino and Schweihs were indicted and convicted of conspiracy and extortion.

Daddino argued on appeal that he withdrew from the conspiracy, and his conviction should be vacated. He said that Wemette told him at one point not to come to his place anymore. Daddino responded, "Okay, buddy," and he never saw Wemette again.[18] Schweihs found someone else to collect payments after this exchange.

The legal issue is whether this action is sufficient to withdraw from the extortion conspiracy. The U.S. Court of Appeals noted that, "withdrawal requires more than a mere cessation of activity on the part of the defendant; it requires some affirmative action which disavows or defeats the purpose of the conspiracy."[19] As the Court had said in an earlier case, "You do not absolve yourself of guilt by walking away from a ticking bomb."[20]

The Court of Appeals concluded in this case:

> Daddino walked away from a ticking bomb. There was no evidence to show that Daddino was no longer associated with Schweihs or the "Outfit." Without evidence of some affirmative action by Daddino, Daddino could continue silently to endorse the extortion plan although he had been relieved of the duty to participate physically by collecting the "street tax" payments.[21]

The Court held that effective withdrawal from a conspiracy requires proof of an "affirmative action" by the defendant that works to defeat the conspiracy. Absent such proof, the defendant has not effectively withdrawn. Daddino's appeal was denied.

The reason why the law is so stringent about withdrawal from a conspiracy is because the object of the conspiracy need not be completed for a conviction. Therefore, if one merely walks away, after being involving in the planning of a crime, something more is needed to absolve one of responsibility for that crime. Otherwise, lower-level criminals who carried out conspiracies would be punished, and the higher-ups involved in the planning could escape prosecution, despite their significant role.

Summarizing the Important Elements of Conspiracy

The most important elements of the crime of conspiracy are of five types. They include: the nature of the agreement, extent of participation, overt acts, voluntariness, and withdrawal. These are summarized in Table 2.2.

Table 2.2
Elements of Conspiracy

Legal Aspects of Conspiracy

1. Two or more people are needed, although no formal agreement is required.

2. Participation need be only slight with reasonable knowledge of the conspiracy's existence, although mere presence by itself is insufficient for liability.

3. An overt act in furtherance of the conspiracy is usually required for liability.

4. Voluntary participation is required, and a person is liable for the acts of co-conspirators.

5. Effective withdrawal from a conspiracy requires an act to either defeat or disavow the purposes of the conspiracy.

As Table 2.2 illustrates, liability for conspiracy generally requires a voluntary agreement between two or more people, the parties do not have to be extensively involved with the conspiracy, withdrawal is not accomplished without actions to defeat the conspiracy, and an overt act in furtherance of the conspiracy is usually required. It can be seen that the crime of conspiracy lies at the heart of organized crime, due to its goal of punishment for those who *organize* to commit a crime.

Provision of Illicit Goods: Drugs and Stolen Property

A second category of organized crime involves the provision of illicit goods. The two most common examples are illicit drugs and stolen property. The term "provision" suggests organization and, as a result, most of the offenses in this category also involve the crime of conspiracy. A person who steals a CD-player from a car possesses stolen property. Until that per-

The scenario that follows describes an actual fact situation, where the courts had to determine whether the law of conspiracy applied. Resolution of this scenario requires proper application of the legal principles discussed above.

The Case of Murder for Hire

Garcia was a drug dealer. He was arrested by the Drug Enforcement Administration in Houston, and cooperated with police officials in exchange for leniency.

Information provided by Garcia led to the subsequent arrest of Antonio for cocaine distribution. Antonio believed Garcia was responsible for his arrest.

An acquaintance of Antonio, named Eugenio, called a friend who had moved to Chicago. This friend, Cabello, was given money to fly to Houston because his help was needed to solve "some problems." Once in Houston, Eugenio offered Cabello $5,000 and gave him a .357 magnum to kill Garcia. Cabello made three unsuccessful attempts to find Garcia's house, and he returned to tell Eugenio.

Eugenio told Cabello he would call his brother-in-law, Hector, to find out where Garcia lived. Eugenio obtained the directions and gave them to Cabello. Cabello left to find Garcia, but still could not find the house. Eugenio called Hector again for more precise directions.

Cabello ultimately found Garcia, and shot him six times, killing him. As Cabello left the murder scene, he ran a stop sign. A sheriff's deputy pulled him over, found the gun, and realized from the smell that it has been fired recently. Cabello was ultimately indicted for murder.

Questions:

1. If the money and gun given to Cabello were provided by Antonio, can Eugenio be held liable for conspiracy to commit murder?

2. If Cabello did not know that Garcia was a witness in a federal case, how would this affect his liability for murder?

3. Can Cabello also be charged with conspiracy, given the facts above?

4. Under what circumstances can Hector be held liable for conspiracy to murder Garcia?

son sells that property, or otherwise organizes to receive or distribute it, it cannot be considered part of organized crime. Therefore, the provision of illicit goods is marked by the crime of conspiracy, due to the need for two or more individuals to engage in this offense on a systematic basis. Several actual cases serve to illustrate the precise nature of these crimes.

Drugs: Liability for the Conduct of Others?

Drugs have been associated with organized crime, especially in recent years. To establish a complete drug trafficking case, it is necessary to identify the source (possessor and/or manufacturer), its method of distribution, and its ultimate arrival to buyers. Identifying the source and method of distribution are the most significant in making organized crime cases, but they also are the most difficult elements to prove in the provision of illicit narcotics. Consider the case of Yonatan Teffera.

Teffera and Thomas Cobb disembarked from a Greyhound Bus that had traveled from New York City to Washington, DC. An FBI agent and detective were working together, and they suspected Teffera and Cobb may be carrying drugs. The detective saw Teffera standing alone, approached him, and identified himself. Teffera gave a false name, and said he was traveling alone. A consensual search of Teffera's person revealed no illegal substances.

After he left, the detective noticed that Cobb had joined Teffera in a cab. The detective approached the cab and identified himself. Cobb said he had not been on the bus, but had picked up his "buddy" Teffera. Cobb agreed to be searched, and the detective found a large plastic bag hidden in the crotch of Cobb's pants that contained chunks of rock cocaine.[22] Cobb was arrested and handcuffed, while Teffera argued, "I don't know him." Teffera was also arrested, and a search found two photos of Teffera and Cobb together and two consecutively numbered bus tickets (later found to have been paid for in cash by one person).

Both Cobb and Teffera were tried for possession of cocaine base with intent to distribute. Expert police testimony at trial linked Cobb and Teffera together in a drug scheme, although Teffera had no drugs. According to this testimony, the person not carrying the drugs:

1. Protects the "mule" (the person carrying the drugs) from being robbed;

2. Insures the mule does not abscond with the drugs; and

3. Diverts police attention from the mule.[23]

Cobb and Teffera were convicted at trial. Teffera appealed, arguing that there was insufficient evidence to show beyond a reasonable doubt that he was guilty of possession with intent to distribute the cocaine in Cobb's pants. The U.S. Court of Appeals delineated the standard for overturning a jury verdict for insufficient evidence:

(a) Viewing the evidence in the light most favorable to the government, could any rational trier of fact have found the essential elements of the crime beyond a reasonable doubt;

(b) The government's evidence need not exclude all reasonable hypotheses of innocence or lead inexorably to the conclusion that the defendant is guilty; and

(c) No distinction is made between direct and circumstantial evidence in evaluating the government's proof.[24]

This is clearly a "daunting" burden for a defendant to have a conviction reversed on these grounds. The question is whether Teffera, found to possess no drugs, could be found guilty of at least aiding and abetting Cobb.

To prove a person aided and abetted the possession of illegal narcotics, the government does not have to show that that person ever "physically possessed" or controlled the movement of the drugs. Instead, the government must only demonstrated "sufficient knowledge and participation to indicate [the person] knowingly and willfully participated in the offense" in an effort to make it succeed.[25]

The government attempted to meet its burden of proof in this case by noting the bus tickets, photos, Teffera's use of a false name, false statements regarding whether he was alone and his destination, and the expert testimony about drug courier methods. The U.S. Court of Appeals reviewed this evidence and concluded, "the government's aiding and abetting theory runs into rough sledding from the outset."[26]

First, the government produced "no direct evidence" that Teffera knew that Cobb possessed the cocaine hidden in his clothes. The government's inference that Teffera's false responses to their questions circumstantially proved his link to Cobb, could also be used to argue the reverse position. Rather than lying to mislead police regarding a drug conspiracy, Teffera may have lied to disassociate himself from Cobb, if he knew that Cobb was frequently in trouble and may be involved in some current illegal activity. Therefore, Teffera's lies could be used to indicate either involvement in a conspiracy *or* a true attempt to disassociate himself from Cobb.

The prosecution had the burden to show that Teffera both *knew* about Cobb's transportation of drugs, but also that Teffera *actually participated* in Cobb's avoiding detection. The Court of Appeals concluded, "this the government has utterly failed to do."[27] The Court found that Teffera's movements in the bus station "are perfectly consistent with innocence and raise no inference that he was a lookout: He got off a bus with a friend, went to get a cab while the friend stopped to pick up a snack, and then met up with the friend again to leave."[28] Simply stated, "the government's problem" in meeting the burden of proof in this case is that Teffera's "misstatements are at least equally consistent with other plausible hypotheses."[29] Even given the expert testimony about drug "mules," the government needed more than this theory alone to link it to Teffera. Teffera's attempt to distance himself from Cobb "is just as consonant with an innocent person's fear of being associated with a guilty person as it is with an intent to help Cobb get out of the station undetected."[30]

In conclusion, the Court of Appeals stated:

> While we recognize that the government's proof need not be so certain as to exclude all inferences of innocence, in a case where the government's overall evidence of guilt is so thin, the alternate hypotheses consistent with innocence become sufficiently strong that they must be deemed to instill a reasonable doubt in our hypothetical juror. Even looking at the government's evidence in the most favorable light, we think that line has been crossed here.[31]

The Court reversed the conviction of Teffera. Although Cobb's guilt is clear by virtue of his transportation and possession of cocaine, the government did not demonstrate effectively any *knowledge* or *behaviors* on Teffera's part that directly or circumstantially made him part of the scheme. In a case like this, the government would have to show that Teffera somehow shared in the control of the drugs, actively took measures to protect them (more than meeting a mule-protector profile), or had other evidence to show Teffera's role in planning, advancing, or being aware of the illegal drug transportation.

This case demonstrates that significant drug cases can be difficult to prove. Proving a street-level sale poses only the problem of direct observation. To prove the existence of a drug distribution conspiracy, significantly more is required. Evidence of planning of the scheme, movement of the drugs, and locating their source are all difficult to do, but are required to prove organized drug conspiracies. They often require long-term surveillance, undercover police work, and other methods that incur large expenditures of police resources. It is possible in the case above, for example, that further observation of the defendant could have linked him to an ultimate drug transaction. Ongoing police training regarding the legal requirements for proving drug conspiracies is as necessary as a willingness to devote adequate time and resources to establishing the existence of significant cases.

Stolen Property: I Didn't Know It was Stolen!

The sale, possession, and distribution of stolen property is rampant in American society. Even otherwise "law-abiding" citizens often have no qualms in obtaining a "hot" stereo, tape player, jewelry, or other merchandise "that happened to fall off a truck" at incredibly low prices. The problem, of course, is that people do not spend much time considering precisely how the prices got so low. When the property is stolen, *any* price becomes a profit, because nothing was paid to manufacture or distribute the product in the first place. How this relates to organized crime is important. Understanding the public willingness to purchase merchandise with "no questions asked," illicit entrepreneurs emerge to cater to that market. Therefore, many people attempt to make a living buying, trading, and in some cases hijacking stolen property in order to make a fast, but illegal, profit. The market for stolen property has supported a number of infamous organized crime figures.[32]

In legal terms, the primary issue that arises in these organized crime cases is knowledge that the property was indeed stolen. Most stolen property statutes require "knowing" that the property is stolen as an element of the offense. This requirement prevents prosecution of those who unknowingly or mistakenly come into contact with stolen property. An interesting example is provided by the case of Peter Rosa in Brooklyn.

Rosa met with David Maniquis at a Brooklyn restaurant on several occasions. Maniquis was introduced through a third party as a source of stolen silver. Over the course of several meetings at the restaurant, Rosa agreed to buy 50 100-ounce bars of silver from Maniquis, after being told the source was a man about to retire from a silver company and being shown a sample of the merchandise. Although he expressed concern that the source, if caught, would turn them in, Rosa agreed to the sale.[33]

Rosa also discussed the possible sale of "warm" watches. Maniquis offered a list watches he had for sale at prices about 20 percent of their actual value.[34] At a subsequent meeting he bought jewelry from Maniquis for 10 to 20 percent of its value. Rosa said at that time, "[T]hey're not gonna put us in jail unless [Maniquis] is wired."[35]

As it turns out, Maniquis was wired, and his conversations with Rosa recorded. Rosa was convicted of conspiring to receive stolen property. He was sentenced to more than four years in prison to be followed by three years of supervised release.[36]

Rosa appealed his conviction arguing, among other things, that the government did not prove that he *knew* the goods were *stolen*. Without such knowledge, he cannot be convicted of this crime, because the mental state (or *mens rea*) required under federal law is whoever receives stolen goods must "know the same to have been stolen."[37]

The U.S. Court of Appeals found "the proof was ample" of Rosa's knowledge he was dealing in stolen property. This proof included his remarks about the source of the silver possibly betraying them to the authorities, his statement about being in trouble if Maniquis was wired, the discussion of "warm" watches, and the price lists supplied by Maniquis that showed the property's sale price to be only 10 to 20 percent of its actual value. These statements, together with the "disparity between stated value and asking price was so great as to create the inference that Rosa and his co-conspirators surely believed they were dealing with stolen goods."[38]

In stolen property cases, therefore, the burden is on the prosecution to show the defendant's knowledge that the property was stolen. The prices of the merchandise, remarks by the defendant, and other circumstantial evidence can be used to demonstrate this knowledge.

In a case in Harrisburg, Pennsylvania, Ben Renfro Stuart was convicted of receiving stolen government property for his involvement in the purchase of more than 100 stolen savings bonds with a face value of $1,000 each. The scheme would pay him 20 cents on the dollar.[39]

Evidence at trial determined that a codefendant gave Stuart a package of bonds wrapped in newspaper and told him to wait at the other end of a hotel parking lot. Stuart was then given instructions by radio to deliver the package and leave, earning $2,000 for this task and for another delivery. As the U.S. Court of Appeals declared, "for this minimal amount of work . . . a jury could well find that Stuart either knew the bonds were stolen or deliberately closed his eyes to that fact."[40]

Most states punish stolen property offenders according to the value of the property involved. In an interesting twist, Stuart argued on appeal that his participation in the scheme netted him $2,000, making that the criterion for determining his sentence. The Court of Appeals determined, however, that under federal sentencing guidelines (and the law in most states) "the loss is the fair market value of the particular property at issue."[41] Therefore, Stuart was punished based on the full $129,000 face value of the bonds recovered, rather than on the $2,000 he made for delivering them.

The provision of illicit goods, such as drugs and stolen property, provides income to support organized crime. This property is often obtained illegally or at incredibly low prices, and then is sold to people who do not show concern about its source or legality. The huge profits that result are demonstrated in the cases just discussed. In this way, otherwise "law-abiding" citizens support organized crime activity in a direct way.

Provision of Illicit Services: Gambling, Loansharking, Sex

The unlawful counterpart to the provision of illicit goods is the provision of illicit services. Like illicit goods, these offenses provide illicit services that are in public demand. In fact, it is the public demand that makes this illicit marketplace possible.

The scenario that follows describes an actual fact situation, where the courts had to determine whether the laws involving stolen property applied. Resolution of this scenario requires proper application of the legal principles discussed in this chapter.

The Case of a Very Good Deal on Carpet

Bill Kunkle was a truck driver for a carpet company. He was assigned to transport a load of carpet from Georgia to California.

He decided during his trip that he was not being paid enough. He started drinking, and resolved to sell the carpet he was carrying in the truck. He sold two rolls to the manager of a truck stop in Oklahoma City. He then stopped at Earl's Bar in Amarillo, Texas and told some patrons that he had carpet for sale. An owner of a carpet store was in the bar and expressed interest.

Kunkle asked the carpet store owner if he was with the police, and the owner said, "no." Kunkle also stated that he was not with the police and that the carpet was not stolen. Kunkle then accepted an offer of $17,500 for the entire load.

After a gambling and cocaine-buying binge, and the report of an abandoned truck at Earl's Bar, authorities contacted Kunkle's employers and obtained numbers located on the backs of the missing carpet rolls. They were found in the carpet store in Amarillo, Texas.

Questions:

1. Kunkle had lawful possession of the carpet in his truck. At what point did it become "stolen" property?

2. The carpet store owner in Texas asked Kunkle if the carpet was stolen, and he said it wasn't. Can the carpet store owner be held liable for receiving stolen property?

3. The carpet store owner paid $17,500 for the carpet. How does this protect him from charges of receiving stolen property?

4. Can Kunkle and the carpet store owner be held liable for conspiracy?

The Unique Problem of Gambling: The Oldest Vice

Crimes associated with gambling pose unique problems in contemporary America, as most states have now legalized at least some forms of gambling. They have done so as a revenue measure, although there continues to be debate regarding its desirability as a government-sponsored enterprise. This debate is not new.

Gambling can be traced back to the beginnings of recorded history. From the very beginning, however, it has been viewed alternately as a moral weakness, a crime, or simple recreation. Given the moral repugnance associated with gambling for the bulk of its history, combined with its enduring popularity, gambling is truly the oldest vice.

Gambling can be defined as games of chance, where luck determines the outcome more than skill. Mention of gambling can be traced to very early history. For example, the Bible provides an account following the crucifixion of Jesus, where four soldiers each wanted Jesus' robe. They resolved the dispute saying, "Let's not tear it; let's throw dice to see who will get it." This story is recounted in three separate books of the New Testament.[42]

Gambling appeared to be popular among Native Americans from early historical accounts. The Onondaga Indians of New York were known to wager their possessions using dice. The Iroquois also played a version of dice.[43] The Narragansett Indians of Rhode Island and Chumash in the Northwest "often gambled for days" in games where "the worldly goods of entire tribes might change hands."[44]

Whereas Indians were known to gamble with dice, or bet on the outcome of sporting contests, early American colonists were most familiar with lotteries. In the early 1600s, the Virginia Company of London experienced financial problems in starting a plantation in Virginia. Given the success of European lotteries, the Virginia Company was given permission to conduct lottery drawings in England (to fund plantations in Virginia). Interestingly, while the Virginia Company attempted to push lottery sales in England, it was attempting to *reduce* gambling back in Virginia. Reports of "gaming, idleness, and vice" were rampant, and anti-gambling ordinances became part of Jamestown's initial legal code.[45] The codes were ineffective in preventing the popularity of gambling.

This peculiar dichotomy where gambling was encouraged for one purpose (public funding), but seen as dissolute for another (recreation), provides an early illustration of the vacillation in attitudes towards gambling throughout history. The Puritans of Massachusetts were widely known for their opposition to gambling on moral grounds. They saw gambling as "an appearance of evil" and therefore irreligious.[46] Like Virginia, though, Massachusetts and other colonies passed laws in an effort to limit or prohibit gambling, but gambling (especially card and dice games) continued in spite of the laws.[47] Nevertheless, when funds were needed for public works during the early 1700s (e.g., schools and roads), many Northeastern colonies started lotteries to raise the required funds. This provides another example of how gambling has been viewed as either a vice or a virtue, depending on how the profits are diverted (i.e., for pleasure or for public works).

Most lotteries were private enterprises, but as they grew the colonies sought to regulate them "motivated by a familiar combination of paternalism and self-interest."[48] By 1750 most states prohibited lotteries that operated without state authorization. The ability of lotteries to raise money, especially among a public outraged by taxation, increased their popularity. In fact, most of the ivy league colleges were first endowed with funds from lotteries. By 1800, there were approximately 2,000 authorized lotteries in existence that grew in size and scope.[49] In addition, brokers were being used to run lotteries for a percentage of the profits.

Horse-racing, cards, and dice games were also popular from colonial times. These games were somewhat more limiting than lotteries, due to the fact that fewer people were able to participate in the same race or game by their local nature. This is in contrast to lotteries that involved entire towns, states, and the nation on several occasions. Like lotteries, these other forms of gambling were viewed with the same measure of alternating acceptance and rejection. Many early colonies and states had prohibitions against horse-racing, card, and dice games, but their general popularity led to widespread disregard of the law.[50]

The allure of gambling has always attracted a disproportionate number of those who are relatively poor for obvious reasons: this is the group who most needs a change in luck, and gambling offers the possibility of an immediate and dramatic change, however slight the odds. Nevertheless, gamblers historically have come from all walks of life. Gambling among the clergy, for example, apparently resulted in a Virginia law in the 1600s that stated, "Ministers shall not give themselves to excess in drinking or yette spend their time idelie by day or by night, playing at dice, cards or any unlawful game."[51] Undergraduates at Harvard played cards unremittingly, ultimately leading to a heavy fine of five shillings if caught. Servants and minors caught gambling with cards in Massachusetts were to be "publicly whipt."[52]

Playing the slot machines at Foxwoods Casino in Ledyard, Connecticut, this woman is among the thousands of people who visit gambling casinos around the country regularly.

AP/WIDE WORLD PHOTOS

Like the drinking of alcoholic beverages, gambling was widely criticized in public but privately enjoyed as a form of recreation or social intercourse. Unlike drinking, however, gambling could be employed for socially constructive purposes (e.g., lotteries to build roads), whereas drinking, prostitution, and narcotics had no redeeming social value. The fact that gambling can be used for social benefits distinguishes it from the other vices. Nevertheless, it did not prevent criticism of those who gambled for recreational purposes. Thomas Jefferson publicly argued that "gaming corrupts our disposition," but he privately gambled. In fact, while he was composing the Declaration of Independence, he made notations in his personal log about winning and losing at backgammon, cards, and bingo.[53] In a similar vein, Benjamin Franklin manufactured playing cards.

Gambling as Vice or Recreation?

The tremendous popularity of gambling in all its forms ultimately contributed to its continuing image as a vice, rather than as a form of recreation. The huge interest and participation in lotteries, cards, dice, and horse racing resulted in the commercialization of these enterprises. Gambling halls, casinos, lottery brokers, and professional gamblers resulted in a growing number of reported instances of fixed games and races, marked cards, loaded dice, dishonest players and operators. The negative public reaction to these reports led to a series of reforms in the mid 1800s that changed the image of gambling. There was less confidence that gambling could be carried out honestly, leading to the prohibition of gambling in many places. This image of gambling as having questionable moral or legal standing has continued for more than one century; and it is an image that the gambling industry still combats today.[54]

There was a great deal of evidence on which the public's growing distrust of gambling was based. Lottery scandals in New York, Pennsylvania, Boston, and elsewhere found instances where $400,000 was collected and no prizes were awarded. One million dollars of fictitious tickets were sold. A lottery broker took $10 million in expenses for a lottery that totaled only $16 million in receipts.[55]

Horse racing suffered from similar scandals. The rise of bookmakers contributed to a concern over profit, rather than thoroughbred breeding. Only a few documented instances of fixed races were enough to shift public opinion to believe that horse racing was a dishonest enterprise.[56] To some extent, this belief continues today.

Cards, dice, and casino games were changed in the public's eye beginning in 1835. In Vicksburg, Mississippi, several professional gamblers and saloon operators were implicated in a political conspiracy. This resulted, although circuitously, in an anti-gambling wave of reform that swept through many parts of the United States. It was this reform movement that most directly led to the rise of organized crime involvement in gambling. The situation in New York is instructive.

The editor of the *New York Tribune*, Horace Greeley, joined with businessmen to form the New York Association for the Suppression of Gambling whose purpose was to "pluck the victim from the gambler's crutches" (i.e., the working classes). After a significant lobbying effort, New York State passed several anti-gambling laws in 1851 that supporters argued, "if faithfully enforced would close every gambling hell within the state."[57] Some commercial gaming enterprises were closed, but "many moved underground and operated by bribing law enforcement officials."[58] Hence, the beginnings of organized crime involvement in gambling can be characterized as the result of a successful campaign by reformers to prohibit gaming enterprises.

Another example is provided by changes in the legal status of lotteries. By the late 1800s, most states had banned lotteries. Policy games (or "numbers") was invented to satisfy those who remained interested in the game after its prohibition. Numbers originally were picked by spinning a wheel, and later became more objective (and less prone to manipulation), using such numbers as the total handle for the day at the racetrack, baseball scores, cattle and customs receipts, or other combinations of numbers that appear in daily newspapers. Policy was very attractive to the poor because bets as small as five cents could be played. Tickets were sold by agents or "runners" who would canvas neighborhoods collecting bets, receiving 15 percent of their sales in return. During the 1880s, it has been reported that New York City had over 700 policy shops, and a cartel called the "Central Organization" operated games in 20 different cities.[59] Policy games were never legalized (except in Louisiana), and they continue to stay in business by paying for "protection" from arrest. In New York City, it is estimated that more than one million people purchase illegal numbers regularly.[60]

The growing intolerance for gambling continued into the early 1900s, fueled by both public figures and religious leaders. Reform administrations in Buffalo, Chicago, Cleveland, Denver, Detroit, New Orleans, New York, Pittsburgh, and San Francisco all raided gambling operations. Local enforcement efforts prompted a number of states to go further in prohibiting gambling. By 1910, Arizona, New Mexico, and Nevada passed laws that even banned card-playing at home! Other states passed laws making it easier to prosecute illegal gaming operators.[61] In fact, the message back then was strikingly similar to the anti-drug messages of today. Consider this statement in a Methodist church in Texas in 1909: "Don't gamble. Don't play cards. Don't bet on race horses. Don't speculate on wheat. Don't speculate on the stock exchange. Don't throw dice. Don't shirk honest labor. Don't be a gambler; once a gambler, always a gambler."[62]

By the 1930s, though, legalized gambling was making a return as a legal form of recreation (or vice). Horse racing returned through a pari-mutuel betting system regulated by the state. Although lotteries were still prohibited, they were re-emerging from one of the same sources of their initial prohibition: churches. During the Depression era, churches turned to bingo and other lottery games as a way to raise funds. Remarkably, Florida legalized slot machines during this same period but church groups successfully lobbied against them, arguing the slot machines were taking the "nickels and dimes of common laborers."[63] The church groups were eventually able to pressure the state legislature to repeal the law and prohibit slot machines in 1937. By 1940, it was estimated that nearly 25 percent of all Americans gambled on church lotteries.[64] As New York Mayor Fiorello LaGuardia observed, "if bingo is unlawful in one place, it cannot be lawful in another."[65] LaGuardia's observation regarding the inherent ironies of legal versus illegal gambling remains unresolved today. The legal/illegal status of gambling today, and the confusion it causes, becomes clear, if one examines some recent cases.

Is Legal Gambling a Constitutionally Protected Right?

By the early 1990s, most states had legalized some form of gambling. Lotteries are the most popular manifestation of legal gaming, although casino gambling and betting on sporting contests are legal in more jurisdictions than ever before.

As legal gaming grows, spurred largely by its ability to generate large revenues with little investment risk, there has arisen conflict between jurisdictions with and without legal games. A classic case was that between North Carolina and Virginia. North Carolina did not a have state-sponsored lottery, but Virginia did. Edge Broadcasting owned and operated a radio station in North Carolina, but was very near the Virginia-North Carolina border. In fact, more than 90 percent of the radio station's listeners were in Virginia with the remainder living in nine North Carolina counties.

The radio station wanted to broadcast Virginia lottery advertisements due to its large Virginia audience. On the other hand, the radio station was located in North Carolina where such lotteries were illegal. Should the radio station be permitted to broadcast the lottery ads?

This debate ended in the U.S. Supreme Court, which considered the case in light of the First Amendment guarantee of freedom of speech. The Supreme Court concluded that "the Government has a substantial interest in supporting the policy of non-lottery States, as well as not interfering with the policy of States that permit lotteries."[66] With regard to the First Amendment, the Court held that "gambling implicates no constitutionally protected right; rather, it falls into a category of 'vice' activity that could be, and frequently has been, banned altogether."[67]

Despite the growing legalization of gambling in a variety of forms, therefore, there is no constitutional right to gamble, nor do radio stations have a right to broadcast advertisements that feature legal gambling to non-gambling states. The U.S. Supreme Court noted that the Constitution "affords a lesser protection to commercial speech," than to other forms of expression under the First Amendment, and that federal laws that prohibit lottery advertising in non-lottery states "directly" serve the governmental interest in "balancing the interests of lottery and non-lottery States."[68] Therefore, legalized gambling continues to be a state prerogative, and not a constitutional right. States without legal gaming are protected from the advertisements of other states so inclined in "balancing" the mutual interests of these states.

What Are the Elements of an Illegal Gambling Business?

Given the dramatic increase in both the forms and number of states now involved in legal gaming, it is not always clear what constitutes *illegal* gambling under current law. An illustrative case is that of John Murray at the Willow Bar in Somerville, Massachusetts.

The case arose out of an internal investigation of a Customs Inspector, who was believed to own a bar without permission of the U.S. Customs Service. The Customs Service placed an undercover agent, Janet Durham, in the bar as a waitress for about four months. Agent Durham observed that a telephone near a corner bar stool at the rear of the Willow Bar was used to accept bets on dog and horse races. While in her undercover role as a waitress, Agent Durham observed several people sit or stand near the corner bar stool, answer the telephone, accept money from customers, and make notations on small pieces of paper. These people included John Murray.

Murray was convicted after trial of conducting and conspiring to conduct a gambling business. Under federal law, it is necessary that a person "conduct, finance, manage, supervise, direct, or own all or part of an illegal gambling business."[69] An illegal business is one that violates state law. Second, the illegal gambling business must involve five or more persons. Third, the illegal gambling business must remain "in substantially continuous operation" for more than 30 days or gross more than $2,000 in a single day.[70] These are the three elements that must be proven to convict someone of involvement in an illegal gambling business under federal law.

On appeal, the U.S. Court of Appeals reversed Murray's conviction. It found that evidence "shows that, at most, four persons operated a gambling business out of the corner bar stool of the Willow Bar for a period in excess of 30 days, and that the identity of those involved frequently changed."[71] The prosecution argued that there were others who participated in the illegal gambling business, increasing the total to five or more as required by law. The Court of Appeals disagreed, however, noting that Agent Durham was inside the Willow Bar for 56 days, and persons answering the telephone and making notes on paper four or fewer times during a 56-day period cannot "be said to have participated in a manner that was necessary or helpful to the gambling business for a period in excess of 30 days," as required by law.[72]

An illegal gambling business is distinguished from a legal gambling business, therefore, in its violation of state law where it operates, the need for meaningful involvement by five or more persons, and the requirement that it last for more than 30 days or gross more than $2,000 per day. This federal statute helps to distinguish gambling as a form or organized crime from gambling that is recreational in nature. This purpose is made clear in the legislative history of this law where Congress intended it to address "illegal gambling activities of major proportions" in order "to reach only those persons who prey systematically upon our citizens and whose syndicated operations are so continuous and so substantial as to be of national concern."[73]

Is Placing a Bet Sufficient for Involvement in an Illegal Gambling Enterprise?

The issue raised in the case of John Murray, discussed above, raises the issue, but does not answer the question, of *how much* participation is required for one to be legally culpable for participation in an illegal gambling enterprise. Does a single bet suffice? Multiple bets? Is other activity supportive of the enterprise needed?

Consider the case of Karin Follin. She and four others were convicted of operating an illegal casino at the Stewart Lodge in Canton, Mississippi. A police investigator visited the casino eight times in five weeks, and observed Follin serving drinks, cooking steaks, wiping off kitchen counters, examining dice, and, on several occasions, wagering bets.[74] As noted in the previous section, at least five persons are necessary to constitute an illegal gambling business under federal law. Follin appealed her conviction arguing that she was only a bettor and, in that capacity, cannot be held to be part of the illegal business.

The U.S. Court of Appeals agreed that the law prohibits "any degree of participation in a gambling operation except participation as a mere bettor."[75] The reason for the exclusion of "mere bettors" from liability under federal law is "to bring within federal criminal legislation not all gambling, but only that above a certain minimum level."[76] The Court also admitted there is "no bright line" that can be drawn to establish what is "necessary or helpful" to a gambling enterprise, as compared to mere betting. It noted that the extent of participation "depends on the facts in a given situation."[77] The Court concluded that Follin's activities "went beyond the realm of a mere bettor" and her conviction was affirmed.[78]

Loansharking

Loansharking, or usury, is lending money at an interest rate that exceeds the legal limit. Its connection with organized crime is closely linked to gambling. The profits reaped from illegal gambling enterprises often have been used to make even more money by lending it to customers at usurious rates. The interest rate is set by law to insure that customers are not exploited by banks or other lenders. The law of usury also deters individuals from incurring unlawful debts, such as those resulting from illegal gambling losses.

Usury: Are Threats Needed for Liability?

An important case that involved charges of loansharking was that of Mario "Murph" Eufrasio, Santo "Sam" Idone, and Gary Iacona. During the 1980s, these persons were alleged to have been part of the Scarfo crime "family," a Philadelphia- and New Jersey-based group of the Cosa Nostra or Mafia. Idone, a "capo" in the Scarfo organization, supervised a group of soldiers and associates that included Eufrasio and Iacona. As the U.S. Court of Appeals noted later, "the function of soldiers and associates, and of the mob generally, was to make money by illegal means."[79]

At trial, intercepted conversations and expert testimony were used to prove that Eufrasio, Idone, and Iacona collected unlawful debts on usurious loans. An "unlawful debt" under federal law is one that is incurred during illegal gambling activity.[80] Therefore, any debts incurred from illegal gambling are unlawful, because the activity itself is unlawful. These debts have no legal standing, so banks cannot lend money to repay these debts, and these debts cannot be collected lawfully either. As a result, loansharks may offer to lend money to those who have no other way to repay gambling losses. The defendants in this case were found to collect debts on "numerous" loans with effective annual interest rates from 78 to 293 percent. One witness testified he borrowed $4,500 from Iacona for 12 weeks, and paid $540 in interest. Idone and Iacona supplied the money and authorized the illegal loans, while Eufrasio was their agent who reported on his crew's loansharking activities to Scarfo.[81] All the defendants were convicted.

AP/WIDE WORLD PHOTOS

Nicodemo "Little Nicky" Scarfo, upon his January, 1984 release from La Tuna Federal Correctional Institute in El Paso, Texas, as he walks down the steps of the prison into a waiting limousine. Scarfo was the leader of the Philadelphia- and New Jersey-based Scarfo crime syndicate.

On appeal, it was argued that the government must prove the defendants were in the "continuous" business of usury to find them guilty on this charge. The U.S. Court of Appeals held that federal law requires an unlawful debt to be collected as part of "the *business* of lending money or a thing or value" at usurious rates, "a 'continuous' business is not required."[82] Only a single act is necessary for liability. Furthermore, an exchange of cash is not required, as long as there exists "a single act which would tend to induce another to repay on an unlawful debt incurred in the business of lending money."[83]

Iacona also appealed on grounds that the government did not prove he threatened people for failure to repay these usurious loans. Such a claim "has no merit" because threats are not an element of the crime of collecting unlawful debts.[84] All that is required is the attempt to collect the debt itself. In fact, the accused's ignorance of the specific interest rate charged on a usurious loan is not a defense either, because it is not an element of the offense. Collecting an unlawful debt is all that is required. Threats incur liability for another crime (extortion), and ignorance of the defendant is not an excuse for any crime (see Chapter 10).

Loansharking is important in understanding the nature of organized crime activity because it shows how illicit profits can be used to generate even more illicit money and, thereby, maintain growing criminal enterprises. It is also related to money laundering, discussed in Chapter 9, in that loansharking provides a means way to move illicit profits away from their initial source, making them difficult to trace.

Sex and Organized Crime

Sex and organized crime are linked in two distinct ways: prostitution and pornography. Organized prostitution has been used to profit from the money made by individual prostitutes in exchange for "protection" or other services offered to prostitutes. Pornography is manufacturing and marketing illicit depictions of sex in the form of photographs and films to a segment of the public that desires them. As in the case of illicit goods and the other illicit services, organized crime involvement in the sex industry is made possible entirely through a continuing public demand for these services. A decreased demand for these services would undoubtedly result in a smaller market for organized crime involvement.

Prostitution: It Was Only a Modeling and Escort Service

Engaging in prostitution is not an organized crime in itself because it fails to fulfill the definition presented in Chapter 1. Simply stated, prostitution often involves little planning or organization in its commission. It becomes a part of organized crime, when it is planned or organized in a systematic way. In the United States, there has been a history of criminal entrepreneurs who "organize" prostitutes and take a percentage of their income as a "commission."

The question that arises in these situations is, Why would a prostitute agree to pay a commission to a "pimp" or "madam," when these people are not necessary to the act? There are two answers to this question. First, there have been instances where prostitutes have been coerced into joining such "prostitution rings" under threat of bodily harm. More often, however, the "pimp" or "madam" provides useful services to the prostitute. These services might include renting a "safe" hotel or rooms for the prostitutes to ply their trade, and screening of customers so that the threat of dangerous, unhealthy, or suspected undercover police officers is reduced. Without these services, street prostitution is a much more dangerous and threatening business.

Actual cases of organized prostitution frequently involve problems in proving that the "pimp," "madam," or other organizer knew of the nature of the enterprise. People simply don't put an advertisement in the paper soliciting customers for prostitutes. These organizers often develop clever ways to disguise their prostitution business as something legitimate. Proving in court that they *knew* it was an illegal enterprise can be difficult.

During the 1980s, Penelope Hatteras operated several businesses in Houston, Dallas, Atlanta, and Denver. These businesses were advertised as "nude modeling and escort services." Customers would call these businesses, and "models" would be dispatched directly to the customer's location. The customer paid by cash or credit card. What was actually occurring was organized prostitution. Once the "model" reached the customer, she would negotiate a monetary agreement in exchange for sex acts.[85]

Hatteras, her accountant Charles Holcomb, and others were eventually arrested and charged with violating the *Mann Act*. This federal law prohibits anyone who "knowingly persuades, induces, entices, or coerces any woman or girl" to travel between states or countries "for the purpose of prostitution or debauchery, or for any other immoral purpose . . . with or without her consent."[86]

Holcomb, the accountant, appealed his conviction, arguing that the evidence against him was insufficient for violation of the Mann Act. As the U.S. Court of Appeals stated, the government cannot establish his guilt under the Mann Act "by simply showing his awareness of prostitution." The government "must also produce some evidence suggesting that Holcomb knowingly agreed with Hatteras that her operation would entice women to cross state lines for the purpose of prostitution."[87]

The government demonstrated at trial that Holcomb set up Hatteras' books, distributed pay to the "models," and that he suspected Hatteras was operating a prostitution ring. But there was no evidence that Holcomb was aware "that the models were crossing state lines," (a requirement of the Mann Act).[88] As a result, Holcomb's conviction was reversed.

It is important to keep in mind that Holcomb's actions would be sufficient to convict him for conspiracy to engage in prostitution under most state laws. A reasonable person would have been aware of what was going on under these circumstances, and Holcomb admitted he had suspicions. The point here is that the federal Mann Act requires *interstate* movement of women for the purposes of prostitution, knowledge of which Holcomb did not possess. Hatteras, and others involved in the enterprise, were convicted in this case, however, for the facts demonstrated their knowledge of interstate movement of women for the purposes of prostitution.

As in all criminal law, *reasonable knowledge* is required for liability for nearly all crimes. In prostitution cases, for instance, *actual* knowledge that prostitution occurred is not necessary, as long as there is evidence that a *reasonable person* should have drawn that conclusion.

In a similar case, Alvin Sigalow was general manager for two massage parlors in New York City. The massage parlors "engaged in the prostitution business," and were actually owned by others who used Sigalow as a "front man."[89] The business advertised through mailings to potential customers in New York, New Jersey, and Connecticut, and also through advertisements in *The Village Voice* newspaper and *Screw* magazine.

Sigalow was convicted of aiding and abetting "the promotion, management, establishment, or carrying on" of a prostitution enterprise in violation of the federal *Travel Act*. This Act prohibits using interstate or foreign commerce in promotion of an illegal activity (including prostitution).[90] In affirming his conviction, the U.S. Court of Appeals held that he can be convicted "so long as he knows that nature of the substantive offense he furthers or promotes."[91] Similar to the "nude modeling" case above, *reasonable knowledge* of the elements of the crime suffices for liability. Actual knowledge need not be proven, as long as a reasonable person would have drawn that conclusion about the nature of the activity.

Distinguishing the Risque from the Obscene

Some people get their sexual gratification vicariously through pornography. Interestingly, the term pornography has no legal meaning. It is a generic term that refers to sexually explicit material. Such material is only illegal when it is also "obscene" under law. Therefore, state and federal laws are directed at "obscene" material, rather than at pornography.

A problem arises when one attempts to define obscenity in an objective manner. The courts have wrestled with this problem for many years, deciding on the current legal definition in 1973. The definition of obscenity is a central issue, of course, in establishing criminal liability.

The U.S. Supreme Court changed the legal standard for obscenity in the case of *Miller v. California*.[92] Marvin Miller conducted a mass mailing to advertise the sale of illustrated books. The brochures advertised four books titled *Intercourse, Man-Woman, Sex Orgies Illustrated*, and *An Illus-trated History of Pornography*. The brochure also featured a film titled *Marital Intercourse*. The brochures consisted primarily of pictures and drawings "very explicitly depicting men and women in groups of two or more engaging in a variety of sexual activities, with genitals often promi-nently displayed."[93] The case resulted from a complaint to the police from a person who had been sent five of these unsolicited brochures. The legal issue was whether these materials were legally obscene and, hence, in vio-lation of the law.

The U.S. Supreme Court admitted that there had been a "somewhat tortured history of the Court's obscenity decisions," but it was able to reach a five-justice majority.[94] The definition of obscenity agreed upon by the Court consisted of three parts. Obscenity was said to exist when the aver-age person, applying contemporary community standards, would find that the work:

(a) Taken as a whole, appeals to the prurient interest in sex,

(b) Portrays sexual conduct (as specifically defined by state law) in a patently offensive way, and

(c) Taken as a whole, lacks serious literary, artistic, political or scientific value.[95]

The majority emphasized that it was not their function to usurp the state prerogative to define obscenity. It did, however, provide examples of what state laws could include as obscenity. The Court felt that "patently offensive representations of ultimate sexual acts, normal or perverted, actual or simulated" as well as "masturbation, excretory functions, and lewd exhibition of the genitals" could be included as obscene "hard-core" sexual conduct.[96] Nevertheless, the Supreme Court ruled that a requirement forcing obscenity proceedings "around evidence of a *national* 'community standard' would be an exercise in futility."[97] It held:

> It is neither realistic nor constitutionally sound to read the First
> Amendment as requiring that the people of Maine or Mississippi
> accept public depiction of conduct found tolerable in Las Vegas,
> or New York City.[98]

Although this definition of obscenity contains several objective elements, it remains difficult to apply in practice. This has made both the prosecution and defense of obscenity cases problematic. Observe how the U.S. Supreme Court has subsequently carved conditions and exceptions to its own defini-tion set forth in *Miller*.

In *Paris Adult Theatre I v. Slaton*,[99] the Supreme Court ruled that the exhibition of obscene films is not protected from prosecution even when viewing is limited to consenting adults. Two films shown in an adult theatre were found to be obscene, despite the fact that minors were excluded and adult patrons were warned of the nature of the material. The Court also held that States have the power to determine whether the exhibition or sale of obscene material "has a tendency to injure the community as a whole, [or] to endanger the public safety," even though the scientific evidence on this point is unsettled.[100]

In another case, Billy Jenkins, a theater manager in Albany, Georgia, exhibited the film *Carnal Knowledge*. The critically acclaimed film was directed by Mike Nichols, and it starred Jack Nicholson, Candice Bergen, and Art Garfunkel. Jenkins was convicted for violating Georgia's obscenity law by showing this film. A jury found it to exceed the "community standards" of Albany, Georgia. Therefore, the film failed a crucial part of the obscenity test set forth in *Miller*. But the U.S. Supreme Court reversed the conviction.[101] The Court was put in the precarious position of having to interfere, only one year after *Miller*, with a state's interpretation of its own community standards. Therefore, the Supreme Court made it clear that the locality does not necessarily have the last word in setting its own "community standards."[102]

The Supreme Court added another caveat to the law of obscenity when a New York City radio station played a recording of comedian George Carlin's monologue titled, "Filthy Words." The monologue dealt with various uses of "seven dirty words" that cannot be said over the airwaves. A man who heard the broadcast while driving with his son complained to the Federal Communications Commission [FCC]. Although the FCC did not find the monologue obscene, it was found to be "patently offensive" and not in the "public interest." It was banned from broadcast.

In a 5 to 4 decision, the U.S. Supreme Court upheld the FCC ruling. It found that the broadcast of "indecent material" was not protected by the First Amendment because it "confronts the citizen not only in public, but in the privacy of the home, where the individual's right to be left alone plainly outweighs the First Amendment rights of an intruder."[103] Also, the majority found that the broadcast media is "uniquely accessible" to children. Interestingly, indecent speech in a non-obscene book would still be protected by the First Amendment, unless it was broadcast over the airwaves. As the majority

AP/WIDE WORLD PHOTOS

Commuters bustle past Show World Center, a high-tech porn palace near Times Square in New York, 1993.

declared, "of all forms of communication, it is broadcasting that has received the most limited First Amendment protection," due to its intrusiveness and accessibility to children.[104]

The Supreme Court ruled in *New York v. Ferber*,[105] that states may prohibit the distribution of material that is not obscene, if it depicts sexual conduct by a juvenile. In its decision, the Court made yet another exception to the *Miller* standard:

> The test for child pornography is separate from the obscenity standard enunciated in *Miller* . . . A trier of fact need not find that the material appeals to the prurient interest of the average person; it is not required that sexual conduct portrayed be done so in a patently offensive manner; and the material at issue need not be considered as a whole.[106]

Therefore, the portrayal of children in *any type* of material dealing with sexual conduct can be defined by the states as obscene, regardless of the *Miller* guidelines.

Finally, the U.S. Supreme Court invalidated a portion of a Washington State obscenity statute in *Brockett v. Spokane Arcades* and its companion case *Eikenberry v. J-R Distributors*.[107] The law included, as part of its definition of obscenity, material that incites "lust or lasciviousness." It was held that "lust" connotes a "normal interest in sex." Therefore, that part of the statute was struck down, because it did not appeal to the "prurient interest."

It can be seen that, once again, a state's interpretation of obscenity law according to "community standards" is ultimately subject to concurrence by the U.S. Supreme Court. As one analysis concluded,

> [a] major myth fostered by the Court is that obscenity can be constitutionally controlled at the local level using local standards. . . . Try as it might, the Supreme Court, under the present approach, cannot escape the need to impose national standards to measure national rights and protections and, in the end, to act as a national censorship board.[108]

The inability of the Court to refrain from continually altering the application of such terms as "serious value," "prurient interest," and "community standards" set forth in *Miller* illustrates the inadequacy of that definition of obscenity. The uncertainty and continuing flux in determining the legal limits of obscenity undoubtedly has affected prosecutions for violations of these laws.

The Attorney General's Commission on Pornography found a "lack of effective enforcement of obscenity laws throughout most parts of the country."[109] This "striking underenforcement" was illustrated by the fact that only 100 individuals were indicted (and 71 convicted) for violation of federal obscenity laws in the eight years preceding the Commission's report.[110]

Some of the blame for this lackluster record was blamed on the low priority given obscenity cases in comparison to other crimes, although the Commission "reject[ed] the view" that a new legal definition of obscenity is needed.[111]

Pornography: I Didn't Know the Model was a Minor

While legislatures and courts continue to struggle with legal definitions of obscenity, there are people making a profit from manufacturing and distributing explicit depictions of sex in books, magazines, videos, and computer software. These people are part of organized crime to the extent they fulfill the definition in Chapter 1, i.e., as part of a continuing criminal enterprise.

A common defense to charges of obscenity is failure to know that the depictions are obscene, or failure to know the models or performers used are minors. Keep in mind, that when minors are used, it does not matter if the pornography exceeds the limits of obscenity to be held criminally liable (see the case in the previous section).

In 1994, the U.S. Supreme Court heard a landmark case involving an alleged violation of the *Protection of Children Against Sexual Exploitation Act* of 1977. This federal law prohibits "knowingly" manufacturing, distributing, or receiving" a visual depiction of "a minor engaging in sexually explicit conduct."[112]

In this case, Rubin Gottesman owned and operated *X-Citement Video*. Undercover police posed as pornography retailers in a sting operation. During the course of this investigation, the media revealed that actress Traci Lords appeared in pornographic films before she was 18 years old. An undercover police officer asked *X-Citement Video* for these videos, and Gottesman sold the officer 49 videotapes featuring Lords before her 18th birthday. Two months later, Gottesman shipped eight more tapes of Lords to the undercover officer in Hawaii.[113]

The two transactions resulted in federal charges against Gottesman and *X-Citement Video* for violating the child pornography act. The defendants argued that the child pornography act is unconstitutional because it does not require that a person *knew* a model or performer was a minor. The U.S. Supreme Court held that the law is constitutional. It "rejects the most natural grammatical reading" of the law, and concluded that a person may be held liable under this law as long as he or she *both* knowingly manufacture, distribute, or receive a depiction of explicit sexual conduct *and* know that depiction is of a minor.[114] Without such knowledge, the Court argued, a drug store that develops film could be held liable for returning photos or for delivering them. On the other hand, proving such knowledge makes it harder to enforce the law. In this case, however, Gottesman knew Traci Lords was underage, so his conviction was affirmed.[115]

The priority given to both prostitution and pornography cases has not been high, especially in terms of its relationship to organized crime. The President's Crime Commission Task Force on Organized Crime, reporting 30 years ago, concluded prostitution plays "a small and declining role in organized crime's operations." This was because prostitution is "difficult to organize and discipline is hard to maintain."[116] Also, a few important convictions of organized crime figures in prostitution cases in the 1930s and 1940s were believed to have a deterrent effect. In recent years, the situation appears to have changed little. The President's Commission on Organized Crime, reporting 10 years ago, gave little explicit attention to prostitution and pornography. A report on "The Income of Organized Crime," completed for the Commission concluded that approximately 20 percent of illegal income from prostitution is related to organized crime.[117] No estimates were made for pornography.

The Attorney General's Commission on Pornography concluded that organized crime "exerts substantial influence and control over the obscenity industry," although it also found "a number of significant producers and distributors are not members" of organized crime groups.[118] These rather contradictory findings summarize the confused state of knowledge in this area. While no one rejects the idea that organized crime is involved in the prostitution and pornography businesses, there is little evidence or consensus regarding precisely how much of it is produced or controlled by organized crime groups.

Extortion

Extortion is an offense that is often associated with organized crime. It involves obtaining property from another using future threats of physical injury, property damage, or exposure to ridicule or criminal charges. Extortion is distinguished from robbery in that robbery is theft using threats of *immediate* harm. An actual case helps to illustrate the scope of the crime of extortion.

Jobs for Sale

The case *United States v. Capo*[119] involved a scheme to sell jobs at Eastman Kodak Company in Rochester, New York. When production needs increased during the 1980s, a Kodak employment counselor, John Baron (an unindicted co-conspirator who testified at trial for the government), began hiring new employees. Because the standard hiring procedure was "laborious and time-consuming," Baron began accepting lists of prospective employees, as well as applications, from supervisors, managers, and other Kodak employees. This practice of hiring from this "referral list" was

The scenario that follows describes an actual fact situation, where the courts had to determine whether the laws involving illegal gambling applied. Resolution of this scenario requires proper application of the legal principles discussed in this chapter.

The Case of Poker for Profit

Undercover police officer Russo attempted to conduct a gambling investigation in Erie, Pennsylvania. In his undercover role, he attempted to enter what he believed to be an illegal gambling operation on the second floor of Dominick's Restaurant.

He was stopped by Lou, and told to wait. Some time later, Billy approached Russo and questioned him about his background and past poker-playing, apparently in an effort to see if he was a police officer. Billy permitted Russo to observe the game that night, taking him to the second floor of the restaurant through three locked doors, protected by buzzers, a surveillance camera, and a look-out.

Once inside, undercover officer Russo observed about 10 people playing poker. Twenty to 25 hands were played each hour, and the "pot" (i.e., total amount wagered) averaged $300 per hand. Two men served drinks and cigarettes, and Lou, Billy, and two others served as "cut men." The cut men took the "rake" from each pot (i.e., a percentage given to the person who runs the game for overhead and profit.) Officer Russo left the game at 4:40 a.m., and 15 people were still playing.

Officer Russo returned and played poker at that location five times over the next six months. He noticed that several of the same people acted as doormen or cutmen during these games.

Ultimately, Billy admitted that he had been operating the game for two years, and that he earned $200 to $300 a night. He also stated that Lou worked for him.

Questions:

1. Can Billy be convicted of running an illegal gambling enterprise under federal law?

2. How does the fact that Billy made only $200 to $300 per game affect his liability?

3. Federal law requires involvement by at least five people. If at no time there were five of the people the same at any given game, how would this affect Billy's liability?

"apparently known to Baron's superiors, and tacitly approved by them." At trial, it became known that prospective employees paid $500 to $1,000 to be hired.

Defendant Robert Capo, for example, was a barber in the area who told friends and customers he could help them get jobs at Kodak for $1,000. On several occasions he received these payments which were passed through intermediaries to John Baron. Each of these applicants was hired.

An inquiry by the FBI was begun and a grand jury convened to investigate allegations concerning the selling of jobs. In testimony before the grand jury the defendants attempted to deny the allegations, or to cast the blame on one another. At one point, "Baron threw several of the gifts he had received, including a stereo and two [video] recorders, into a dumpster" to escape the attention of the investigators.

The conspiracy to extort money for jobs ultimately collapsed when several people, some of whom had paid for jobs but were not hired, testified before the grand jury. For example, FBI agents interviewed one of the codefendants about three $500 checks from two job applicants. The defendant [Walter] told them he had worked on the car of one, charging $1,000, and the other $500 was payment for winning the Super Bowl pool. When it was pointed out that the $500 check was written prior to the Super Bowl, Walter stated, "Well, maybe she knew I was going to win." When the FBI later questioned the two job applicants, they denied any involvement in a Super Bowl pool, or that Walter had worked on her car.

On appeal from their convictions, one of the claims made by the defendants was that their conduct did not amount to extortion. The U.S. Court of Appeals disagreed.

> The essence of extortion . . . is the extraction of property from another through the wrongful use of fear. The victim's fear need not be fear of bodily harm but may be fear of a loss that is purely economic.[120]

Furthermore, the Court held that the federal extortion law [*the Hobbs Act*] "has been held [in prior cases] to reach conduct threatening the loss of a status that would produce future assets." The Court explained the application of the law in this case.

> The loss of an opportunity to obtain employment as a wage or salary earner constitutes no less an "economic loss" than does the loss of an opportunity to obtain a one-time contract for the supply of materials or services. The amounts at stake for the victim may differ; the time periods during which the victims would receive benefits may differ. But the nature of the loss is the same. We conclude that the fear that a job opportunity will be lost is the type of fear whose extortionate exploitation is within the reach of the Hobbs Act.[121]

As a result, the U.S. Court of Appeals upheld the convictions for extortion in this job-selling scheme at Kodak. Extortion may be defined, therefore, as purposely obtaining property from another, with his consent, that is induced by wrongful use of force or fear, or under color of official right. Extortion is sometimes called blackmail. It is clear that the crime of extortion characterizes the infiltration of legitimate business by organized crime, in the same way that conspiracy characterizes the systematic provision of illicit goods and services.

Under Color of Official Right

Extortion "under color of official right" involves misconduct by government officials. In these cases, a public official solicits bribes to influence his or her exercise of duties.[122] Under the Hobbs Act property is "extorted" under law when a public official "asserts that his official conduct will be controlled" due to an action or promise. These actions or promises might include a favorable vote, failure to write a ticket, or other miscarriage of official responsibility.[123]

In a Louisiana case, a bail bondsman and local police department were charged with extorting money from travelers who passed through town in exchange for reducing or dismissing DWI charges.[124] In New York, inspectors for the New York City Taxi and Limousine Commission pled guilty to extortion for taking bribes for overlooking defects and certifying inspections for taxicabs that were never inspected. Most were sentenced to two or three years in prison, followed by supervised release and restitution.[125] Clearly, the law of extortion applies to a variety of behaviors all of which involve obtaining property by way of *coercion* or *threats*, implied or explicit, of some future harm.

Racketeering

The crime of racketeering was established in 1970 as part of the Organized Crime Control Act. The *Racketeer Influenced and Corrupt Organizations* (RICO) section of that Act makes it unlawful to acquire, operate, or receive income from an *enterprise* through a *pattern* of *racketeering activity*. Racketeering is defined broadly in the federal statute and most felonies suffice for liability, if conducted as part of an enterprise and pattern. The pattern is two or more felonies committed within a 10-year period (excluding any periods of imprisonment). An enterprise can be any individual or group that commits these crimes.

Therefore, the RICO law attaches extended penalties (up to 20 years imprisonment) for crimes committed in "racketeering" fashion, i.e., as part of a criminal enterprise and as part of a pattern. These RICO provisions

Critical Thinking Exercise

The scenario that follows describes an actual fact situation, where the courts had to determine whether or not the laws involving extortion applied. Resolution of this scenario requires proper application of the legal principles discussed in this chapter.

The Case of Collecting a Debt

Isaac loaned money to Melvin several times over the course of two years. The amounts usually ranged from $5,000 to $30,000, and the total amount loaned was approximately $100,000 over the span. At the time of each loan, Melvin agreed to repay the loan amount plus 20 percent interest within 10 weeks.

Melvin made periodic payments, but had difficulty meeting his commitments to Isaac. Isaac confronted him on several occasions and stated he would use physical force if Melvin failed to repay the loans, even if Isaac had to "do 20 years." Isaac's threats caused Melvin to make out a will, buy a gun for protection, and carry it when he met with him. A third party recorded some of Isaac's threats during a collection attempt.

Questions:

1. Given the facts above, can Isaac be found liable for extortion?

2. Assume that Isaac only intimidated Melvin, but never struck him. How would that affect his liability?

3. Assume that the interest rate charged by Isaac was within the legal limit allowed by law. How does that affect his liability?

were established to attack organized crime groups and their operations. Chapter 9 provides information on the use of RICO as a prosecution tool.

Hidden Ownership and Skimming Profits

The precise scope and meaning of "enterprise," "pattern," and activities that suffice for "racketeering" have been developed through a series of court challenges and interpretations. Although passed in 1970, the RICO law was used infrequently until the 1980s, probably due to its complexity and the need to develop complicated and detailed cases to prosecute under these provisions. The court challenges to the law have upheld its provisions and have further broadened its scope. A few examples illustrate this.

Matthew Ianniello and Benjamin Cohen were part of a group that skimmed profits from bars and restaurants they owned in New York City. These bars and restaurants were ostensibly owned by others and liquor licenses were obtained in the names of others, but they were really "fronts" for Ianniello and Cohen. The skimming involved taking cash paid by customers and keeping it for themselves. This entailed keeping false accounting records (that under-counted the true income of the bars and restaurants), and filing false income and sales tax returns that also failed to reflect the actual income of these enterprises.[126]

Ianniello, Cohen, and their associates, were convicted of racketeering by violating the Racketeer Influenced and Corrupt Organization provisions of the Organized Crime Control Act. They were also convicted of mail fraud and tax evasion. They appealed, arguing that there must be "a combination of relationship and continuity between separate acts" in order to establish a "pattern" necessary for a RICO conviction. The U.S. Court of Appeals held, and the U.S. Supreme Court denied review, that when a person commits two felonies "that have the common purpose of furthering a continuing criminal enterprise with which that person is associated," the elements of "relatedness and continuity" are satisfied.[127] The convictions of Ianniello and Cohen were affirmed.

In another case, evidence at trial linked a defendant's involvement in stolen property transactions and a murder as part of a criminal enterprise, rather than as isolated incidents. It was found that the murder was performed to consolidate the power of the enterprise and enrich its members, and the stolen property was taken by an associate of the enterprise. This permitted a conviction under RICO.[128]

These court findings help to make clear the distinction between felonies committed as part of an ongoing criminal enterprise, and those isolated crimes that may be committed by a repeat offender. These cases show how the terms "racketeering," "pattern," and "enterprise" must be interrelated for a RICO conviction. It is necessary to show a person's law violations in association with a criminal enterprise ("racketeering"), the existence of the ongoing enterprise itself ("enterprise"), and that the offenses have a common purpose in furthering the enterprise ("pattern"). This illustrates the distinction between "street" crimes and organized crime. A habitual offender is not necessarily a RICO offender, if his or her offenses are unrelated to each other, or are not associated with an ongoing criminal enterprise. Therefore, many organized crime figures are also career criminals, but not all career criminals are members of organized crime, because their acts do not constitute racketeering.

I Didn't Know My Property was a Crackhouse

Growing concern about drugs has led to an attack on all its manifestations, including the places where people actually take the drugs. Congress passed the "Crackhouse" statute in response to negligent landlords who ignored or abandoned their property, allowing it to become a place where drug-users stayed, sold, bought, and ingested illegal narcotics.

The crackhouse statute prohibits "knowingly" maintaining "any place" for the purpose of manufacturing, distributing, or using controlled drugs. It also prohibits managing or controlling in any way a building or room "and knowingly and intentionally rent, lease, or make available for use with or without compensation" that property to manufacture, distribute or use drugs.[129]

Take the case of Randolph Lancaster who owned a house in Washington, D.C. Over the course of six months, the house was searched a number of times by several different law enforcement agencies. On each occasion, police found "large groups of individuals" inside with drugs and drug paraphernalia. Prosecuted under the "crackhouse" law, Lancaster was convicted for maintaining a crackhouse. He was sentenced to prison, and his house was seized by the government. His appeal challenging his conviction, and the constitutionality of the crackhouse law, was denied.[130]

In a related case, Mei-Fen Chen owned the Della Motel in Houston. She claimed she was unaware that drug transactions were taking place there, although four former tenants testified that she had witnessed drug transactions, alerted tenants when police were coming, and encouraged drug sales by providing storage, and loaning them money. Chen admitted seeing syringes in the parking lot of the motel, but claimed "she believed they came from a nearby hospital."[131] Prosecuted under the crackhouse law, she claimed she was unaware of drug transactions at her motel. The U.S. Court of Appeals held, however, "all the circumstances . . . support either a finding of actual knowledge or willful blindness on the part of Chen."[132]

These cases illustrate that the crackhouse law holds landlords and owners liable for what they know, or failed to know due to deliberate ignorance, about illegal activities occurring. In essence, the crackhouse law extends the concept of racketeering to those who provide the *forum* to engage in criminal activity, in addition to those who actually carry it out. This extension of complicity in ongoing criminal activity is designed to curtail that activity by reducing the number of "safe havens" that exist for it.

The Ephemeral Nature of Criminal Enterprise

Unlike legitimate business, criminal enterprises are secretive by their nature. It is sometimes possible to arrest a criminal for multiple crimes, but it is more difficult to link them together as part of a pattern connected to an ongoing enterprise.

Consider the case of Albert Tocco, the alleged "boss" of Chicago Heights. He and others, extorted money from people who were engaged in criminal activity, such as chop shops that disassembled stolen cars, illegal gambling operations, and houses of prostitution. In some ways, these are desirable targets for extortion because the victims are unwilling to go to the police for fear of exposing their own criminal activity. Based on the testimony of informants, Tocco was implicated in numerous acts of extortion, and also in four murders. He was ultimately located after fleeing to Greece, returned to the United States, convicted of 34 crimes, and sentenced to 200 years imprisonment.[133]

Given this plethora of criminal activity, it is still difficult to put it all together. Even with the testimony of former "insiders," electronic surveillance, and undercover officers in some cases, the evidence of an ongoing enterprise is often fragmentary. The RICO provisions have extended penalties, as noted above, and this offers an incentive for prosecutors to attempt to connect individual crimes to something larger. In the Tocco case above, the U.S. Court of Appeals held that "the government is entitled to try to provide all the racketeering acts making up the pattern of racketeering, so that it may obtain a conviction even if the jury rejects some of its theories."[134] Therefore, even if a jury ultimately rejects the existence of an ongoing criminal enterprise, it may still convict on the individual crimes charged.

RICO is a sweeping law with far-reaching consequences for the defendant. On the other hand, it is a tool for the government to fight the "organizations" that maintain organized crime, rather than prosecution of individuals for isolated acts. It was observed more than 60 years ago that "racketeering cannot exist without protection."[135] The RICO provisions attempt to remove some of the protection that surrounds criminal enterprises by exposing those involved to extended penalties beyond that entailed by the crimes themselves. The RICO law provides civil remedies as well. These are discussed in Chapter 9.

Summary

This chapter has defined the scope of organized crime activity. Based on the typology of organized crime presented in Chapter 1, it can be seen that the provision of illicit goods, illicit services, and the infiltration of legitimate business can be characterized by the crimes of conspiracy, extortion, and racketeering. In addition, the substantive elements of the offenses involving illegal drugs, stolen property, gambling, loansharking, and sex were detailed.

Organized crime engenders a plethora of activity, but this chapter has shown that it can be categorized and defined in explicit terms. The nature of the offenses discussed here provides the groundwork for the remainder of the book. The causes, investigation, prosecution, defense, and sentencing of organized crime, explained in subsequent chapters, rely on a specific understanding of organized criminal activity itself.

References to Chapter 2

[1] *United States v. Auerbach and Helish*, 913 F.2d 407 (7th Cir. 1990) at 409.

[2] Ibid. at 409-410.

[3] at 414-5 and *United States v. Anderson*, 896, F.2d 1076 (7th Cir. 1990).

[4] *United States v. Douglas*, 818 F.2d 1317 (7th Cir. 1987) and *United States v. Marks*, 816 F.2d 1207 (7th Cir. 1987).

[5] *United States v. Auerbach and Helish*, at 415.

[6] *United States v. Bourjaily*, 781 F.2d 539 (6th Cir. 1986), 197 S. Ct. 2775 (1987).

[7] at 544.

[8] at 545.

[9] From the general conspiracy statute, 18 U.S.C. 371.

[10] *United States v. Shabani*, 993 F.2d 1419 (9th Cir. 1993).

[11] at 1420.

[12] at 1422.

[13] Comprehensive Drug Abuse Prevention and Control Act of 1970, Pub. L. 91-513, 84 Stat. 1236, at 1265. This Act was amended by the Anti-Drug Abuse Act of 1988, Pub. L. 100-690, 102 Stat. 4377, 21 U.S.C. 846, but the drug conspiracy elements were not altered.

[14] Organized Crime Control Act of 1970, Pub. L. 91-452, 84 Stat. 922, 18 U.S.C. 1511.

[15] *United States v. Shabani*, 114 S. Ct. 1048.

[16] at 1052.

[17] *United States v. Schweihs and Daddino*, 971 F.2d 1302 (7th Cir. 1992) at 1309.

[18] at 1323.

[19] Ibid.

[20] *United States v. Patel*, 879 F.2d 294 (7th Cir. 1989), *cert. denied*, 110 S. Ct. 1318.

[21] *United States v. Schweihs and Daddino*, 971 F.2d 1302 (7th Cir. 1992) at 1323.

[22] *United States v. Teffera*, 985 F.2d 1082 (D.C. Cir. 1993).

[23] at 1085.

[24] See *United States v. Lam Kwong-Wah*, 924 F.2d 298 (D.C. Cir. 1991).

[25] *United States v. Raper*, 676 F.2d 841 (D.C. Cir. 1982).

[26] *United States v. Teffera*, 985 F.2d 1086 (D.C. Cir. 1993).

[27] at 1087.

[28] Ibid.

[29] at 1088.

[30] Ibid.

[31] Ibid.

[32] See, for example, the biography of Henry Hill, whose life was depicted in the film *Goodfellas*. Nicholas Pileggi, *Wiseguys* (New York: Simon and Schuster, 1985).

[33] *United States v. Rosa*, 17 F.2d 1531 (2d Cir. 1994).

[34] *United States v. Rosa*, 17 F.2d 1538 (2d Cir. 1994).

[35] Ibid.

[36] at 1537.

[37] 18 U.S.C. Sec. 2315.

[38] at 1547.

[39] *United States v. Stuart*, 22 F.3d 76 (3d Cir. 1994).

[40] at 81.

[41] at 82.

[42] Mark 15:24, Luke 23:34, John 19:24.

[43] Henry Chafetz, *Play the Devil* (New York: Potter Publishing, 1960), p. 8.

[44] John Rosecrance, *Gambling Without Guilt: The Legitimation of an American Pastime* (Belmont, CA: Brooks/Cole, 1988), p. 12.

[45] Ibid., pp. 12-13.

[46] Gilbert Geis, *Not the Law's Business* (New York: Schocken, 1979), p. 223.

[47] *Play the Devil*, p. 17.

[48] *Gambling Without Guilt*, p. 13.

[49] Herbert Ashbury, *Sucker's Progress: An Informal History of Gambling from the Colonies to Canfield* [First Published in 1938] (Montclair, NJ: Patterson Smith, 1969), pp. 76-78.

[50] William H.P. Robertson, *The History of Thoroughbred Racing in America* (Englewood Cliffs, NJ: Prentice Hall, 1964), p. 8; Stephen Longstreet, *Win or Lose: A Social History of Gambling* (Indianapolis: Bobbs-Merrill, 1977).

[51] *Play the Devil*, p. 13.

[52] *Win or Lose*, p. 37.

[53] Ibid., p. 37.

[54] Jerome Skolnick, *House of Cards* (Boston: Little, Brown, 1978).

[55] John S. Ezell, *Fortune's Merry Wheel* (Cambridge, MA: Harvard University Press, 1960).

[56] John M. Findlay, *People of Chance* (New York: Oxford University Press, 1986).

[57] *Play the Devil*, p. 94.

[58] *Gambling Without Guilt*, p. 23.

[59] *Sucker's Progress*, pp. 88-106.

60 *Gambling Without Guilt*, p. 24-5.

61 *Gambling Without Guilt*, p. 36-7.

62 *Sucker's Progress*, p. 451.

63 *Gambling Without Guilt*, p. 41.

64 Ibid., p. 38.

65 *Fortune's Merry Wheel*, p. 279.

66 *United States v. Edge Broadcasting Co.*, 113 S. Ct. 2696 (1993) at 2703.

67 Ibid.

68 Ibid., pp. 2703-2704.

69 U.S.C. Sec. 1955(b)(1).

70 U.S.C. Sec. 1955(b)(1)(iii).

71 *United States v. Murray*, 928 F.2d 1242 (1st Cir. 1991) at 1246.

72 Ibid., at 1249.

73 H.R.Rep. No.91-1549, 91st Congress, 2d Session (1970) and 1970 U.S.C. *Congressional and Administrative News*, at 4007, 4029.

74 *United States v. Follin*, 979 F.2d 369 (5th Cir. 1992) at 372.

75 Ibid., at 373.

76 *United States v. Bridges*, 493 F.2d 918 (5th Cir. 1974) at 922.

77 *United States v. Follin*, 979 F.2d (5th Cir. 1992) at 373.

78 Ibid.

79 *United States v. Eufrasio*, 935 F.2d 553 (3d Cir. 1991) at 559.

80 18 U.S.C. Sec. 1961(6).

81 *United States v. Eufrasio*, 935 F.2d 553 (3d Cir. 1991) at 562.

82 Ibid. at 576.

83 Ibid.

84 Ibid. at 577.

85 *United States v. Holcomb*, 797 F.2d 1320 (5th Cir. 1986).

86 18 U.S.C. Sec. 2422.

87 *United States v. Holcomb*, 797 F.2d 1327.

88 Ibid.

89 *United States v. Sigalow*, 812 F.2d 783 (2d Cir. 1987).

90 18 U.S.C. Sec. 1952.

91 *United States v. Sigalow*, 812 F.2d 786.

92 93 S. Ct. 2607.

[93] at 2611-12.

[94] at 2612-13.

[95] at 2615.

[96] at 2615.

[97] at 2618.

[98] at 2619.

[99] 93 S. Ct. 2628 (1973).

[100] at 2621. For a review of this evidence, see Edward Donnerstein, Daniel Linz, and Steven Penrod, *The Question of Pornography: Research Findings and Policy Implications* (New York: The Free Press, 1987).

[101] *Jenkins v. Georgia*, 94 S. Ct. 2750.

[102] Harvey L. Zuckman and Martin J. Gaynes, *Mass Communications Law* second edition (St. Paul, MN: West Publishing, 1983).

[103] *FCC v. Pacifica Foundation*, 98 S. Ct. 3026, at 3040.

[104] Ibid.

[105] 102 S. Ct. 3348.

[106] at 3358.

[107] 105 S. Ct. 2794.

[108] Zuckman and Gaynes, p. 141.

[109] U.S. Attorney General's Commission on Pornography, *Final Report* (Washington, DC: U.S. Government Printing Office, 1986), p. 366.

[110] Ibid., p. 367.

[111] at 366.

[112] 18 U.S.C. 2252.

[113] *United States v. X-Citement Video*, 114 S. Ct. 8061 (1994).

[114] at 8601.

[115] Tony Mauro, "Burden of Proof Made More Difficult in Child-Porn Cases," *USA Today*, (November 30, 1994), p. 3.

[116] President's Commission on Law Enforcement and Administration of Justice, *Task Force Report: Organized Crime* (Washington, DC: U.S. Government Printing Office, 1967), p. 4.

[117] Sima Fishman, Kathleen Rodenrys, and George Schink, "The Income of Organized Crime," in President's Commission on Organized Crime, *Organized Crime Today* (Washington, DC: U.S. Government Printing Office, 1987), p. 463.

[118] U.S. Attorney General's Commission on Pornography, *Final Report* (Washington, DC: U.S. Government Printing Office, 1986), p. 1053.

[119] 791 F.2d 1054 (2d Cir. 1986).

[120] at 1061.

[121] at 1062.

[122] *United States v. Allen*, 10 F.3d 405 (7th Cir. 1993).

[123] 18 U.S.C.A. Sec. 1951; *McCormick v. United States*, 111 S. Ct. 2807 (1991).

[124] *United States v. Stephens*, 964 F.2d 424 (5th Cir. 1992).

[125] *United States v. Abbadessa*, 848 F. Supp. 369 (E.D.N.Y. 1994).

[126] *United States v. Ianniello and Cohen*, 808 F.2d 184 (2nd Cir. 1986), *cert. denied*, 107 S. Ct. 3229.

[127] at 192.

[128] *United States v. Minicone*, 960 F.2d 1099 (2d Cir. 1992), *cert. denied*, 112 S. Ct. 1511.

[129] 21 U.S.C. Sec. 856.

[130] *United States v. Lancaster*, 968 F.2d 1250 (D.C. Cir. 1992).

[131] *United States v. Chen*, 913 F.2d 183 (5th Cir. 1990) at 186.

[132] at 192.

[133] *United States v. Crockett and Tocco*, 979 F.2d 1204 (7th Cir. 1992).

[134] at 1211.

[135] Henry Barrett Chamberlin, "Some Observations Concerning Organized Crime," *Journal of Criminal Law and Criminology*, vol. 22, no. 5 (January, 1932), p. 667.

Chapter 3

Causes of
Organized Crime

It is not the thief who is hanged, but one who is caught stealing.

Czech Proverb

The causes of crime comprise one of the two fundamental issues in the study of criminology and criminal justice. (The other issue is what to do with offenders.) A large body of literature has developed over the centuries that attempts to explain the existence of crime. The bad news is that crime exists in all societies of all types. As Emile Durkheim pointed out a century ago, "Crime is not present only in the majority of societies of one particular species but in all societies of all types. There is no society that is not confronted with the problem of criminality."[1]

The good news is that levels of crime vary dramatically both within and among nations. The United States is at the high end of crime rates around the world, and there is great variation in crime even within the United States. Therefore, there is room for improvement and there are examples within the United States and around the world to study.

Is Organized Crime Unique?

Unfortunately, very little attention has been paid to the causes of organized crime as a special kind of criminal behavior. As we shall see, some have argued that explanations of crime should be universal, while others argue that different manifestations of crime may require different explanations. In either case, it is obvious that different people commit different crimes for different reasons. Therefore, more than one explanation is likely needed to explain the crimes of many diverse people.

Organized crime is distinguished from most other forms of crime in that it is usually a *career pattern*. Most organized criminals engage in persistent criminal activity over a long period of time. This is not the case with most types of crime. Studies of delinquency have found (and common experience suggests), for example, that most juveniles engage in delinquency but very few become frequent or serious offenders.[2] Furthermore, the vast majority do not go on to become adult offenders.

Organized crime is also distinguished from other kinds of criminal behavior in its organization. As explained in Chapter 1, most criminal behavior is spontaneous or involves very little planning. Organized crime, on the other hand, *requires organization* in order for it to be effective and successful (especially as a long-term activity).

The long-term nature of organized crimes, together with the organization required for the acts themselves, suggest that organized crime is unique as a criminal choice. White-collar crime requires organization, but it is almost never a career pattern. Some street crimes are committed by career criminals, but these offenses usually require little organization. These examples point to important distinctions between organized crime and other forms of criminal behavior.

The question remains, however, as to whether the *causes* of organized crime are different from these other types of crime. This chapter offers a four-part typology of existing explanations of crime: positivism, classicism, structural, and ethical. Actual case studies will be used in an effort to show how these explanations of crime may, or may not, apply to individual instances of organized crime.

Positivism: Social and Economic Influences

Positivism in criminology corresponds with the rise of social science and the scientific method in the late 1800s. Positivism looks to internal or external influences as the cause of criminal behavior. Many attempts to explain crime and delinquency have been attempted over the last century, employing some combination of psychological, social, economic, and biological factors, although most rely on social factors.[3] All these theories have in common the assumption that changes in these conditions will reduce or prevent criminal behavior.

None of these theories specifically addressed the two features unique to organized crime: a career criminal pattern and organization in the crimes themselves. The theory that comes closest, however, is that of Richard Cloward and Lloyd Ohlin. Their book, *Delinquency and Opportunity*, attempts to formulate a theory of delinquent gangs.[4] Although they focus on juvenile delinquency, their theory has direct implications for organized crime. The authors argue, as Robert Merton did before them,[5] that crime results from lack of access to legitimate means (i.e., "blocked opportunity") for achieving social goals (e.g., making a good living, having a family). They also believe, however, that even *illegitimate* means for obtaining social goals are not available to everyone. As a result, some lower-class neighborhoods provide greater opportunity for illegal gain than do others.

Cloward and Ohlin conclude that three types of criminal subcultures develop when young people withdraw legitimacy from middle-class standards (i.e., social goals) because they lack the means to achieve them (e.g., unequal employment opportunities or inability to go to college). The three subcultures they identify are: criminal, conflict, and retreatist. The criminal subculture is the result when these young people associate with, and go on to become, adult criminals. The conflict subculture is where fighting gangs develop and status is obtained by violence and coercion. The retreatist subculture is comprised of those who lack opportunity or the ability to gain status in the criminal or conflict subcultures. These people drop out and may become drug addicts.[6]

Most relevant to the causes of organized crime is the criminal subculture. Cloward and Ohlin provide the example of the "fence," a dealer in stolen property, who exists in many lower-class neighborhoods. The fence often "encourages delinquent activities," by leading young people to steal "in the most lucrative and least risky directions." They believe the same point "may be made of junk dealers in some areas," and "racketeers who permit minors to run errands."[7] Therefore, the "apprentice criminal" moves from one status to another in the "illegitimate opportunity system," developing "an ever-widening set of relationships with members of the semi-legitimate and legitimate world." In this way, the young person becomes socialized into the criminal subculture, a process made possible, according to Cloward and Ohlin, by blocked opportunities for success in legitimate society.

If a person cannot successfully gain access or status in the criminal subculture, "the possibility of a stable, protected criminal style of life is effectively precluded."[8] Therefore, blocked opportunity does not lead directly to a life of crime, according to this theory. Instead, there must exist *both* opportunities to form the relationships with the criminal subculture, as well as the personal ability to gain status in this milieu. This merging of age-groups and "value integration" is necessary for young people to become part of the adult criminal subculture. James O'Kane found this theory of "blocked opportunity" useful in explaining the organized crime involvement of ethnic minorities in the United States.[9]

Other sociological theories of crime use similar techniques to explain how a young person becomes an adult criminal. One theory places emphasis on the "delinquent traditions" found in lower-class neighborhoods.[10] Another theory gives most importance to "learning" through personal associations that crime is acceptable behavior.[11] Still another points to peer group pressure, and how young people attempt to "neutralize" the guilt they feel about their criminal behavior by rationalizing it.[12] Cloward and Ohlin's theory makes an effort to address each of these factors at least implicitly, and therefore is the most complete as a positivistic explanation for the emergence of an organized criminal.

The life histories of organized crime figures often show a pattern similar to that described by Cloward and Ohlin. Henry Hill, whose life has been the subject of a best-selling biography (*Wiseguy*) and film (*Goodfellas*), is illustrative. Henry came from a large, working-class family in a poor neighborhood in Brooklyn. He took his first job at age 12 at a cabstand across the street. It was there he was socialized into the criminal subculture. He was taught how to pass counterfeit $20 bills, deal in stolen property, illegal gambling, and a host of other illegal activities.

> At Christmas, Tuddy [Vito Vario] taught me how to drill holes in the trunks of junk Christmas trees he'd get for nothing, and then I'd stuff the holes with loose branches. I'd stuff so many branches into those holes that even those miserable spindly trees looked full. Then we'd sell them for premium prices, usually at night and mostly around the Euclid Avenue subway stop. It took a day or two before the branches came loose and began to fall apart. The trees would collapse even faster once they were weighed down with decorations.[13]

The scams ranged from small to large, but they had common elements: he was taught by adult criminals, and his acceptance grew as he performed small errands well for these people. From the perspective of Cloward and Ohlin's positivistic approach, Henry's ultimate entrance into the criminal subculture of organized crime grew directly from the limited opportunities he faced in his neighborhood and the countervailing possibility for success in the criminal subculture just across the street. In the words of Henry Hill:

> To me being a wiseguy was better than being President of the United States. It meant power among people that had no privileges. To be a wiseguy was to own the world. I dreamed about being a wiseguy that way other kids dreamed about being doctors or movie stars, or firemen or ballplayers.[14]

The problem with Cloward and Ohlin's explanation, and all positivistic explanations of criminal behavior, is that they place too much emphasis on external (or internal) influences on behavior, and give too little consideration to the criminal decision. That is to say, despite all influences in one's life, a person must still make a *criminal decision* to violate the law. Poor neighborhoods, bad associates, and improper supervision of young people certainly make it difficult to become a law-abiding adult, yet it happens all the time. So in some ways, positivistic explanations of crime beg the question. There is a long list of influences that help us to *understand* why a person may have chosen to commit crimes, but this does not *determine* that decision. Therefore, positivistic explanations point to conditions that make a criminal lifestyle an easy choice, but they do not explain *why or how* that choice is made in the face of competing choices, such as redoubling one's energies in a noncriminal direction.

Classicism: Hedonism and the Odds of Apprehension

In many ways, classicism is the converse of positivism. Rather than focusing on influential factors that *contribute* to crime, as positivism does, classicists see crime the result of a *free-will decision* to choose it. This free-will decision is guided by the pain-pleasure principle: that is, people always will act in a way that maximizes pleasure and minimizes pain.

Classicists believe that people are hedonistic, and will naturally seek pleasure at every opportunity and avoid pain. The way to prevent crime in this view is through deterrence. Criminal behavior is prevented, therefore, when the pain associated with criminal conduct (i.e., likelihood of apprehension and punishment) is greater than the pleasure derived from the crime (usually economic gain).

Michael Gottfredson and Travis Hirschi offer a classical explanation that they intend to explain "all crime," including organized crime.[15] They believe that crime results from "the tendency of individuals to pursue short-term gratification in the most direct way with little consideration for the long-term consequences of their acts." This tendency is associated with impulsiveness, aggression, and lack of empathy. They base this theory on the classical assumption that "human behavior is motivated by the self-interested pursuit of pleasure and avoidance of pain."[16] Following the classical view, the only effective way to prevent criminal behavior is through the threat of apprehension and punishment that will outweigh (at least in the mind of the offender) the pleasure derived from the criminal conduct.

The problem with this theory, and the classical viewpoint in general, is an overemphasis on the impact of penalties for crime prevention. Deterrence is not very effective in criminal justice. Second, the hedonism, or "tendencies" toward short-term gratification, must come from somewhere. If they are innate, what prevents the majority of us from engaging in a life of crime? If only some of us have these tendencies, where do they come from? Classical explanations have difficulty with these questions.

Another example drawn from the biography of Henry Hill illustrates these points. First, it can be argued that, despite his social surroundings, Henry Hill made a free-will choice to engage in a life of crime that was guided by the pain-pleasure principle. Before he worked at the cabstand in Brooklyn, Henry had made observations and drawn conclusions about the advantages of a criminal lifestyle.

> The men at the cabstand were not like anyone else from the neighborhood. They wore silk suits in the morning and would drape the fenders of their cars with handkerchiefs before leaning back for a talk. He had watched them double-park their cars and never get tickets, even when they parked smack in front of a fire hydrant . . . And the men at the cabstand were rich. They

> flashed wads of $20 bills as round as softballs and they sported diamond pinky rings the size of walnuts. The sight of all that wealth, and power, and girth was intoxicating.[17]

This suggests Henry Hill was making a conscious choice to join the organized crime group, due to the benefits (pleasure) it would bring. When his father objected to his employment at the cabstand the following year, Henry "wouldn't listen to what he said." His father "worked hard his whole life" as an electrical worker, but could never get ahead. Henry said, "we could never move out of our crummy three-bedroom house jammed with seven kids," and he decided, "my old man's life wasn't going to be my life."[18] He chose the criminal lifestyle available at the cabstand. It can be seen that positivists focus on what factors might have *influenced* his decisionmaking, whereas classicists focus on the decision itself.

Classicists would also argue that Henry Hill's life of crime may never have gotten started, or would have been quite brief, if the odds of apprehension and punishment been greater. This may be true, although the odds of criminal apprehension for unplanned, street crimes reported to police, such as burglary and larceny, is only about 15 percent. Given the fact that most of these crimes are never reported to police, the true odds are less than 10 percent.[19] It is reasonable to surmise that the odds of apprehension for *planned* crimes, such as those Henry Hill was committing, are even lower. Compounding this is the *volume* of criminal activity committed by career criminals. At one time, Henry Hill saw several police cars outside a lounge he frequented, so he went instead to his girlfriend's house. He did not know what he was wanted for until he turned on the radio.[20] The odds of apprehension were so low, he had engaged in a great deal of criminal activity without ever being caught. When people like him are ultimately caught, the penalty or prison time are seen as a long-term cost of doing business, rather than a penalty for a specific act. Classicism places much importance on the free-will decision to engage in crime, but its solution (deterrence) in untenable, given the low odds of apprehension.

Structural: Capitalism and Arbitrary Laws

"It remains a matter of controversy whether it is the criminal structure that creates the need for illicit goods and services or whether, on the contrary, it is a widespread demand for these things that stimulates and nourishes the illegal activities of organised crime groups."[21] It is this conundrum that forms the basis for the structural view of crime causation. This approach focuses less on individual behavior and more on how acts come to be defined as criminal. Social, economic, and political circumstances cause certain behaviors to be defined as criminal, resulting in a great deal of "marginal" criminal behavior, according to the structuralists. Examples would include gambling, prostitution, loansharking, and pornography. Structuralists would argue that we *create* some of our own crime problem by prohibiting gambling *unless* the state is running the game, or disallowing prostitution *unless* it is sanctioned by the state, or lending money at high rates *unless* the high interest rate is approved by the state. These inconsistencies are viewed by structuralists as a mechanism by which we create illicit markets, and then prosecute people for catering to the demand that the state manufactured.

Structuralists also argue that the American capitalist ideology, that equates success with income accumulation, encourages people to disregard the rights of others who stand in their way. The line between a successful businessperson, a white-collar criminal, and an organized crime figure, according to this view, is narrow indeed, distinguished only by the *method* (legal or illegal) by which the money was obtained, and not by who may have been exploited in garnering it.

As Alan Block and William Chambliss explain, the structuralist perspective links capitalism and crime to class conflict.

> the structure of capitalism creates both the desire to consume and—for a large mass of people—an inability to earn the money necessary to purchase the items they have been taught to want . . . Another fundamental contradiction of capitalism derives from the fact that the division of a society into a ruling class that owns the means of production and a subservient class that works for wages leads to conflict between the two classes . . . It follows that as capitalism develops and conflicts between social classes continue . . . more and more acts will be defined as criminal and the amount of crime will increase.[22]

In this view, capitalism promotes organized crime by placing a premium on income generation, and the ensuing conflict between the working class and those who control the legitimate market. Crimes are created to control the working class, according to the structuralists.

If the capitalist ideology lies at the root of organized crime, it can be argued that socialist economies would have less organized crime. As Chapter 7 indicates, however, this is not the case. In his study of the Neapolitan Camorra in Italy, for example, Vincenzo Ruggerio argues that "one cannot assert that organised crime prospers where there is little sense of a state; on the contrary, it prospers where there is too much state, or at least where the state is present in formal bureaucratic details, routine, hypertrophied and predatory."[23] This may be true of organized crime that involves corruption of government processes, but the emergence of Cosa Nostra in Sicily argues the reverse: entrenched organized crime groups arose from the weak central government in Italy that was unable to enforce contracts, creating the opportunity for private enforcers called "gambellotto or mafiosi" (see Chapter 5). This was also the case with the Camorra in Italy at the time of the unification of the Italian peninsula in 1860. The Camorra was entrusted with the task of maintaining order to the Camorra when the regular police has been sent to back up the army.[24] The Camorra played the "role of Broker" mediating disputes as private individuals assumed a government role. Therefore, organized crime has emerged both in situations where the political and economic control exercised by the government is strong, and also where it has been weak.

The structural view helps to understand the inconsistencies in our laws regulating gambling, sex, and other consensual "vices." On the other hand, it offers little help in understanding the behavior of individuals who violate the law. Our case study of Henry Hill shows that he cared most about self-enrichment. He and his associates "wanted money, they wanted power, and they were willing to do anything necessary to achieve their ends."[25] How does this differ from the motivations of a legitimate businessperson who wants the same things, and will do anything necessary *and legal* to achieve those ends? The structuralists do not provide an explanation, other than the economic inequalities faced by Hill from an early age (already addressed by the positivists), and the fact the many (but not all) of the crimes committed by Hill involved the vices, where the law is inconsistent across jurisdictions.

Ethical: When Crime Brings Pleasure, Not Guilt

An ethical explanation of criminal conduct addresses the limitations of the positivist, classical, and structural explanations of crime. These can be summarized in three propositions:

1. External factors play a role in influencing some people to engage in crime, but these factors do not *cause* the crime by themselves.

2. A freely-willed decision lies at the base of virtually all criminal behavior, but there is no hedonistic "tendency" to engage in crime controlled only by the risk of apprehension.

3. This free-will decision is more effectively guided by the failure of a crime to bring pleasure, than the classical reliance on pain (apprehension and punishment).

What is lacking in virtually all contemporary discussions of crime causation is ethics and morality. Crime is the study of good and evil, yet it is rarely characterized in these terms. Why are most people good? Why are some people evil? This is the choice that is made when people harm others without legal justification.

Classicists are correct in emphasizing the free-will choice that underlies all behavior. If behavior was *determined* by internal or external influences, we would be no different than the lower animals. Yet pain versus pleasure is not what guides our behavior. If it did, most of us would be criminals. If the odds of apprehension and punishment were the only obstacles that stood in the way of you committing a crime, you are probably a criminal already. As noted earlier, the odds of apprehension and punishment are quite low. Over the years, they have fallen further.[26] Therefore, there is more at work in conforming behavior than the threat of police and criminal penalties.

Likewise, the positivists get only part of the picture. There is no doubt that bad economic and social conditions affect opportunities for success in legitimate society. A civilized society should be measured by number and quality of opportunities it provides for legitimate success. On the other hand, if your behavior was *determined* by your opportunities, there would be no successful people from disadvantaged backgrounds, and everyone in prison would be from socially or economically deprived areas. This is clearly not the case. Many people emerge successfully from disadvantaged backgrounds, and a number of people in prison are "white collar" offenders who had every advantage in life. Therefore, more is at work in explaining crime than social and economic conditions.

Third, the structuralists point to the inconsistencies in American criminal law, where we criminalize and decriminalize behaviors for political and economic reasons, often unrelated to social harm. This should be avoided to the extent possible, because consistency in law helps promote consistency in expectations for behavior of citizens. Also, laws implemented for symbolic reasons, rather than for reasons of public safety, can result in the creation of illicit markets and criminal opportunities that outweigh any benefit intended by the law. Nevertheless, structuralists do not help us explain why some individuals choose to exploit an illicit market created by gambling laws, for example, while most of us do not.

The ethical perspective sees crime as a moral failure in decisionmaking. When a crime is committed, a person has acted in a manner that harms another individual or the state. Placing one's own self-interest above the interests of others is a fundamental violation of ethical principles. The ethics of virtue, for example, dates back to Aristotle.[27] Moral virtue consists of wanting what is really good for you (as a human being) and nothing else. It is guided by the four cardinal virtues: temperance, fortitude, prudence, and justice. In fact, there are only about 10 real goods that exist in the pursuit of happiness.[28] From an ethical standpoint, a person refrains from criminal behavior because it does not bring pleasure. Any short-term gain for the offender is far outweighed by the harm it causes to the victim or state. Therefore, criminal behavior is undesirable because it works against the achievement of real human goods and it violates the four cardinal virtues.

This brief discussion of ethics may seem a bit unfamiliar, but that is the point. Education in ethics and ethical decisionmaking is extremely uncommon in American society. We have confused education with the accumulation of facts, and the accumulation of facts with the knowledge of what to do with them. Ethical decisionmaking and reinforcement from an early age would help to inculcate the notion of personal and social responsibility for one's own behavior. This is something that is lacking today in American government, business and, not surprisingly, organized crime.

The biography of Henry Hill illustrates how the failure to possess an ethical outlook results in a twisted, and often self-centered, world view:

> Anyone who stood waiting his turn on the American pay line was beneath contempt . . . They were the timid, law-abiding, pension-plan creatures neutered by compliance and awaiting their turn to die. To wiseguys, "working guys" were already dead. Henry and his pals had long ago dismissed the idea of security and the relative tranquility that went with obeying the law.[29]

This contempt for law-abiding citizens is made possible by the failure to feel guilt when it is appropriate. Similar to many other criminals, Hill and his associates felt pleasure when most people properly feel guilt.

> It was just that stuff that was stolen always tasted better than anything bought . . . Paulie [Vario] was always asking me for stolen credit cards whenever he and his wife, Phyllis, were going out for the night . . . The fact that a guy like Paul Vario, a *capo* in the Lucchese crime family, would even consider going out on a social occasion with his wife and run the risk of getting caught using a stolen credit card might surprise some people. But if you knew wiseguys you would know right away that the best part of the night for Paulie came from the fact that he was getting over on somebody . . . The real thrill of the night for Paulie, his biggest pleasure, was that he was robbing someone and getting away with it.[30]

In this case, crime brings pleasure, not guilt. The value system is upside-down. It serves as an example of a complete dearth of ethics. Ethics focuses inculcation of moral values that would re-emphasize the responsibility every person has for his or her own decisions, and that there exist objective ethical guidelines by which these decisions should be made and prioritized. The failure of individuals to comprehend, feel guilty about, and gauge their actions by the long-term consequences of their conduct lies at the heart of the ethical view of criminal behavior.

The scenario that follows describes an actual situation that describes the circumstances of an organized crime figure. Respond to the questions below, employing the principles from this chapter.

The Case of the Irish Mob

The so-called "Westies" were an Irish organized crime group in the Hell's Kitchen neighborhood on the West side of Manhattan. They were prosecuted virtually into extinction during the 1980's.

The group that formed the nucleus of the Westies were high school dropouts from working class homes. They were known "more for their nerve than their brains," emulating existing gangs, such as that of Mickey Spillane, which grew out of the same neighborhood culture. The Westies were different, however, in that they were motivated almost entirely by profit, rather than respect for their neighborhood or heritage. Incidents of fighting and violence were common among the Westies, and they often fought among themselves. A reputation for violence served to enhance a person's standing in the neighborhood.

On a "typical" day, two of the group's leaders, Jimmy Coonan (the leader) and Mickey Featherstone (the enforcer), would pick-up money for numbers gambling, loansharking debts, and extortion payments from the union at the piers. They were known in the neighborhood for violence to intimidate their victims.

Ultimately, the Westies self-destructed due to greed and reckless violence. After a trial for racketeering and murder, Coonan was sentenced to 75 years in prison without parole, based in part on the testimony of Featherstone who had become a government informant to reduce his own sentence.

Source: T.J. English, *The Westies: The Irish Mob* (New York: St. Martin's, 1991).

Questions:

1.   Explain the criminal behavior of the Westies using a positivistic explanation.

2.   Explain the crimes of the Westies using a classical approach.

3.   Explain the crimes of the Westies using an ethical explanation.

4.   Which of these explanations appear to explain the Westies' crimes most adequately?

Summary

This chapter has presented a four-part typology of explanations of organized crime: positivistic, classical, structural, and ethical. Within in each type, a specific example was chosen to illustrate how it attempts to account for criminal behavior in the context of organized crime. The biography of Henry Hill, an organized crime figure, was used in each section of this chapter to demonstrate how these explanations may be applied in actual cases. Table 3.1 summarizes the four-part typology of explanations, and an additional case study is presented as a critical thinking question for student evaluation.

Table 3.1
Four Approaches to Criminal Behavior

Approach to Crime Causation	Primary Cause of Crime	Prescribed Remedy
Positive	External factors (usually social and economic)	Rehabilitation or reform by changing social and economic conditions, or changing someone's reaction to them.
Classical	Free-will decision (guided by hedonistic tendency to maximize pleasure and minimize pain).	Deterrence through threat of apprehension and punishment.
Structural	Political and economic conditions promote a culture of competitive individualism where individual gain becomes more important than the social good.	More equitable distribution of power and wealth in society, and fewer arbitrary laws, so that all individuals have a greater stake in a better society.
Ethical	Free-will decision is guided by ethical principles (that involve prioritizing of values in unclear situations based on the failure of illegal conduct to bring pleasure).	Education and reinforcement in ethical decision-making from an early age. Reduction to the extent possible the external factors that promote unethical decisions.

References to Chapter 3

[1] Emile Durkheim, *The Rules of Sociological Method* (1895) (New York: Free Press, 1964), p. 65.

[2] Jay S. Albanese, *Dealing with Delinquency: The Future of Juvenile Justice* second edition (Chicago: Nelson-Hall, 1993), ch. 2.

[3] For a summary, see Albanese, *Dealing with Delinquency*, ch. 3.

[4] Richard A. Cloward and Lloyd E. Ohlin, *Delinquency and Opportunity: A Theory of Delinquent Gangs* (New York: Free Press, 1960).

[5] Robert K. Merton, "Social Structure and Anomie," *American Sociological Review*, 3 (1938), pp. 672-682.

[6] Cloward and Ohlin, *Delinquency and Opportunity*, pp. 22-27.

[7] Cloward and Ohlin, pp. 165-166.

[8] Ibid., p. 166.

[9] James M. O'Kane, *Crooked Ladder: Gangsters, Ethnicity, and the American Dream* (New Brunswick, NJ: Transaction Publishers, 1992), pp. 27-28.

[10] Clifford R. Shaw and Henry D. McKay, *Juvenile Delinquency and Urban Areas* (1932) (Chicago: University of Chicago Press, 1969).

[11] Edwin H. Sutherland, *Principles of Criminology* (Philadelphia: Lippincott, 1939).

[12] David Matza, *Delinquency and Drift* (New York: Wiley, 1964).

[13] Nicholas Pileggi, *Wiseguy: Life in a Mafia Family* (New York: Simon and Schuster, 1985).

[14] Pileggi, *Wiseguy*, p. 19.

[15] Michael Gottfredson and Travis Hirschi, *A General Theory of Crime* (Stanford, CA: Stanford University Press, 1990), p. 117.

[16] Travis Hirschi and Michael Gottfredson, "Causes of White-Collar Crime," *Criminology* 25 (November, 1989), p. 959.

[17] Nicholas Pileggi, *Wiseguy*, pp. 13-14.

[18] Ibid., p. 21.

[19] Jay S. Albanese, *Myths & Realities of Crime and Justice*, Third edition (Niagara Falls, NY: Apocalypse, 1990), ch. 2.

[20] Pileggi, *Wiseguy*, p. 141-142.

[21] Vincenzo Ruggiero, "The Camorra: 'Clean' Capital and Organised Crime," in Frank Pearce and Michael Woodiwiss, eds. *Global Crime Connections: Dynamics and Control* (Buffalo: University of Toronto Press, 1993), p. 142.

[22] Alan A. Block and William J. Chambliss, *Organizing Crime* (New York: Elsevier, 1981), pp. 9-10.

[23] Ruggerio, p. 157.

[24] Ruggerio, p. 145.

[25] Pileggi, *Wiseguy*, p. 39.

[26]   Federal Bureau of Investigation, *Crime in the United States - Uniform Crime Report* (Washington, DC: U.S. Government Printing Office, published annually).

[27]   Aristotle, *Ethics* (325 B.C.) (New York: Penguin Books, 1976).

[28]   The real goods include: nourishment, shelter, health, wealth (to live decently), pleasure, knowledge, liberty, friendship, civil peace, and leisure. See Mortimer J. Adler, *Desires Right and Wrong: The Ethics of Enough* (New York: Macmillan, 1991).

[29]   Pileggi, *Wiseguy*, p. 38-39.

[30]   Pileggi, *Wiseguy*, p. 24-25.

Chapter 4

Paradigms of Organized Crime[†]

Your salary is $5,375.82.
Where did you get that
Rolls Royce?"
Richard Sparks (1976)

Everyone knows the story of the blind men asked to identify an object that was actually an elephant. One grabbed the tail and guessed the animal was a snake. Another touched its tusks and thought it was a smooth stone instead. A third held its ear and surmised it was a large piece of leather. In each case, the perception was based on logical deductions, but the conclusion was wrong.

Models, or paradigms, of organized crime have developed in much the same way. Government investigators, researchers, and scholars have examined various manifestations of organized crime using informants, electronic surveillance, court records, participant-observation, interviews with convicted offenders, economic analyses, and historical accounts. By and large, these investigations have been conducted with integrity and true interest in discovering the actual nature of organized crime. Often the perceptions of these individuals have been correct, but the conclusions drawn misleading. Why?

What is a Model of Organized Crime?

A model, or paradigm, is an effort to make a picture of a piece of reality in order to understand it better. We make physical models of the structure of the solar system in order to see how it is organized at a level difficult to observe otherwise, due to its immense size. We have modeled distinct stages of child development to illustrate the maturation process that is difficult to observe otherwise due to its slow, gradual process. In each case, we try to simply "freeze" a model in time and space, even though the objects we are modeling are constantly moving and changing. As a result, models are limited but still useful. They make physical objects too large (or too small) to observe, visible. Objects too fast or too slow to capture, understandable. This ability to capture the essence of an object, system, or process without actually witnessing it makes models the most useful of all educational tools.

As noted in Chapter 1, what U.S. Supreme Court Justice Potter Stewart said about obscene material holds equally true for organized crime: I might not know precisely what it is, but "I know it when I see it."[1] Everyone has perceptions of what organized crime is, even when it is difficult to explain in a comprehensive or systematic way. There have been a great number of efforts to model organized crime, most occurring during the last three decades. In every case the goal has been to capture the essence of organized crime in the form of a model because it is so difficult to observe otherwise.

Like the blind men who attempted to identify the elephant, the outcome of efforts to model organized crime invariably reflect the perspective of the investigator. Economists model it in terms of economic factors. Government investigators model organized crime as a hierarchical government-like enterprise. Social scientists view it as a social phenomenon. In too many cases the perceptions are based in reality, but the conclusions drawn either inaccurate or overgeneralized. Just as in the case of the blind men who disagreed in their conclusions, the elephant still existed in a distinct form. They simply did not identify it correctly. Even though investigators may model organized crime inaccurately, organized crime continues to exist. The failure of a model to capture the true nature of organized crime should not be construed as proof, one way or the other, about its existence. Too often in the past a model shown to have shortcomings in its depiction of organized crime is rejected in its entirety. This overlooks the fact that the investigator's perceptions may have been correct, but the conclusions wrong. As a result, it is important to distinguish between the *facts and perceptions* on which models are based and the *conclusions drawn* from those facts and perceptions. The deduction of wrong conclusions does not mean necessarily that the facts and perceptions on which they are based are also inaccurate.[2]

Models of organized crime can be grouped into three general types: those that focus on hierarchical structure, those that emphasize local ethnic or cultural connections, and those that emphasize the economic nature of organized crime. As we will see, none of these models excludes consideration of the others, as some overlap clearly exists. Nevertheless, the development and structure of these models is distinct and will be treated separately.

Hierarchical Models of Organized Crime

Hierarchical is defined in the dictionary as "a group of persons or things arranged in order of rank or grade." Various authors over the years have termed this the "bureaucratic," "national conspiracy," or "corporate" model of organized crime. Stated most simply, this model of organized crime characterizes it as a government-like structure, where organized illegal activities are conducted with the approval of superiors, "policy" is set by higher-ups, and illicit activities are "protected" through the influence of the hierarchy.

This model of organized crime was put forth first in these terms by Estes Kefauver, a U.S. Senator who conducted hearings on the subject of organized crime in 1950. His committee concluded that "there is a sinister criminal organization known as the Mafia operating throughout the country with ties in other nations in the opinion of this committee."[3] Unfortunately, Kefauver had little more than the opinions of law enforcement officials to support his contention. The fact that he drew such sweeping conclusions without independent corroboration has been pointed out in several serious critiques of the Kefauver Committee.[4]

It was not until 1963 that evidence was produced that supported the notion that organized crime operated as a hierarchical structure. U.S. Senator John McClellan held public hearings during this period at which the government introduced the first "insider" in organized crime. His name was Joseph Valachi, then serving a prison sentence, and agreeing to testify as part of a deal to avoid a possible death sentence for a murder he committed while in prison. Valachi's testimony became the basis for the hierarchical model of organized crime.

Valachi testified that a nationwide criminal organization did exist, as Estes Kefauver had argued in 1950. Unlike Kefauver, Valachi said the organization's name was "Cosa Nostra," rather than Mafia. Valachi claimed he had never heard of the term Mafia, while no law enforcement official who testified had heard of Cosa Nostra. The Senate Committee treated the two names for this apparently identical organization interchangeably.[5] Valachi claimed this organization arose out of a gangland war in New York City during the early 1930s. The main stake in this so-called Castellammarese War, which was said to have lasted 14 months, was "absolute control of the large segment of the underworld then in the hands of gang leaders of Italian nativity or lineage."[6]

Valachi described the organizational structure, established after this gangland war, as consisting of "the individual bosses of the individual families, and then we had an underboss, and then we had what we call a caporegima which is a lieutenant, and then we have what we call soldiers."[7] In this way territory and criminal enterprises were divided among "families" of men of Italian descent. According to Valachi, membership was restricted by Lucky Luciano after the Castellammarese War, to "Sicilians from the turn of the century through the 1920s," and then it was confined to "full Italians," requiring Italian parentage on both sides of a man's family. This restriction lasted until 1954, when membership was opened to others not meeting these requirements.[8]

Based primarily on Valachi's testimony and the statements of law enforcement officials from some large cities, the McClellan Committee concluded that "there exists . . . today a criminal organization that is directly descended from and is patterned upon the centuries-old Sicilian terrorist society, the Mafia. This organization, also known as Cosa Nostra, operates vast illegal enterprises that produce an annual income of many billions of dollars. This combine has so much power and influence that it may be described as a private government of organized crime."[9] This characterization of organized crime as a large, centrally controlled, highly organized entity, forms the basis for the hierarchical model of organized crime. The major attributes of organized crime according to this model are highlighted in Table 4.1.

Table 4.1
Hierarchical Model of Organized Crime

Structure (That Forms the Basis for Criminal Activity)
1. "Family" structure with graded ranks of authority from boss down to soldiers.
2. Bosses oversee the activities of family members.
3. A "commission" of bosses handles inter-family relations and disputes.

As Table 4.1 indicates, the hierarchical model posits a "family" structure with several military-style ranks from the boss down to soldiers. The bosses control the activities of the family. Valachi also testified that there exists a "commission" of bosses from approximately 12 families in large cities around the country.[10] This commission handles inter-family relations and disputes, according to the McClellan Committee's conclusions. The source of this information was largely Joseph Valachi and other criminal informants used by police agencies who also provided testimony at the McClellan hearings.

Over the last 30 years, the hierarchical model has been criticized for its imprecision. Inaccuracies in several important factors to the hierarchical model were believed by some to render the model useless. Problems with the hierarchical model included: (1) the inability to confirm historically that any type of gangland war occurred during the early 1930s,[11] (2) information provided by Valachi himself, and others after him, that the "family" actually plays very little role in directing the lives and activities of its members,[12] (3) subsequent informants, such as Jimmy Fratianno, differed widely in their testimony about the size and structure of Cosa Nostra.[13] Most investigations that produced findings that contradicted parts of the hierarchical model were historical in nature, relying on court records, testimony, interviews, and archival data. The number, method, and similarity in conclusions of these investigations suggest that they raise valid criticisms of parts of the hierarchical model. What they failed to establish, and perhaps were not intended to prove, is that the hierarchical model is invalid as a description of at least some parts of organized crime.[14] It is true that Valachi's history was faulty, and it is unfortunate that the Senate and subsequent investigators for the President's Crime Commission in 1967 did not assess Valachi's statements more carefully. The President's Commission Task Force on Organized Crime essentially repeated Valachi's testimony and added little new insight.[15] Nevertheless, the most important question remains unanswered: are the errors arising from the McClellan hearings incidental, or do they warrant an abandonment of the hierarchical model altogether?

The decade of the 1970s witnessed a growing body of scholarly research into the nature of organized crime. It began with sociologist Joseph Albini in 1971 and continued with anthropologists Francis Ianni and Elizabeth Reuss-Ianni in 1972, and was followed by others. In every case the researchers were unable to find any connection between the individuals and groups they studied and a larger, controlling hierarchy. This led to growing doubts about the existence of a national crime syndicate, and led to the emergence of a second model of organized crime, discussed later.

Not until the decade of the 1980s was information available that showed conclusively that the hierarchical model accurately portrayed at least some manifestations of organized crime. The "mob trials" of the 1980s and 1990s were the most significant organized crime prosecution efforts in the history of the United States. Several hundred high-level organized crime figures were convicted, based on electronic surveillance and protected witnesses that provided documentary evidence of how organized crime operates in some areas. The "Commission" trial of 1986 was perhaps the most notable of the mob trial because it involved the alleged "bosses" of the five New York City "families" of the Cosa Nostra as defendants. The defense conceded that the "Mafia exists and has members," and "there is a commission" which was mentioned in the wiretapped conversations of the defendants. The defendants tried to argued that their membership was not synonymous with criminal activity, but they were each convicted and sentenced to 100 years in prison for various crimes.[16] Interestingly, the defendants argued that the purpose of the "commission" was to resolve disputes, rather than to plan crimes, an argument not unlike that made by Joseph Valachi in the 1960s who characterized the commission as a mechanism for dispute resolution between families. The defense stipulations, wiretap evidence, and jury findings in the commission trial and in the successful prosecution of John Gotti in 1992 make it clear that the hierarchical model clearly characterizes at least some part of organized crime in the United States.[17] Consider the testimony of Salvatore (Sammy the Bull) Gravano in the trial of John Gotti:

> ASSISTANT U.S. ATTORNEY GLEESON: Have you ever heard the term "administration"?
>
> GRAVANO: Yes.
>
> GLEESON: To you what does that mean?
>
> GRAVANO: There is the boss, the underboss, and the *consigliere*, it's the higher up in the family. The administration.
>
> GLEESON: Were you part of the administration?
>
> GRAVANO: Yes.
>
> GLEESON: Who was the rest of the administration?
>
> GRAVANO: John (Gotti) was the boss, I was the underboss, and Frank— and Joe Piney was the *consigliere*, Frankie was acting *consigliere* . . .
>
> GLEESON: What's below the administration?
>
> GRAVANO: Captains.

This testimony from Gravano, a criminal informant of higher "rank" than Valachi, is remarkably similar to Valachi's testimony nearly 30 years earlier.[18] Gravano's description of his "induction" ceremony into the Cosa Nostra, and the "commission" made up of leaders of various "families," is quite similar to Valachi's version in 1963.[19] There is no apparent cause or reason for Gravano, or the other criminal informants from the decade of the 1980s, to model their testimony after that of Valachi, so it reasonably can be said that the structure of Cosa Nostra (at least within New York City) is based on the same hierarchical model described by Valachi in the early 1960s.

Given the available evidence to date, it is clear the hierarchical model characterizes organized crime among Italian-Americans in the New York City area who are connected to the Cosa Nostra. There is also evidence from other cities in New England and elsewhere that *at least within* those cities a significant part of organized crime is controlled by organized criminals of Italian-American roots. The hierarchical model fits best in its description of how the group functions in accord with respect for position, and in partnerships and deference to other "connected" individuals in organized crime.

The hierarchical model is weakest, given the evidence to date, in describing whether there exists a true connection among organized crime groups in different cities, and in specifying the role of Cosa Nostra in the lives of its members. The commission trial in New York City established how the various "families" operate and divide their criminal activities there. The trial sheds little light, however, on (1) the existence and nature of connections among organized crime groups in different cities, (2) the extent of the connections between Italian and non-Italian groups in the same cities, or (3) whether organized crime *not* connected with Cosa Nostra is structured in similar fashion. Contemporary investigations suggest that organized crime activities, both within and outside the Cosa Nostra, might be becoming less hierarchical and more entrepreneurial in nature.[20]

Local, Ethnic Models of Organized Crime

It was said by some during the 1980s that once free-market competition was introduced into the U.S. telephone system, the price of making a telephone call would drop considerably. The government was ultimately successful in adding competition to the long-distance telephone marketplace, but the results were far from dramatic. A similar logical, but incorrect, prediction often arises from the hierarchical model of organized crime.

Perhaps the biggest problem with the hierarchical model of organized crime is that it leads to the conclusion that prosecution of the "bosses" and others in control will make organized crime less prevalent and less threatening. The successful prosecutions of the 1980s and 1990s illustrate that this is not necessarily the case, in that the demand for drugs, gambling, stolen property, combined with a weak regulatory system provoke the emergence of illicit entrepreneurs to cater to the illegal markets or to exploit the legal marketplace. Once these entrepreneurs are removed by arrest or incarceration, others emerge because the demand remains, as do the opportunities for criminal exploitation of the legitimate marketplace.[21]

Social scientists became involved in the study of organized crime in a significant way in the 1970s. For the first time a series of independent studies appeared that relied on information from sources outside the government. The first was conducted by sociologist Joseph Albini who found that individuals involved in organized crime "do not belong to an organization." Rather than a "criminal secret society, a criminal syndicate consists of a system of loosely structured relationships" that develops so each person can maximize profits.[22] The following year anthropologists Francis and Elizabeth Reuss-Ianni conducted a two-year study of one specific organized crime "family" in Brooklyn. Francis Ianni became a participant-observer and based on his observations, and those made of two other criminal groups he studied, he found these groups not to be "bureaucratic." In fact, he found them to have "no structure . . . independent of their current 'personnel'."[23]

Unlike the prevailing view at the time that organized crime operated as "a private government," both Albini and the Ianni's found little organization, and that friendships based on cultural (i.e., Italian) and economic ties formed the basis for organized crime activities. These authors' findings are limited, of course, by the areas and groups they studied, much in the same way that Valachi was limited in his knowledge about organized crime outside the New York area. The primary difference between Valachi's model of organized crime, and the newer local, ethnic model developed by social scientists centers on the degree of organization within and between organized criminal groups.

The body of social science evidence continued to grow from the 1970s to the present. Now numerous studies exist of organized crime groups in various locales around the country that all have found: (1) cultural and ethnic ties link organized criminals together, rather than a hierarchy, and (2) the groups studied appear to be local in nature without apparent connections to a national crime syndicate.[24]

Table 4.2
Local, Ethnic Model of Organized Crime

Structure (that Forms the Context for Criminal Activity)
1.   Cultural and ethnic ties bind the group together, rather than a hierarchical structure.
2.   Individuals control their own activities and take partners as they wish.
3.   No evidence of connection of these groups with a national crime syndicate in most cases.

This model, outlined in Table 4.2, has obvious differences to the hierarchical model first detailed by Joseph Valachi, but there are similarities as well. All these studies highlight the importance of heritage (i.e., racial, ethnic, or other cultural ties) in forming the basis for working relationships, and from Valachi forward it has been clear that even those organized crime members who are part of Cosa Nostra obtain relatively little direction in their day-to-day activities. Consider Valachi's statement at the McClellan hearings in 1963:

> SENATOR JAVITS: That is the function of the family . . . that is mutual protection?
> MR. VALACHI: Right.
> SENATOR JAVITS: Otherwise, everybody operates by himself. They may take partners but that is their option.
> MR. VALACHI: Right.

This exchange shows that the organization of organized crime, even as a member of the Genovese crime family, as Valachi claimed, is rather loose.[25] Therefore, the differences between the hierarchical and local, ethnic models appear to lie entirely in *how* illicit relationships are structured, rather than in the nature or extent of the criminal activity itself.

A third model of organized crime developed in the late 1970s, when the economics of organized crime drew interest among researchers and policymakers. Rather than focusing on the *personal relationships* that form the basis for organized crime, this group of investigations focused on the *economic relationships* that drive the business of organized crime.

Organized Crime as a Business Enterprise

The enterprise model of organized crime grew out of dissatisfaction with both the hierarchical and local ethnic models. A growing number of investigations had found that *relationships between individuals* (hierarchical, ethnic, racial, or friendship) were the genesis of *organized* crime activity (as opposed to individual, less organized forms of criminal behavior). The view was that if the factors causing these illicit relationships to form (i.e., conspiracies) could be isolated, a determination might be made about the true causes of organized crime. It is the conspiratorial nature of organized crime that makes it serious. It is not the individual drug dealer and illegal casino operator that causes public concern, as much as how these individuals *organize* their customers, suppliers, and functionaries to provide illicit goods and services for a profit.

The realization that organized crime operates as a business spurred a series of studies in an effort to isolate those factors that contribute most significantly to the formation of criminal enterprises. Dwight Smith was among the first to attempt to explain the economic origins of organized crime in a systematic manner. In his book *The Mafia Mystique*, and in his subsequent publications he developed a "spectrum-based theory of enterprise."[26] Applying general organization theory to criminal activity, Smith found that organized crime stems from "the same fundamental assumptions that govern entrepreneurship in the legitimate marketplace: a necessity to maintain and extend one's share of the market." According to this view, organized crime groups form and thrive in the same way that legitimate businesses do: they respond to the needs and demands of suppliers, customers, regulators, and competitors. The only difference between organized crime and legitimate business, according to Smith, is that organized criminals deal in illegal products, whereas legitimate businesses generally do not.

The business enterprise model of organized crime focuses on how *economic* considerations, rather than *hierarchical* or *ethnic* considerations, lie at the base of the formation and success of organized crime groups. Regardless of ethnicity or hierarchy, the enterprise model labels economic concerns as the primary cause of organized criminal behavior. A number of empirical studies of specific organized crime operations support this perspective. Patricia Adler's study of illicit drug sales in the southwest as a participant-observer found that "dealers and smugglers I studied operated within an illicit market that was largely competitive, or disorganized, rather than visibly structured." Disputes were settled in "a spontaneous and unrestricted manner."[27] She concluded that the drug markets she observed consisted of "individual entrepreneurs and small organizations rather than massive, centralized bureaucracies," that were "competitive" rather than "monopolistic" in nature.[28] In a study of bookmaking, loansharking, and numbers gambling in New York City, Peter Reuter found them "not monopolies in the classic sense or subject to control by some external organization." Instead, he observed that "economic forces arising from the illegality of the product tend to fragment the market," making it difficult to control or centralize these illegal activities on large scale.[29]

Studies like these typify the enterprise model of organized crime. Rather than the product of illicit relationships based on hierarchical or ethnic relationships, this model sees organized crime as the product of market forces, similar to those that cause legitimate businesses to flourish or die in the legal sector of the economy. The major characteristics of the enterprise model are summarized in Table 4.3.

Table 4.3
Enterprise Model of Organized Crime

Structure (Incidental to the Criminal Opportunities)
1. Organized crime and legitimate business involve similar activities on different ends of "spectrum of legitimacy" of business enterprise.
2. Operations not ethnically exclusive or very violent in order to enhance profit.
3. Rarely centrally organized due to the nature of the markets and activities involved.

Table 4.3 shows that it is *economic relationships*, rather than *personal relationships* (based either in hierarchy or in ethnicity), that form the basis for organized crime activity. Organized crime activity is seen as a deviant variation of legitimate business activity, that is often inter-ethnic and nonviolent, because these latter two factors enhance profit-maximization.

Several studies have found that organized crime can be inter-ethnic in nature and also less violent than is commonly believed. Historian Alan Block saw that, although Jews dominated the cocaine trade in New York City during the early 1900s, there was also notable "evidence of interethnic cooperation" involving Italians, Greeks, Irish, and Black participants.[30] A contemporary account of the Irish mob "The Westies" on Manhattan's West Side saw that they cooperate occasionally with Cosa Nostra groups to further mutual interests.[31] Annelise Anderson's analysis of a single organized crime "family" indicated that there was "no strong evidence" of violence in its legitimate businesses, and the use of force to encourage payments from loanshark customers was "almost nonexistent."[32] An investigation of organized crime infiltration of the New York City construction industry showed that "actual violence is only rarely necessary."[33] Reuter, Rubinstein, and Wynn noted that vending machine and waste collection industries in the New York City area had "outgrown the racketeers," inasmuch as "there is no point in a racketeer using force to control machine placement in a bar or restaurant unless he is also able to provide the patrons with the games they desire. If he cannot, the patrons will just move to another bar."[34] Each study demonstrates that organized crime activity operates according to economic factors faced by any business enterprise (i.e., the pressures of suppliers, customers, regulators, and competitors). The enterprise model clearly places these business-related concerns as more significant than hierarchical obligations or ethnic links in the genesis and continuation of organized crime.

Fitting the Models Together

Thus, there is evidence to support each of the three models of organized crime in certain respects. Clear evidence from criminal informants, electronic surveillance, and jury findings indicate that the hierarchical model characterizes relationships among the New York City Cosa Nostra families and some groups in other cities. The mob trials of the 1980s and 1990s removed any doubt that existed after the Valachi testimony in the 1960s. Yet there is clear evidence that much organized crime remains unconnected to Cosa Nostra activity. This evidence has been derived largely from independent case studies (cited earlier) of organized crime groups in a number of different cities. In many cases these groups are locally based and bound by ethnic or cultural ties, groups that are often non-Italian. Finally, there is clear evidence that economic considerations are a significant factor in the development and maintenance of criminal enterprises. These findings stem largely from economic analyses of organized crime markets (cited earlier) in different regions of the country.

To what extent do these three models overlap? There are three distinct ways in which these models merge. Cosa Nostra groups are hierarchical (if loosely so), ethnically bound, and perhaps also maintained by market forces. Ethnically bound organized crime groups exist that are *not* hierarchical in structure, but rather are driven by economic concerns. There are also organized crime groups *not* hierarchical *or* ethnically bound that engage in criminal activities corresponding to the nature of the available market. These three possibilities point out the major similarities and differences in the three models of organized crime and suggest how organized crime might be addressed more effectively in the future.

Both the hierarchical and local ethnic models focus on how organized crime *groups are organized*; the enterprise model focuses on how organized crime *activities are organized*. This is why the three models do not conflict in any significant way. While it is important to understand how a criminal group is organized, if one is to develop a criminal conspiracy case, it is not always necessary to understand the group structure to understand how and why it engages in the activities it does. Perhaps Mark Haller said it best, "it makes little sense, for instance, to compare an Italian-American crime family to a Jamaican cocaine distribution group. One is largely a social group that serves its members' business interests; the other is a business group distributing illegal drugs."[35] The Jamaican group, in Haller's view, exists simply as a mechanism to engage in the drug business with little in the way of structure or cultural ties beyond the drug business itself. On the other hand, the Cosa Nostra group has both preexisting hierarchical and cultural ties that form the basis for launching illicit enterprises. As Haller puts it, it's like "comparing a Rotary Club and a department store. It is more appropriate to compare stores with stores, and Rotary Clubs with other social organizations."[36]

The perceived inconsistencies among the hierarchical, ethnic, and enterprise models of organized crime are incidental for the purposes of both study and crime control. Once one recognizes, as the organized crime literature clearly indicates, that (1) some organized crime is hierarchical in nature, and that much is not; (2) some is locally based and ethnically bound in nature, and that much is not; and (3) that all organized crime activity is entrepreneurial in nature; the differences among the models become less significant.

Organized crime is studied most fruitfully as an economic activity, and prosecuted on the basis of the relationship among its participants. For the scholar, the *economic activity* is paramount inasmuch as it provides more leads to understanding the genesis and maintenance of the illegal acts. For the law enforcement official, the *structure of the group* is paramount inasmuch as it provides more leads for prosecution purposes. Hopefully, an appreciation of each of these models will enable both scholars and the law enforcement community to understand that the apparent tension among the various models of organized crime is inconsequential, rather than contentious.

The enterprise model characterizes all organized crime activity, whereas the precise structure of particular organized crime groups becomes more or less important depending on the group in question (esp. whether it predated the current illicit activity, or whether it merely arose in response to the criminal opportunity). Future investigations should take greater care to appreciate the dynamic and better distinguish between organized crime *activities* and organized crime *group characteristics* as recognized in the three models of organized crime. Just as the three blind men who examined various parts of the elephant had good instincts and made logical judgments, their conclusions were still wrong. When it comes to understanding the true nature of organized crime, it is equally important not to lose sight of the "elephant," as one studies its various structures and activities.

Critical Thinking Exercise

The scenario below reports on an actual investigation of organized crime activity. Using the information provided in this chapter, answer the questions below.

The Case of Morrisburg

"Morrisburg" (a pseudonym) is an industrial "rust-belt" city that once had booming coal, steel, and railroad industries. Vice and organized crime activity are prevalent, and have been throughout most of the city's history. The illicit activities include gambling, loansharking, stolen property, drug trafficking, and prostitution. These activities do not appear to be controlled by a single group, but rather through a number of independent groups and individuals. A single ethnic group characterizes most of those involved, but no one group is dominant.

New groups periodically enter the mix of illegal activities, but older groups do not withdraw. The new groups are merely added to the existing mixture.

Money is generated and laundered through a confusing combination of illegal operations and legitimate businesses that make illegal funds difficult to trace. Activities are protected through political contributions and corruption of individuals in both criminal justice and government agencies.

Source: Gary W. Potter, *Criminal Organizations: Vice, Racketeering, and Politics in an American City* (Prospect Heights, IL: Waveland Publishing, 1994).

Questions:

1. Which model of organized crime appears to account for the organized crime in Morrisburg most comprehensively?

2. What strategies do you believe would have the most long-term impact in Morrisburg?

References to Chapter 4

[1] *Jacobellis v. Ohio*, 84 S. Ct. 1676 (1964).

[2] Charles H. Rogovin and Frederick T. Martens, "The Evil That Men Do," *Journal of Contemporary Criminal Justice*, 8 (February, 1992), pp. 62-79.

[3] U.S. Senate Special Committee to Investigate Organized Crime in Interstate Commerce, *Third Interim Report* (Washington, DC: U.S. Government Printing Office, 1951), p. 2.

[4] Daniel Bell, "Crime as an American Way of Life," *The Antioch Review*, 13 (June, 1953), pp. 131-154; William H. Moore *The Kefauver Committee and the Politics of Crime, 1950-1952* (Columbia: University of Missouri Press, 1974).

[5] U.S. Senate Committee on Government Operations Permanent Subcommittee on Investigations, *Report on Organized Crime and Illicit Traffic in Narcotics* (Washington, DC: U.S. Government Printing Office, 1965), p. 117.

[6] Ibid. p. 12.

[7] U.S. Senate Committee on Government Operations Permanent Subcommittee on Investigations, *Organized Crime and Illicit Traffic in Narcotics: Hearings Part I* (Washington, DC: U.S. Government Printing Office), pp. 80, 215.

[8] Ibid. p. 13.

[9] U.S. Senate, *Report on Organized Crime and Illicit Traffic in Narcotics*, p. 117.

[10] Ibid.

[11] Alan A. Block, "History and the Study of Organized Crime," *Urban Life*, 6 (1978), pp. 455-474; Humbert S. Nelli *The Business of Crime: Italians and Syndicate Crime in the United States* (Chicago: University of Chicago Press, 1981).

[12] Annelise G. Anderson *The Business of Organized Crime* (Stanford, CA: Hoover Institution Press, 1979), p. 44; Mark H. Haller, *Life Under Bruno: The Economics of an Organized Crime Family* (Conshohocken: Pennsylvania Crime Commission, 1991).

[13] Albanese, *Organized Crime in America*, p. 46-62; Ovid Demaris, *The Last Mafioso* (New York: Bantam, 1981), pp. 20-22; U.S. Senate Committee on Governmental Affairs Permanent Subcommittee on Investigations, *Organized Crime and Violence: Hearings Part I* (Washington, DC: U.S. Government Printing Office, 1980), p. 88.

[14] see Robert J. Kelly, "Trapped in the Folds of Discourse: Theorizing about the Underworld," *Journal of Contemporary Criminal Justice*, 8 (February, 1992), pp. 11-35.

[15] President's Commission on Law Enforcement and Administration of Justice, *Task Force Report: Organized Crime* (Washington, DC: U.S. Government Printing Office, 1967); Donald R. Cressey, *Theft of the Nation* (New York: Harper & Row, 1969).

[16] Albanese, *Organized Crime in America*, pp. 62-69.

[17] John Gotti, *The Gotti Tapes* (New York: Time Books, 1992).

[18] *The Gotti Tapes*, pp. 134-135.

[19] *The Gotti Tapes*, pp. 146-149.

[20] Peter Reuter, *Disorganized Crime: The Economics of the Visible Hand* (Cambridge: MIT Press, 1983; Patricia A. Adler, *Wheeling and Dealing: An Ethnography of an Upper-Level Drug Dealing and Smuggling Community* (New York: Columbia University Press, 1985); Pino Arlacchi, *Mafia Business: The Mafia Ethic and the Spirit of Capitalism* (London: Verso, 1986).

[21] Howard Abadinsky, *The Mafia in America: An Oral History* (New York: Praeger, 1981); Joseph L. Albini, *The American Mafia: Genesis of a Legend* (New York: Irvington, 1971), p. 289; Peter Reuter, Jonathan Rubinstein, and Simon Wynn, *Racketeering in Legitimate Industries: Two Case Studies* (Washington, DC: National Institute of Justice, 1983); Dwight C. Smith, "Organized Crime and Entrepreneurship," *International Journal of Criminology and Penology* 6 (1978), pp. 161-177.

[22] Albini, *The American Mafia: Genesis of a Legend*, p. 288.

[23] Francis A.J. Ianni with Elizabeth Reuss-Ianni, *A Family Business: Kinship and Social Control in Organized Crime* (New York: New American Library, 1972), p. 20.

[24] Abadinsky, *The Mafia in America*; Albini, *The American Mafia*; Anderson, *The Business of Organized Crime*; Ianni and Reuss-Ianni, *A Family Business*; Adler, *Wheeling and Dealing*.

[25] U.S. Senate, *Organized Crime and Illicit Traffic in Narcotics: Hearings Part I*, pp. 116, 194.

[26] Smith, "Organized Crime and Entrepreneurship," pp. 161-177; Dwight C. Smith, "Paragons, Pariahs, and Pirates: A Spectrum-Based Theory of Enterprise," *Crime & Delinquency*, 26 (July, 1980), pp. 358-386; Dwight C. Smith, *The Mafia Mystique*, revised edition (Lanham, MD: University Press of America, 1990).

[27] Adler, *Wheeling and Dealing*, p. 80.

[28] Adler, *Wheeling and Dealing*, p. 82.

[29] Reuter, *Disorganized Crime*, p. 176.

[30] Alan A. Block, "The Snowman Cometh: Coke in Progressive New York," *Criminology*, 17 (May, 1979), pp. 75-99.

[31] T.J. English, *The Westies* (New York: St. Martin's, 1991), pp. 136-178.

[32] Anderson, *The Business of Organized Crime*, pp. 66, 117.

[33] Ronald Goldstock, Martin Marcus, Thomas D. Thacher, and James B. Jacobs, *Corruption and Racketeering in the New York City Construction Industry* (New York: New York University Press, 1990), p. 31.

[34] Reuter, Rubinstein, and Wynn, *Racketeering in Legitimate Industries*, p. 33.

[35] Haller, "Bureaucracy and the Mafia," p. 7.

[36] Haller, "Bureaucracy and the Mafia," p. 8; Haller, *Life Under Bruno*, p. 227.

†   Portions of this chapter consist of revised material from a chapter written by Dr. Jay Albanese that appeared in *Handbook of Organized Crime* (1994), edited by Robert Kelly. An imprint of Greenwood Publishing Group, Inc., Westport, CT. Reprinted with permission.

Chapter 5

The Mafia: 100 Years of Historical Facts and Myths

How many things which
served us yesterday as arti-
cles of faith, are fables for
us today.
Michel De Montaigne
(1580)

When did the "Mafia" first arise? How did it come about? What is the evidence that supports this history? The answers to these questions are imperative if an accurate understanding of organized crime is to be established. This chapter examines the origins of the "Mafia" link to organized crime in North America, and it attempts to separate the myth from the reality on the basis of first-hand investigations of the historical record.

Hennessey Murder in New Orleans, 1890

Interest in a "Mafia" in the United States can be traced to the murder of David Hennessey in 1890. Hennessey was Superintendent of Police in New Orleans when he was shot and fatally wounded on his front doorstep by a group of unknown assassins. His deathbed statement was said to be either "Sicilians have done for me," or "Dagoes," which was interpreted as indicating an Italian connection with his death.

Seventeen Italian immigrants were arrested as a result of this alleged statement, and they were called part of a "Sicilian Assassination League." The prime count of murder against nine of the defendants was the first to come to trial. Before the trial, however, the prosecution dropped its case against one of the defendants, and the judge directed a verdict of acquittal against another due to a lack of evidence. Nevertheless, it was widely assumed that the other seven suspects would be convicted.[1]

On March 13, 1891 the jury acquitted four of them and a mistrial was declared in the case of the other three. The citizens of New Orleans were outraged by this apparent miscarriage of justice. Soon after the trial, a mass meeting of the town was called, which turned into an angry mob. The crowd marched on the jail, broke into it, shot nine of the 17 defendants, and publicly hung two others. In response, the Italian government recalled its foreign minister to the United States in protest. Diplomatic relations were resumed, however, when the United States made an indemnity payment to the Italian government.

Most contemporary explanations that rely on verifiable evidence now indicate that Hennessey's death was actually the result of a business rivalry between two Italian families: the Matrangas and the Provenzanos.[2] The Provenzanos controlled the dock areas of New Orleans, but the Matrangas had begun to take business away from them.

In early 1890, several of Matranga's workers were killed or wounded. The Provenzanos were accused. In July, 1890 several of the Provenzanos were convicted, but a new trial was subsequently ordered due to inconclusive identification of the suspects. The Matrangas objected to this and were especially unhappy with Police Chief Hennessey, who supported the Provenzanos during the trial and who was thought to have influenced the judge in setting aside the verdict.

At the retrial of the Provenzanos, Hennessey was scheduled to testify against the Matrangas to the effect that they were part of a "Mafia" in New Orleans. Hennessey was, of course, killed before he testified, and many concluded that his death proved that a "Mafia" existed.

In the eventual retrial of the Provenzanos, however, the Mafia issue was never raised, and there has never been any hint that Hennessey ever had any evidence of a "Mafia" in New Orleans. If such evidence existed, it never came out either before or after his death.

During this period, many people in North America generally assumed that some sort of "Mafia" existed in Italy (or Sicily). As a corollary to this belief, it was commonly held that if there was a "Mafia" there, some of its members were probably included in the mass of immigrants from southern Italy during the 1880s.[3] As a result, a common explanation given for these murders was lax immigration controls that permitted entry to North America of numerous ex-convicts and criminals escaping from Italian justice.[4]

The Italian Connection

From a historical perspective, it appears that a desire to believe in a local "Mafia" outstripped any facts that were available to support its existence. For example, it was claimed that there were many unsolved murders of Italians in New Orleans during this period. However, less than four Italian deaths per year have been documented. As Dwight Smith has observed,

> In retrospect, it appears that a desire to believe in a local Mafia
> society outstripped any objective investigation of fact. Shreds of
> evidence—even hearsay assertions—that would support the the-
> ory were accepted without reservation, and contrary evidence
> was ignored.[5]

In addition, local feelings were very much anti-immigrant during this period; so it would not be surprising that Hennessey's death caused an anti-
Italian campaign. It was said during this period that over 1,000 Italian
immigrants with criminal records in Italy had come to the United States
during the previous few years. However, a grand jury investigation of the
lynching of the Italians charged with Hennessey's murder found that only
about 300 Italian immigrants had been offenders in Italy, and most were
petty offenders. In any case, this total of 300 was less than one percent of
the Italian population of New Orleans.

Despite these facts, many people continue to believe, even today, that a
"Mafia" was somehow imported to North America from Italy. Now, it is
only possible to examine this claim through historical investigations. Fortu-
nately, a number of investigations have been conducted to determine the
existence of a "Mafia" in Italy and/or its importation to North America.

Sociologist Joseph Albini conducted an investigation based on archival
data and information provided by confidential informants gathered in both
Italy and the United States. Published in 1971, his book was titled, *The
American Mafia: Genesis of a Legend*. It attempted, among other objectives,
to examine the historical basis for the popular belief that a "Mafia" exists in
Sicily that somehow formed the basis for a similar organization in the United
States. Albini found no formal organization that could be called a "Mafia."

> It is not a centralized, highly complex national and international
> organization with a supreme head in Palermo. It does not have a
> rigidly defined hierarchy of positions. It does not have specific
> rules and rituals. In other words it has none of the characteristics
> generally attributed to it in popular and clandestine descriptions.
> In noting the absence of these characteristics the author is not
> alone, as evidenced by the agreement found in the works of
> Pitre [1904], Barzini [1954], Bruno [1900], Sladen [1907],
> Hood [1916], King and Okey [1901], Neville [1964], Candida
> [1964], Maxwell [1960], Paton [1900], Monroe [1909], Pantale-
> one [1966] to mention only a few.[6]

As Albini notes, numerous authors before him found a similar result; there
appears to be no organization called "Mafia" in Italy. Instead, there is
much evidence to indicate that persons considered "mafioso" came about
during the 1800s in Sicily, when feudalism was legally abolished. This
resulted in a large class of landowners (who had land to be cultivated) and
a large class of peasants (who could now cultivate the land if they paid rent

to the landowner). This situation led to the demand for a person who could: (1) make sure that the landowner received an adequate yearly rent for his land, and (2) provide protection for the landowner because the government could not guarantee it. As a result, there emerged a middleman called a "gabellotto" or "mafioso" who provided protection for landowners, while insuring that the peasants paid for their use of the land. As Albini discovered,

> By using violence, by subjugating the tenant into accepting impossible leases, by extorting the small farmer with threats of attacks upon person and property, the "gabellotto" entrenched himself in a patronage system which continues today. As a client to his landowner in return for certain favors he promised continued suppression of the peasant. As a patron to the peasant he promised work and the continuation of contracts.[7]

This system of protection and patronage provided by the "gambelotto" or "mafioso" was not found to be a centralized or organized system. In fact, Albini found no evidence of an organization called "Mafia." Rather, "Mafia" merely refers to the role of the mafioso in Sicilian society.

> "Mafia" then is not an organization. It is a system of patron-client relationships that interweaves legitimate and illegitimate segments of Sicilian society. "Mafioso" is not a rank or position within a secret organization. Rather it represents a type of position within the patron-client relationship of Sicilian society itself.[8]

Although the work of Albini, and the many others before him cited above, found no evidence of a Mafia in Italy, it is useful to examine the work of subsequent investigators who used slightly different methods in their research.

Criminologist Henner Hess published the results of his historical investigation into a "Mafia" in Italy in 1973. Titled, *Mafia and Mafiosi: The Structure of Power,* he examined Sicilian archives of police reports and trial transcripts from the period 1880-1890. Hess found that, ". . . there is no organisation, no secret society called *mafia.*"[9] Rather than a "Mafia" organization, there was, instead, the mafioso type, which existed in Sicily due to Italy's weak central government which was located far from Sicily. "The moral, social, economic and geographical conditions of Western Sicily, combined with the decisive political factor of a weak central power situated outside Sicily, thus led to the emergence and continued existence of a *mafioso* self-help which stepped into a power vacuum" to enforce contracts and other relationships that the state could not effectively carry out.[10] Hess concluded, that "Mafia is neither an organisation nor a secret society, but a method."[11] Like Albini, Hess sees the idea of a "Mafia" as a general term applied to these individuals who provided "protection" and other services to citizens that the government was unable to provide.

In a subsequent update of his archival investigation, Hess found more evidence to support his conclusions. He found that it is "easy to misinterpret [the actions of mafiosi] as actions planned and supervised by a single command group." This is because these individuals have similar interests. His investigation uncovered no evidence of a *central organization* that controlled those who acted as mafiosi; rather, he found evidence if *individual mafiosi* who shared "the same profession and the same problems" and who occasionally "turn to each other as to colleagues for help."[12]

Anton Blok published an anthropological study of a Sicilian village titled, *The Mafia of a Sicilian Village, 1860-1960*. Blok's study followed the emergence of the concept and role of "Mafia" through an examination of archival data.

Similar to the findings of Albini and Hess, Blok found the emergence of "Mafia" in Italy to be the result of tensions among the central government of Italy, landowners, and peasants.

> *Mafia* emerged in the early nineteenth century when the Bourbon State tried to curb the power of the traditional landowning aristocracy and encouraged the emancipation of the peasantry . . . Feudal rights and privileges were abolished by law, and the peasants were offered a prospect of land which had become marketable. This so-called anti-feudal policy touched off tensions between the central government and the landowners, who sought to maintain their control over both the land and the peasants . . . "mafiosi" were recruited from the ranks of the peasantry to provide the large estate owners with armed staffs to confront both the impact of the State and the restive peasants, especially in the inland areas of the island where the Bourbon State failed to monopolize the use of physical power.[13]

According to Blok, therefore, mafiosi came about due to the need for power-brokers to mediate between the weak central government, which was attempting to alter the long-standing privileges of the landowners and, on the other hand, between the landowners and the peasants, whom the government was attempting to liberate.

> Even after the unification of Italy, the State failed to monopolize the use of physical force in large areas of western Sicily and, therefore, could not hope to enforce legislation . . . "Mafia" was born of the tensions between the central government and local landowners on the one hand, and between the latter and peasants on the other.[14]

Blok found no evidence of a full-fledged organization called the "Mafia," but only uncovered evidence of private citizens who found themselves in a position for gain by using violence to control a political situation.

As a result, Albini, Hess, and Blok each found the "mafia" to be a term applied to individuals who were employed by private citizens for protection. In none of these investigations was there any evidence that these "mafiosi" were coordinated or organized in any systematic way.

Still another investigation, titled *Mafioso*, was published by journalist Gaia Servadio. The book attempted to assess the historical accuracy of a belief in an Italian Mafia. Interestingly, Servadio's findings concur with those of previous investigators.

> When Sicily became part of the new-born state of Italy in 1860 it had been under continual foreign occupation for more than two thousand years . . . To the outsider, Sicilian society appeared brutal, corrupt and secretive. It was not difficult to lump these qualities together, and in fact it was during the decade of 1860-70 that the myth of a 'secret society' was born and baptized. Italy, and soon Europe, discovered 'the Mafia'.[15]

Like Albini, Hess, and Blok, Servadio saw "the Mafia" as the result of the inability of a central government to effectively deal with the people of Sicily who, historically, had resisted foreign occupation by an outside government. She goes on to note how the idea of a secret society may have come about.

> For an administrator or policeman confronted with the complex criminal machinery of Sicilian society the conspiratorial notion of a mysterious secret entity made a kind of sense, and glossed over any more far-reaching speculations. They saw the symptoms, but diagnosed the wrong disease. If the Mafia were in fact a secret society, it would be long defunct. Even a weak police force would have uncovered names and details of its organization, and the Mafia whose rise we have traced is not secret: on the contrary, it thrives on publicity.[16]

As Servadio points out, it is improbable that a secret society could have survived, especially when the acts of mafiosi thrive on publicity (i.e., violence or murders are rarely kept secret. Under most circumstances, it is desired that the evidence be discovered to serve as an example of influence or power).[17]

Servadio concludes that destruction of the "Mafia" will never come about because no such organization exists. "The Mafia cannot be eliminated because, as a single entity it does not exist, it is not a 'thing,' not a secret society."[18] Servadio goes on to note that only through more equal distribution of wealth will the undesirable activities of mafiosi be eliminated. As she suggests, their services as power-brokers among the landowners, the government, and peasants would no longer be needed if disputes over property ownership were resolved.

A fifth historical investigation of the roots of the "Mafia" was published by Italian sociologist Pino Arlacchi. Using archival data that included official inquiries and court records, he found the "mafia was a form of behaviour and a kind of power, not a formal organization."[19] Arlacchi found, like the investigators before him, that individuals, called *mafioso*, emerged as power-brokers due to a weak central government. Given the conditions "typical of the local community, there was very little security of property, wealth or person, anyone who owned anything had to entrust its protection to the leading *mafioso* of the area."[20] Those refusing to pay protection money suffered from fires, robberies, vandalism and, occasionally, murder. Therefore, Arlacchi's investigation of the origins of the "Mafia" drew similar conclusions to those of Albini, Hess, Blok, and Servadio: the term "Mafia" describes a criminal lifestyle, not an organization.

A sixth historical investigation was conducted of the origins of organized crime in northern Italy, rather than in Sicily. Sociologist James Walston examined court records, police archives, newspaper sources, and conducted interviews to examine the nature of organized crime in Naples, Italy during the nineteenth and twentieth centuries. Walston examined the origins of the "Camorra," a term used to describe Neapolitan organized crime. Walston found that "there has been organized crime in Naples since the beginning of the 19th century." He discovered that the "rise to a position of power and prestige of Neapolitan gangsters has not changed" over the years and, in fact, "it is a similar path taken by mafiosi and gangsters everywhere."[21]

Nevertheless, it was found that "Neapolitan society is too fragmented, as indeed one would expect a city of two million people to be, to allow a single figure [or group] to control the whole or even a fractional part of the whole" of political power necessary for the protection of organized crime activities. In the villages around Naples, Walston found "gangsters might control the local council . . . But in the city and region as a whole there is too great a heterogeneity for one social group to gain control."[22]

Although there is much evidence of continuing organized crime activity by "Camorra" groups, Walston expressed doubts about the existence of a "strictly ordered secret society" that has continued for several hundred years. First, the education level of the organized criminals and very high illiteracy rate casts doubt that they are "sufficiently literate" to write or read rules. Second, an ordered society governed by "codes" or internal "laws" would be quite vulnerable to police discovery once the "secret is out." Third, the "supposed submissiveness of members" to a "code" ignores the fact that "internal conflict within the society" did occur, and continues to occur.[23] Indeed, a continuing "gang war" has resulted in the trials of several hundred defendants originally recruited as members while in prison. Conflicts among these Neapolitan groups have arisen due to resistance to an attempted organization along geographical lines, the profitability of the narcotics trade, and disagreements over control of various illicit markets, such as cigarette smuggling.[24]

Testimony from Tommaso Buscetta, a Sicilian organized crime figure who became a government informant in 1985, revealed that there was no central organization of criminal groups in Sicily until the 1950s. Interestingly, the suggestion for such an organization, according to Buscetta, was made by Joseph Bonanno, a well-known American organized crime figure. The purpose for the organization of criminal groups (via a "commission") was "to resolve disputes" among the various criminal groups.[25] The "commission" in Sicily did not last very long, however, and continuing disputes among criminal groups over both territory, control, and markets resulted in mass trials of defendants there during the 1980s.

Each of the six separate historical investigations by Albini, Hess, Blok, Servadio, Arlacchi, Walston, as well as others,[26] has ended with similar conclusions. First, none found evidence of a *single* organization called "Mafia" in Italy. Rather, it is a "collection of groups."[27] Second, the violence attributed to a "Mafia" in Italy appears to have resulted from individuals filling the need for power-brokers among the conflicting interests of the government, landowners, and peasants.

In recent years, the organization of the Mafia in Sicily has taken on newfound importance. The so-called "Pizza Connection" case in New York established that Sicilian Mafia figures had conspired with American Mafia figures to import heroin through pizza parlors in the United States. Tons of morphine were smuggled from Turkey to Sicily, processed there into heroin, and then smuggled through U.S. airports.[28] This case prompted a realization on the part of U.S. investigators that, regardless of the form, organized criminals did engage in mutually beneficial arrangements, and sometimes on an international scale.[29] The mafia "maxitrial" in Sicily opened in 1986, charging 464 defendants with multiple murders and with operation of a worldwide heroin ring covering the years 1975-1985. In Italy, this was momentous for two reasons: mafia members and names were made public, and never before had such a huge trial occurred. Tomasso Buscetta testified, as he did in the Pizza Connection trial in New York. A total of 1,337 witnesses testified, and 342 of the defendants were convicted. From the Italian point of view, "this was the first serious assault ever made on the entire, infinitely complex Mafia phenomenon."[30] It also prompted recognition that, regardless of its structure, some Sicilian organized crime figures were now operating worldwide. This prosecution effort has continued with the conviction of 97 members of the 'Ndrangheta crime "family," after a four-year trial. This Mafia group operated out of Calabria in southern Italy. They were found guilty of 20 murders, extortion, drug smuggling, and other crimes. Thirteen of the members received life terms, and the others sentences that totaled 460 years.[31]

Most Italian organized crime, like its American counterpart, remains primarily local in nature. The confession of Antonio Calderone, an alleged "boss" of a Mafia group in Sicily, illustrates this. The city of Palermo has long been known to be the most active Mafia city in Sicily, and Calderone claims "there are more than 50 of them [mafia families], at least one for each neighborhood" in Palermo.[32] But he claims, "a family is autonomous in its own territory."[33] Therefore, the organization of organized crime can be characterized as locally based, but its activities, especially in recent years, can span the globe. According to the U.S. Drug Enforcement Administration, alliances have been struck between several Sicilian Mafia "families" and the Cali and Medellin drug cartels in Colombia.[34]

From City Gangs to a National Conspiracy

After the Hennessey murder in 1890, and the subsequent lynchings of the Italian suspects, public interest in a "Mafia" quickly faded. In fact, during the 25-year period from 1918 to 1943 the word "Mafia" appeared in the *New York Times* only four times.

During the early 1900s, there existed concern about organized crime, but not about the Mafia. John Landesco's work for the Illinois Crime Survey in 1929 is illustrative. His examination of "Organized Crime in Chicago" found crime "organized on a scale and with resources unprecedented in the history of Chicago." He found the "leading gangsters were practically immune from punishment," and that organized crime had corrupted local politicians.[35] This report identified by name the gangsters of whom it spoke. Big Jim Colosimo who ran the rackets up until his murder in 1920, followed by John Torrio, who organized a bootlegging syndicate from 1920-24, followed by Al Capone, who consolidated all forms of commercialized vice and gambling in Chicago during the late 1920s.[36]

Ironically, concern about these "gangsters" was seen as a local phenomenon, rather than a problem of any national significance. A similar situation existed in New York during the early 1900s. Keep in mind that this was the era of prohibition, which was probably responsible more than any single event for the emergence of strong organized crime groups. Organized crime developed around the black market created by the void left between public demand for alcoholic beverages (and the other vices of gambling and prostitution) and the prohibition of them.

Illegal alcohol manufacturing, smuggling, and operation of speakeasies were predominant forms of organized crime during this period as prohibition took effect in January, 1920. Brewers of alcoholic beverages had a choice in 1920: shut down, convert their equipment to make legal one-half percent liquor, or do business as usual by becoming partners with questionable people who would market their product. Organized crime groups slowly evolved into more sophisticated criminal enterprises, as was made necessary by competition from other criminal entrepreneurs, to evade law enforcement, and to bribe public officials when necessary. This evolution was slow as is witnessed by the fact that most local crime leaders during this period did not die a natural death. Gang warfare was common, as mostly uneducated, first- or second-generation immigrants attempted to make their fortune. In Chicago, "Big Jim" Colosimo was murdered by

Johnny Torrio's people before prohibition was six months old. Torrio was later to be shot five times, but lived as his assassin ran out of bullets. He left for New York to become a mentor to the up-and-coming Lucky Luciano. Hymie Weis controlled part of Chicago's vices with Al Capone, his primary competitor. Weis was killed by Al Capone's gang in 1926.[37]

In New York, the story was similar. Arnold Rothstein organized the vices there, and mentored such infamous figures as Frank Costello and Jack "Legs" Diamond.[38] An attempt on the life of Frank Costello failed. Legs Diamond was shot and recovered, only to be challenged by Dutch Schultz. Rothstein himself was ultimately murdered in 1928, a crime blamed on Legs Diamond.[39] Dutch Schultz was later murdered by Charles "Lucky" Luciano in 1935.[40]

It may be difficult to remember who murdered who,[41] but the point is clear. Organized crime in the early 1900s was centered around the vices (especially alcohol), involved a great deal of corruption to maintain a degree of immunity from law enforcement, and the competition to control these vices was violent, at least in selected large cities. This violence, and the reign of these gangs, declined somewhat as the Great Depression took hold in 1930, law enforcement slowly became professionalized and more effective, followed by the end of Prohibition in December, 1933.[42] The Depression took many of their customers' spendable income, and the repeal of Prohibition dried up the huge illegal alcohol market. In spite of these set-backs, however, many organized crime groups maintained themselves largely on the illicit profits to be made by gambling.

The Kefauver Hearings, 1950

It was not until 1950 that "Mafia" made a dramatic return to the head-lines. U.S. Senator Estes Kefauver chaired the Special Senate Committee to Investigate Organized Crime in the United States (Kefauver Committee). The Committee spent 12 months holding public hearings in major cities across the country. Kefauver's investigation received much attention because there was live television coverage of the hearings. A number of law enforcement officials testified, as did a number of individuals with criminal records. Interestingly, all the criminal offenders denied membership in, or knowledge of, a "Mafia," while the law enforcement officials claimed there existed such an organization, although they offered no objective evidence to substantiate their belief. Despite these conflicting views and lack of evidence, the Kefauver Committee concluded,

> There is a sinister criminal organization known as the Mafia operating throughout the country with ties in other nations in the opinion of the committee. The Mafia is a direct descendant of a criminal organization of the same name originating in the

island of Sicily . . . The Mafia is a loose-knit organization . . . the
binder which ties together the two major criminal syndicates as
well as numerous other criminal groups throughout the country.[43]

William Moore, a historian, conducted an extensive investigation of the
Kefauver Committee, and he found that the political environment at the
time worked against the possibility of conducting any significant investigation into the true nature of organized crime. Because the Committee was
created at a time when there were "rampant fears and rumors about politi-
co-criminal conspiracies," Moore found that the Kefauver Committee did
not investigate the problem so much as it dramatized it.

> Particularly in the case of the Mafia, the senators lacked ade-
> quate evidence for their conclusions. Because such groups as the
> press and the academic community failed to point out the weak-
> nesses in the Committee's overblown and unfounded statements,
> the public accepted them, and the popular myths and misunder-
> standings grew stronger, buttressed by the "proofs" of the
> Kefauver Committee. Sensational journalists and publishers
> enjoyed a field day . . . gangster movies and television programs
> dramatized variations of the same theme . . . Even after the ini-
> tial shock and novelty of the Kefauver findings had lifted and
> critics began to question the more sweeping Committee state-
> ments, the public at large continued to hold to the older conspir-
> acy view, thus making more difficult an intelligent appraisal of
> organized crime.[44]

Kefauver's conclusions about the nature of organized crime in the United States were very similar to those at the turn of the century. The Committee adopted the conspiratorial view that most organized crime was controlled by a single "Mafia." It "implied that [the Mafia] essentially originated outside of American society and was imposed upon the public by a
group of immoral men, bound together by a mysterious ethnic conspiracy."
As William Moore also discovered, the Kefauver Committee "unquestion-
ably exaggerated the degree of centralization in the underworld." Treating
organized crime as a conspiracy, rather than as a social and economic problem, allowed the Committee to focus on legal remedies and to dismiss
underlying circumstances that give rise to organized crime. In discussing
gambling, the Kefauver Committee even suggested that "those who supported legalization might themselves be part of an underworld plot."[45]
    As recognized by Henner Hess, such a view of organized crime as an
alien conspiracy is much easier for the public and government officials to
accept (and legislate against) than is the proposition that organized crime
may result from social and economic disparities within American society
(which do not provide for simple answers). Even more disconcerting, in the
view of historian William Moore, is the fact that the Kefauver Committee

misled the public to believe that a thorough investigation of organized crime had taken place when, in fact, it had not.

> If it is unfair to criticize the Committee for an investigation it did not make, it is hardly unjust to point out that they did not make it and that the scope of their authoritative judgment should have been lessened by that failure. The real tragedy, of course, is that the public thought such a study had been made, and popular opinion being set, later investigations enjoyed less flexibility for reeducating the public.[46]

As a result, the Kefauver Committee, largely through its televised hearings in various parts of the country, brought the concept of "Mafia" to the forefront of public concern, but added nothing to what little was known about the nature and causes of organized crime in America. As Joseph Albini has remarked, Kefauver did not prove the existence of "the Mafia." Rather, he "merely assumed its existence."[47]

Other investigations have subsequently examined the evidence that exists to support the claims of the Kefauver Committee. One of the early critics was sociologist Daniel Bell.

> Unfortunately for a good story—and the existence of the Mafia would be a whale of a story—neither the Senate Crime Committee in its testimony, nor Kefauver in his book, presented any real evidence that the Mafia exists as a functioning organization. One finds police officials asserting before the Kefauver Committee their "belief" in the Mafia; the Narcotics Bureau "thinks" that a worldwide dope ring allegedly run by Luciano is part of the Mafia; but the only other real evidence presented . . . is that certain crimes bear "the earmarks of the Mafia."[48]

Bell's conclusion was corroborated by Burton Turkus, a New York prosecutor who broke up the "Murder, Inc." ring, who denied the existence of the Mafia.[49]

In place of this conspiratorial view, Daniel Bell offered an alternative explanation for the existence of organized crime, based on ethnic succession into positions of political power. Bell argued that it was necessary to look at the waves of immigrant groups that have entered the United States. During the middle 1800s, for example, the Irish comprised the largest group of immigrants, the late 1800s were characterized by German-Jews, and the early 1900s saw a large number of Italian immigrants. Bell claims that as these ethnic groups attempted to enter the mainstream of American life, some of them did so through illegal means. He provides examples of well-known Irish criminals in politics and in the trucking industry, as well as Jewish gangsters in the garment industry in years past. According to Bell, as each ethnic group became established in American life, the next wave of immigrants received the bulk of attention when crimes were perpetrated.

> There is little question that men of Italian origin appeared in
> most of the leading roles in the high drama of gambling and
> mobs, just as twenty years ago the children of East European
> Jews were the most prominent figures in organized crime, and
> before that individuals of Irish decent were similarly prominent.
> To some extent statistical accident and the tendency of newspa-
> pers to emphasize the few sensational figures gives a greater
> illusion about the domination of illicit activities by a single eth-
> nic group than all the facts warrant.[50]

Ultimately, following the year-long hearings of the Kefauver Committee,
the rediscovered interest in the "Mafia" was not lasting, either in terms of
public interest or legislative response. But the idea of "Mafia" was to return
to the public spotlight for good in 1957.

The Apalachin Incident, 1957

On November 19, 1957 *The New York Times* had a page one story head-
lined, "65 Hoodlums Seized in a Raid and Run Out of Upstate Village." As
it turned out, 58 Italians, some with criminal records, were gathered at the
home of Joseph Barbara in Apalachin, New York. The incident itself was
unremarkable. Speculation about the event was fueled primarily by the lack
of information.

> New York State Police Sergeant Edgar Croswell had set up a
> roadblock on the only route away from the Barbara home, because
> a large number of guests [most of whom were unknown to him
> then] were visiting a local resident about whom he had long held
> suspicions of illegal activity. But he had no charges to bring
> against the men he detained or against those who were found later
> inexplicably in the woods adjoining the Barbara property. He
> learned the names, addresses, and stated occupations of fifty-eight
> men [including the Barbaras, father and son] and was able to
> determine through teletype networks whether any were wanted by
> police in New York State or in their home jurisdictions; he
> checked those who drove cars for valid operator licenses and
> those who might be armed for pistol permits, and he searched
> each vehicle and its occupants [the principal result being a report
> of how much money each was carrying]. Beyond those bare
> essentials there was little Croswell could do except let them go. It
> was a baffling event, and we can appreciate why, amid all the tan-
> talizing news stories in the first few days after the incident, there
> were few government leaders willing to be quoted.[51]

There was great interest, sparked by election year publicity-seeking in New
York State, in finding out what this supposed meeting was all about. None

of the 65 men at Barbara's house would talk to government officials or say that it was anything more than a friendly visit, but John Cusack, New York district director of the Federal Narcotics Bureau, believed it was a meeting with a purpose.

AP/WIDE WORLD PHOTOS

Front view of the hilltop estate of Joseph Barbara in Apalachin, New York. This is the site of the police raid November 14, 1957, that broke up a meeting of 58 men.

In early 1958, Cusack testified before a committee of the New York State legislature. Rather than discuss the fact that eight of the men at Joseph Barbara's house had previous narcotics convictions, he attempted to link the meeting with a "Mafia." Not other witness mentioned the Mafia, but it raised the specter of Mafia in a government forum for the first time since the Kefauver hearings.[52]

The New York State committee incorporated Cusack's allegations in its interim report, claiming that "the Apalachin meeting . . . is strong evidence that there exists in this country an active association or organization of criminals whose operations are nationwide and international."[53] When the report was submitted to the New York State Legislature in April, 1958, the media reported that the Apalachin incident was considered to be a "gathering of the Grand Council of the Mafia." In this way, Cusack's unsupported allegations were eventually interpreted as the conclusions of an official government investigation.

Despite Cusack's assertions, which were picked up by the media, the most striking feature of the entire Apalachin incident was the unwillingness of those gathered to testify before a grand jury or investigative committee about their purpose. Most of Barbara's guests employed the Fifth Amendment protection against self-incrimination and refused to testify.

In the 1983 autobiography of reputed organized crime figure Joseph Bonanno, he claimed that the Apalachin incident in 1957 was a meeting of leaders of organized crime groups in the New York area to discuss the implications of the recent murder of Albert Anastasia. This account may, or may not, be accurate as Joseph Bonanno did not attend the meeting, and it is not clear whether any meeting ever took place at Apalachin.

In May 1958, New York State established the Temporary State Commission of Investigation to uncover the purpose of the meeting at Apalachin. The Commission had subpoena power to force the appearance of reluctant witnesses, and it had the power to grant immunity to prevent witnesses from invoking the Fifth Amendment when testifying about incriminating activities. Of those men that appeared, most refused to testify and were jailed for contempt. Those that did testify gave unsatisfactory answers to the Commission, explaining their presence as a "wrong turn" or as a visit to a sick friend. The Commission hoped that by jailing the reluctant witnesses for refusing to testify under a grant of immunity, they would eventually hear what they were looking for. Unfortunately, the Commission's efforts were unsuccessful.

By 1959, 14 men had been subpoenaed, eight were jailed, two were fugitives, one was contesting the subpoena, and only three had chosen to answer the Commission's questions. In March, 1959, New York State's highest court upheld the jailing of the first seven men. As a result, the men began to answer the questions posed by the Commission. Their responses, however, were considered to be "inherently incredible," and the Commission continued to hold the men in contempt and held them in jail. In October, 1959, New York State's Court of Appeals held that the Commission could not continue to hold the men in jail just because it did not like the answers given. The Court found, "it has not been established that the answers to questions are so preposterous as to offer not the slightest possibility of truthfulness." To hold these men in jail indefinitely it was thought could result "in life imprisonment without trial by jury."[54]

Following this decision, the remaining five witnesses also won their release, the last being released after nearly two years of confinement. In February 1963, the Temporary State Commission of Investigation released its final report which reflected the lack of success of its tactics.

> Apalachin attendees subpoenaed to testify at the Commission's public hearings, who refused to answer Commission questions, were confined to jail for various periods ranging up to sixteen months—the only prison term ever served by these major racketeers. Although the full story as to the purpose of the meeting has not been divulged by any participant, much was accomplished by this investigation to shake up the members of this criminal syndicate; many have departed from the State, others have gone into full or semi-retirement and their over-all strength and influence in this State has been diminished substantially.[55]

It is clear that the Commission attempted, in vain, to justify its actions by referring to the witnesses as "major racketeers," even though none had prison records and no conviction resulting from the Commission investigation withstood court review. The Apalachin incident did not die easily, however.

In May 1959, 27 of the men at Barbara's house were indicted for conspiracy to obstruct justice through their failure to explain the meeting at Apalachin. Thirty-six other attendees were named as co-conspirators. The trial lasted eight weeks and consisted of testimony from 69 prosecution witnesses. None of the defendants took the stand. The case went to the jury in December 1959, and all the defendants were found guilty. In June 1960, however, the U.S. Court of Appeals unanimously reversed the convictions. An excerpt from the opinion of Chief Judge Lumbard provides an indication of the court's rationale.

> The fact that none of those present admitted that he was asked to attend a meeting for other than social purposes and that at least some of those present must have lied, does not warrant a jury's conclusion that any or all lies were told pursuant to an agreement made [among the attendees]. There is nothing in the record or in common experience to suggest that it is not just as likely that each one present decided for himself that it would be wiser not to discuss all that he knew.
>
> Indeed, the pervasive innuendo throughout this case that this was a gathering of bad people for an evil purpose would seem to us to rebut any possible argument that only as a result of group action would any individual lie. Even an otherwise law-abiding citizen who is stopped and interrogated by police, and who is given no reason for his detention and questioning, may feel it his right to give as little information as possible and even perhaps to respond evasively if he believe he might thereby by earlier rid of police inquiry . . .

The other judges also expressed concern about the apparently indiscriminate round-up of citizens without cause, and the supposed link to organized crime, that "was given unusual and disturbing publicity." As the Court concluded,

> This is vastly unfortunate; not only does it go beyond the judicial record necessary for its support, but it suggests that the administration of the criminal law is in such dire straits that crash methods have become a necessity. But it seems we should have known better, and a prosecution framed on such a doubtful basis should never have been allowed to proceed so far. For in America we still respect the dignity of the individual, and even an unsavory character is not to be imprisoned except on definite proof of specific crime. And nothing in present criminal law administration suggests or justifies sharp relaxation of traditional standards.[56]

The result of the Apalachin episode is much more far-reaching than the substance of the event. Like the Kefauver hearings, a great deal of publicity surrounded the Apalachin incident, and it went a long way toward cementing public attitudes about the nature of organized crime, despite the absence of hard information assembled by either of these events. A new event in 1963 held the spotlight on organized crime.

The Valachi Hearings and the Cosa Nostra, 1963

In September 1963, Joseph Valachi appeared before the U.S. Senate Subcommittee on Investigations and testified to the existence of a nationwide organization involved in widespread criminal activity. Valachi was an admitted lower-level criminal associated with the Genovese crime "family" in New York City. This testimony, together with more detailed information obtained by federal investigators during months of interviews with Valachi, constituted the first time someone had ever admitted "belonging to or

openly talk[ing] about a huge criminal conspiracy in this country, indeed an entire subculture of evil . . . the Cosa Nostra."[57] In addition to providing his view of the structure of organized crime in the United States, Valachi also discussed the processes by which this structure engaged in crime in a systematic manner.

Valachi's testimony is significant because, unlike the Kefauver hearings and the Apalachin incident, it resulted in far-reaching new laws designed to combat organized crime more effectively. His accounts became part of the rationale for legislation permitting widespread use of wiretaps, special grand juries, witness immunity, and other prosecution tools.

When Valachi testified, he told of the existence of activities and organization not previously known by the United States government. His willingness to testify resulted, not because of his involvement in these activities, but due to circumstances beyond his control. Valachi felt he was marked to be killed in prison by his "boss," and in order to prevent that from happening, he killed a fellow inmate who turned out to be an inno-

AP/WIDE WORLD PHOTOS

Joseph Valachi sits at the witness table as he waits to begin another round of testimony before the U.S. Senate Subcommittee on Investigations, October 8, 1963. Valachi turned government informant after he was marked for assassination by the crime syndicate (the Genovese crime "family" in New York City) of which he was a member. During his testimony, Valachi told of gangland wars in New York City, and implicated his former boss, Vito Genovese, in widespread illegal activity.

cent bystander. To escape the death penalty for his crime, and feeling betrayed by his organization, Valachi agreed to cooperate with federal investigators.

Valachi's testimony before the Permanent Subcommittee on Investigations of the Senate Committee on Government Operations described a number of activities and an organization that provided new information about the nature and extent of organized crime in the United States. The two major subjects covered by Valachi were:

1. A power struggle among Italian-American gangs that took place during the early 1930s, called the Castellammarese War.

2. The existence of a structured organization whose principal activity is to pursue crime, called La Cosa Nostra.

In addition, Valachi gave the details of a number of murders in New York City that were confirmed as previously "open" cases by the New York City Police Department.

The veracity of Valachi's testimony became an important issue because of his unsavory past and also because he was facing a murder charge. The primary method used to establish his truthfulness was the confirmation by police that the murders he described did indeed occur. During the so-called Castellammarese War, for example, Valachi stated that up to 60 killings may have taken place. He was only able to name a few, however. Valachi also claimed the Castellammarese War was national in scope, but provided no evidence that this was actually the case.

> MR. ALDERMAN (Counsel to the Committee): Did Masseria declare or condemn anybody who came from that area (the Castellammarese area of Sicily), no matter where they came from in the United States, to death?
>
> MR. VALACHI: All Castellammarese. That is the way I was told. I never found out the reason. I never asked for the reason. All I understand is that all the Castellammarese were sentenced to death.
>
> SENATOR McCLELLAN: That is when all-out war was declared by the other side?
>
> MR. VALACHI: That is, I would put it, national.
>
> SENATOR McCLELLAN: It was made national.
>
> MR. VALACHI: It was made in all cities, wherever the members were—in Chicago, Cleveland, and California.[58]

The question that arises is, how is this incident a national war when only a handful of sites are mentioned, and actual events can only be described in one location (New York City)? This was not pursued further by the Subcommittee. Neither was an alternative account of the same killings given a decade earlier.[59] Inexplicably, there was not even a check as to whether 60 people were killed during this period in the manner Valachi described. Two separate historical investigations have subsequently confirmed only four or five deaths, and no evidence of a national "gangland war."[60]

Valachi's version of events was accepted by Senate investigators (and the Justice Department) even though law enforcement officials had not even heard of a "Cosa Nostra" prior to his testimony. Furthermore, his version was accepted in spite of available conflicting evidence. This is a serious concern as Valachi's testimony to the existence and structure of Cosa Nostra, and the Castellammarese War as its immediate precursor, became the basis for the conclusions drawn about organized crime by the President's Crime Commission and by others.[61]

Valachi described the organizational structure as consisting of "the individual bosses of the individual families, and then we had an underboss, and then we had what we call a caporegima which is a lieutenant, and then we have what we call soldiers."[62] When it came to specifying the role of the organization in the lives of its members, however, the Cosa Nostra appears less organized.[63]

> SENATOR JAVITS: Now, what he (Vito Genovese) got out of it then, your actions and these of other members of the family, was to kill off or otherwise deal with people who were bothering him; is that right?
>
> MR. VALACHI: Anybody bothering him, naturally he has the soldiers.
>
> SENATOR JAVITS: That is the function of the family?
>
> MR. VALACHI: Right.
>
> SENATOR JAVITS: That is mutual protection?
>
> MR. VALACHI: Right.
>
> SENATOR JAVITS: Otherwise, everybody operates by himself. They may take partners but that is their option.
>
> MR. VALACHI: Right.

Given this scenario, it appears that if an organization existed at all, it was a very loose association.

Valachi also provided information about the members of Cosa Nostra "families" in the New York area. While all the law enforcement personnel who testified, including Attorney General Robert Kennedy, claimed that a nationwide criminal organization existed, no one could provide supporting information independent of Valachi.

> SENATOR MUSKIE: Would it have been possible for you to reconstruct these charts (of Cosa Nostra families) without his testimony?
>
> MR. SHANLEY (of the Intelligence Unit of the New York City Police Department): No, sir.

Another important question about Valachi's testimony is why it did not result in convictions of organized crime figures.[64] The willingness to accept Valachi's often uncorroborated testimony could be explained by the Senate committee wanting to hear Valachi's version because it corresponded with the preconceptions established by the Kefauver hearings and the Apalachin incident. As Dwight Smith explains, "It was a case of the story being true because it sounded like what ought to be heard."[65]

Fratianno, The FBI and The *Tieri* Trial, 1980

Gordon Hawkins has argued that, like the existence of God, the history of organized crime has been based largely on unprovable assumptions. He claimed that to the believer in a "Mafia" or "Cosa Nostra," no evidence is enough to prove its nonexistence.

> Thus, denials of membership in, or knowledge of, the syndicate can not only be dismissed as self-evidently false, but also adduced as evidence of what they deny. If there is gang warfare, this indicates that "an internal struggle for dominance over the entire organization" is going on; and also provides "a somber illustration of how cruel and calculating the underworld continues to be." If peace prevails this may be taken either as evidence of the power of the syndicate leadership and the fear in which it is held; or alternatively as reflecting the development of "the sophisticated and polished control of rackets that now characterize that organization." In the end, it is difficult to resist the conclusion that one is not dealing with an empirical phenomenon at all, but with an article of faith.[66]

Hawkins, of course, did not believe that organized crime does not exist. To believe this would mean that all crime is the product of the random or unplanned acts of individuals. Clearly, this is not the case. The point Hawkins attempted to make was that although belief in God relies essentially on faith, believers in a North American "Mafia" or "Cosa Nostra" expect others also to believe it based on a similar leap of faith.

At the time of Hawkins' writing in 1969, the only "independent" evidence that had been produced in support of a North American criminal conspiracy was the testimony of Joseph Valachi in 1963. As discussed in the last section, Valachi was a criminal who became a government informant and testified to the existence of a nationwide criminal conspiracy that he said controlled the bulk of the illegal gambling, prostitution, and narcotics trade in North America. Although the 1967 President's Crime Commission, and many subsequent writers, have accepted Valachi's description of organized crime as fact, Hawkins and many others have pointed to a number of inconsistencies that cast doubt on the veracity of Valachi's testimony.

In 1980, this debate over the true nature of organized crime was rekindled with the introduction of another criminal-turned government informant, Jimmy Fratianno. The testimony of Fratianno was seen by many as being more important than Valachi's because, unlike Valachi, Fratianno was said to be (1) a high-ranking member of an organized criminal group, and (2) his testimony appeared to be resulting in the conviction of a number of suspected organized criminals.

As a result, it is appropriate to re-evaluate Hawkins' thesis to determine whether the uncorroborated assertions of Valachi were supported or refuted by Fratianno. Fratianno testified at several trials that have ended in convictions, one of which was selected for discussion here. The case of *United States v. Frank Tieri* took place in federal district court Manhattan in 1980. After a month-long trial, Frank Tieri was convicted of racketeering and conspiracy and was, according to court records, the first person ever proven to be "boss" of a Cosa Nostra "Family." This case was chosen here for its focus on proving the existence of a national conspiracy of organized criminals.

Frank Tieri was originally indicted on charges of racketeering, conspiracy, bankruptcy fraud, and income tax evasion under the Racketeer Influenced and Corrupt Organization (RICO) provisions of the Organized Crime Control Act. This statute is particularly important to the *Tieri* case is that the "enterprise" he was alleged to have illegally operated or received income from was the Cosa Nostra. According to the indictment, the grand jury alleged that,

Jimmy "The Weasel" Fratianno, right, is escorted by an agent into the San Francisco FBI office on November 23, 1977, after surrendering to authorities. Fratianno, then 64, was indicted along with four other men by a Los Angeles federal grand jury, for conspiring to extort a pornographic film business that was a decoy operation set up by the FBI.

> a criminal organization known by various names including La Cosa Nostra was a criminal group which operated throughout the United States through entities known as "Families" with each "Family" having as its leader a person known as a "Boss." At all times relevant to this Indictment, the defendant Frank

> Tieri, a.k.a. "Funzi Tieri," a.k.a. "Funzuola," a.k.a. "The Old
> Man," was the "boss" of one of five New York City "Families"
> of La Cosa Nostra and which "Family" constituted and contin-
> ues to constitute an "enterprise," as defined by [the Organized
> Crime Control Act of 1970].

The significance of this case, therefore, lies in its attempt to prove in court
the existence of the Cosa Nostra as a continuing illegal enterprise, that
Tieri was the "boss" of one of its families, and that he committed various
organized crimes in that capacity.

Fratianno's role in this case was not only to testify to the existence of
the Cosa Nostra, but also to implicate Tieri in at least two indictable offenses during the last 10 years in order to establish the "pattern" of racketeering activity necessary for conviction under RICO. One of the illegal acts
about which Fratianno testified was Tieri's alleged involvement in a bankruptcy fraud of the Westchester Premier Theatre in New York State. The
presiding federal trial judge acknowledged during a conversation with
prosecution and defense counsel (while the jury was excused) how important Fratianno's testimony was to the prosecution's case, and how much the
jury had to rely on his "fragmentary" testimony.[67]

> COURT: So, this may be absolutely far out, but I wonder if there
> is somebody who really is an expert on the relationship
> [between] crime families who could—you see, I don't really
> know. I know nothing about the subject virtually, and I don't
> know whether it is part of the protocol or part of the custom and
> usage to have two families involved in one operation. Now, there
> was that very fragmentary testimony of Fratianno. You know, it's
> two questions or one question or whatever, and it doesn't solve
> very much. He said what he said. But it's almost a subject you'd
> like a Yale professor to come in and . . .
>
> MR. GOLDBERG: Harvard.
>
> COURT: Harvard. You know, I will take any one of those modern
> schools, and come in and explain to me—I would like to know.
>
> MR. GOLDBERG: Maybe I can do it. I was on both sides.
>
> COURT: But what is it, because it may be that people who
> know about this know that it is impossible to have a situation
> where you've got the kind of relationship the government is talk-
> ing about. Maybe that's just an impossibility. On the other hand,
> maybe there is enough of a fraternity between the different fam-
> ilies, if they are families, there is enough of a fraternity that they
> go to each other's wakes, they will go to each other's theatres,
> they will lend each other money, and if Frank Sinatra comes to
> the Westchester Premier Theatre it wouldn't be unusual to have
> Mr. Tieri, who is not a high profile type, he is in the background
> controlling it, maybe the Gambino people are a little more, you

know, social, and they go to the theatre and they get pho-
tographed with Sinatra and all this goes on. Maybe this is perfectly standard. I haven't the faintest idea, and what do I have?
That's a one-liner. It's a one-liner by Mr. Fratianno. I don't know.

Later that same day the trial was nearing completion, but the prosecutor's
request to charge (i.e., recommendations to the judge for his legal instructions to the jury for their deliberations) claimed that Fratianno's testimony
about the Westchester case was *not* essential for a conviction.

> MR. GOLDBERG: Judge, before he offers an expert, will he
> have an offer of proof?
> COURT: You mean expert testimony by Cantalupo?
> MR. GOLDBERG: No. He's going to have expert testimony by
> an FBI agent about the interrelationship of families, no doubt
> plugging up the holes created by Mr. Fratianno.
> COURT: He didn't say that.
> MR. ACKERMAN: No.
> COURT: No.[68]

It can be seen from these two excerpts from the trial record that Fratianno's testimony was significant, yet uncertain.[69] It is clear from these
exchanges that the credibility of Fratianno's testimony had not been well
established at this point.

The most important aspect of the *Tieri* case was the government's
effort to prove the existence of the Cosa Nostra. This effort was based
entirely on the testimony of Fratianno.

> MR. ACKERMAN: Now, directing your attention to late 1947,
> early 1946, did you become a member of any organization?
> MR. FRATIANNO: Yes, sir.
> MR. ACKERMAN: What is the name of that organization?
> MR. FRATIANNO: La Cosa Nostra.
> MR. ACKERMAN: How long have you been a member of La
> Cosa Nostra?
> MR. FRATIANNO: Thirty-two years, sir.
> MR. ACKERMAN: Would you tell the jury what La Cosa Nos-
> tra is?
> MR. FRATIANNO: Well, I would say it is a secret organiza-
> tion, sir.
> MR. ACKERMAN: What does it do, primarily?
> MR. FRATIANNO: Well, it engages in different businesses,
> illegal activities.
> MR. ACKERMAN: What kinds of illegal activities?

> MR. FRATIANNO: I'd say shylocking, bookmaking, taking
> bets on horses, football games, baseball games, labor racketeer-
> ing, all sorts of illegal activity . . .
>
> MR. ACKERMAN: Mr. Fratianno, would you please tell the
> jury what requirements there are for one to become a member
> of La Cosa Nostra?
>
> MR. FRATIANNO: Well, you are more or less proposed by
> somebody. Sometimes you do something significant. Then there
> is times when you have a brother or a father in it, and you get in
> that way. There's different ways, sir.
>
> MR. ACKERMAN: Is there any kind of background require-
> ment that's necessary?
>
> MR. FRATIANNO: You have to be Italian, sir.
>
> MR. ACKERMAN: Would you please tell the jury where La
> Cosa Nostra is located?
>
> MR. FRATIANNO: Well, it is located in different parts of the
> United States, sir, most of the big cities.
>
> MR. ACKERMAN: How is this national organization broken
> down with respect to the big cities?
>
> MR. FRATIANNO: It is broken down into families, sir.
>
> MR. ACKERMAN: Now, I am going to put up a map of the
> United States which has been marked as Government's Exhibit
> 4 for identification. Mr. Fratianno, starting from the West Coast,
> could you tell the jury where there are families, and which cities
> have families of La Cosa Nostra?[70]

Fratianno went on to claim that "families" of La Cosa Nostra exist in 25 cities including San Francisco, San Jose, Los Angeles, Denver, Dallas, Kansas City (Missouri), Chicago, Detroit, Cleveland, Buffalo, St. Louis, Pittsburgh, Steubenville (Ohio), Milwaukee, Philadelphia, Pittston (Pennsylvania), New Orleans, Tampa, an unknown city in Connecticut, Providence, and five families in New York City. He also testified that he met Frank Tieri in 1976 when Tieri was boss of one of the New York City "families."

Unfortunately, problems with Fratianno's account of the Cosa Nostra begin here. The head of the FBI's organized crime operations testified before the Senate Permanent Subcommittee on Investigations in April, 1980, and said there exist 26 "active" families of La Cosa Nostra (LCN) in the United States. Interestingly, he claimed there were LCN families in Tucson (Arizona), Rockford (Illinois), Madison (Wisconsin), and Elizabeth-Newark (New Jersey) that Fratianno did not acknowledge. Further, the FBI agent did not acknowledge in his testimony that any families existed in Steubenville, Ohio or in Connecticut, or that there was an active group in Dallas, as Fratianno had testified.[71]

A comparison of the Fratianno and FBI testimony both in 1980, weighed against Valachi's 1963 testimony about the cities where LCN "families" supposedly exist, reveals some further unaccountable differences.

MR. ALDERMAN (Counsel to the Senate Subcommittee): Mr. Valachi, we have covered New York rather extensively. Now are there any other members, any other families outside of the area of New York?

MR. VALACHI: You mean like Chicago, Boston?

MR. ALDERMAN: Yes. Could you mention the cities where other families exist of the Cosa Nostra, and if you know, the numbers of the members as you know them, could you mention them?

MR. VALACHI: I will start with Philadelphia. In Philadelphia I would say about 100. Boston, when I left the streets, was about 20, 18 or 20. Chicago, about 150. Cleveland, about 40 or 50. Los Angeles, about 40. Tampa, about 10. Newark, about 100. Detroit, I am not familiar at all with Detroit . . .

MR. ALDERMAN: How about Buffalo?

MR. VALACHI: Buffalo, about 100 to 125.

MR. ALDERMAN: Utica, N.Y.?

MR. VALACHI: Utica, 80 to 100.

MR. ALDERMAN: I think you covered New Orleans, did you?

MR. VALACHI: No, I didn't cover New Orleans. Very few in New Orleans.

MR. ALDERMAN: Now you mentioned you don't know any in Detroit. Do you know if any families exist there?

MR. VALACHI: Yes, they exist.

MR. ALDERMAN: But do you know the number they have there?

MR. VALACHI: I have no idea of Detroit.

MR. ALDERMAN: Did you mention Tampa?

MR. VALACHI: Tampa, I did, yes, about 10. When I left the streets.

MR. ALDERMAN: In other words, the 10 cities (sic) are Boston, Chicago, Los Angeles, San Francisco, New Orleans, Tampa, Buffalo, Utica, Philadelphia, Cleveland, and Detroit?

MR. VALACHI: Right.[72]

Counting the five New York City families, Valachi identified a total of 16 LCN groups in the United States. Fratianno dropped two cities from Valachi's list, but added nine others for a total of 25 LCN cities. The FBI testified to the existence of 26 LCN groups, disagreeing with two of the cities Fratianno included, while adding four others. The disparate claims of Valachi, Fratianno, and the FBI are summarized in Table 5.1.

Whether one chooses to believe Fratianno or the FBI, the number of LCN groups has apparently increased from between 40 to 60 percent since 1963. If this is true, however, their subsequent testimony as to the size of La Cosa Nostra must be false. At the beginning of the same 1980 Senate

Table 5.1
Cities Where Families of La Cosa Nostra Are Alleged to Exist

Valachi (1963)	Fratianno (1980)	FBI (1980)
Boston	xx	Boston-Providence
Buffalo	Buffalo	Buffalo
Chicago	Chicago	Chicago
Cleveland	Cleveland	Cleveland
Detroit	Detroit	Detroit
Los Angeles	Los Angeles	Los Angeles
New York (5)	New York (5)	New York (5)
New Orleans	New Orleans	New Orleans
Philadelphia	Philadelphia	Philadelphia
San Francisco	San Francisco	San Francisco
Tampa	Tampa	Tampa
Utica, NY	xx	xx
xx	San Jose	San Jose
xx	Denver	Denver-Pueblo
xx	Dallas	(Inactive)
xx	Kansas City, MO	Kansas City, MO
xx	Pittsburgh	Pittsburgh
xx	Milwaukee	Milwaukee
xx	Providence	(See Boston)
xx	St. Louis	St. Louis
xx	Pittston, PA	Pittston-Cranston-Wilkes-Barre, PA
xx	Steubenville, OH	xx
xx	Connecticut (1 city)	xx
xx	xx	Tucson
xx	xx	Rockford, IL
xx	xx	Madison, WI
xx	xx	Elizabeth-Newark, NJ
xx	xx	Springfield, IL (Inactive)

xx = no family reported.

hearings, the FBI director and his unit chief responsible for organized crime investigations gave testimony as to the "family" structure and size of the Cosa Nostra.

> SENATOR COHEN: May I also ask for a clarification for the record that, when you say "families" that does not necessarily intimate they are blood relations, although there may be blood relations within the "family"—
>
> MR. NELSON (FBI unit chief): That is correct, there may be blood relationships, but "family" comes from the Italian

"famiglia" and it does not necessarily mean that they are blood related. In most cases, of course, they are not.

MR. STEINBERG (Counsel to the Senate Committee): Mr. Nelson, how many members of La Cosa Nostra exist today?

MR. NELSON: There are approximately 2,000 members. However, I must say that is probably the most misleading figure I could throw out because these are the initiated members, the people who are considered by other people as part of the organization. Our most conservative estimate is that for every initiated member, there are approximately at least 10 people aligned with them and associated with them on a daily basis whose day-to-day activities are criminal and associated with La Cosa Nostra. So the conservative figure of the number of people in this country who are doing La Cosa Nostra's work is 20,000, and that is conservative.[73]

Compare this 1980 description of the size of La Cosa Nostra with Valachi's original description in 1963.

MR. ALDERMAN: Mr. Valachi, along those lines, how many active members do you feel there are in the New York area that belong to the various families? . . . All of the five families.

MR. VALACHI: About 2,000.

MR. ALDERMAN: Those whom you have been able to identify in the five families, you have marked with stars on these charts?

MR. VALACHI: Yes.

MR. ALDERMAN: But they do not represent all of the members of families? I mean in any family you don't know all of the members of the family?

MR. VALACHI: Well, I tell you, I am off the street for about 4 years. I am sure I know more than what I have got up there.

MR. ALDERMAN: These charts portray something over 400 names.

MR. VALACHI: Something like that.

MR. ALDERMAN: You say there are 2,000 members. So there are quite a number of members whom you do not know.

MR. VALACHI: Yes, there is quite a number, yes.

MR. ALDERMAN: How many inactive members are there?

MR. VALACHI: I would say about 2,500 or 3,000.

MR. ALDERMAN: You are just talking about New York City alone?

MR. VALACHI: I am talking about New York, including Newark.[74]

If Valachi estimates LCN membership in the New York City area alone to be 2,000 in 1963, and the FBI says that the *nationwide* membership is only 2,000 in 1980, it is difficult to argue that Italian-American organized crime has grown. Even if we choose to accept both Valachi's and the FBI's *upper* estimates of LCN participants, a New York City-only membership of 5,000 in 1963, compared to a nationwide estimate of 20,000 in 1980, certainly does not indicate growth in the size of La Cosa Nostra (considering that the FBI counts only five New York City families out of a nationwide total of 26). Furthermore, if the LCN has not increased in size between 1963 and 1980, how could it have established "families" in 7 to 10 additional cities during that period?

As a result, there not only appears to be contradictions between Fratianno and the FBI's testimony in 1980, but the Justice Department claims about the Cosa Nostra in 1980 cannot be believed if we are also expected to believe the claims of their 1963 witness, Joseph Valachi. A final note of concern relates to how the Cosa Nostra is organized. At the Tieri trial, Fratianno testified about the organization of LCN "families."

> MR. ACKERMAN: Now, is there any structure in La Cosa Nostra above the families which are located in the cities as we have in Government's Exhibit 4?
>
> MR. FRATIANNO: Yes, sir.
>
> MR. ACKERMAN: What is the name of that structure?
>
> MR. FRATIANNO: Well, they have a commission, sir.
>
> MR. ACKERMAN: Now, who comprises the commission?
>
> MR. FRATIANNO: The five bosses of the New York family plus the boss of the Chicago family, sir.
>
> MR. ACKERMAN: Now, what is the purpose of the commission?
>
> MR. FRATIANNO: Well, they more or less handle disputes with other families. If you have a problem with another family, they more or less handle it, sir.
>
> MR. ACKERMAN: Now, when a new boss is selected by a family, who is notified?
>
> MR. FRATIANNO: The commission is notified, sir.
>
> MR. ACKERMAN: Would you describe to the jury how a family of La Cosa Nostra is actually run?
>
> MR. FRATIANNO: Well, it's run by the boss. He's the main one. And then they have an underboss. They have a consigliere, and then they have capos . . .
>
> MR. ACKERMAN: What is the consigliere's job in the family?
>
> MR. FRATIANNO: Well, he is more or less the counselor of the family, you know.
>
> MR. ACKERMAN: You mentioned the capos. What are they?
>
> MR. FRATIANNO: Well, they are like captains. They more or less—they break the soldiers into units and they belong to the capos, certain capos.

> MR. ACKERMAN: You referred to soldiers. Is everybody who
> is not a capo, a boss, underboss, and consigliere, a soldier in La
> Cosa Nostra?
> MR. FRATIANNO: That's correct.[75]

Therefore, each "family" has ranks from "soldier" up to "boss," and the
families are, according to Fratianno, regulated by a six-member commission of six "family" bosses (of the five New York City families and Chicago). When the FBI unit chief testified before the Senate the same year,
however, he arrived at a different formulation.

> At that time [when the commission was allegedly formed in
> 1931], there were seven members on the Mafia Commission,
> the La Cosa Nostra Commission . . . Currently, there are nine. It
> is made up of the five bosses of the New York families, the boss
> in Philadelphia, the boss in Buffalo, the boss in Detroit, and the
> boss in Chicago.[76]

This confusion over the existence and size of the "commission" is further
amplified when Fratianno's 1981 biography offers still a *third* version of the
commission structure. In it, the commission is said to be comprised of 10
Cosa Nostra bosses. Fratianno's credibility suffers again, not only due to
his self-contradiction, but also because he admits in his biography that he
was *told* of the family and commission structure by someone else in 1947.[77]
This inconsistency is especially disturbing because Fratianno claims he was
the one-time "boss" of the Los Angeles "family." Therefore, Fratianno's testimony on this subject is not only inconsistent, but it is also hearsay.

Fratianno's testimony is suspect on other grounds as well. At other
points during the *Tieri* trial, Fratianno was found to have contradicted his
prior grand jury testimony, admitted violation of the "family" code in setting up a fellow member to be murdered, admitted lying under oath in the
past, and he admitted defrauding the FBI while receiving money as a paid
informant. These facts, in addition to his unsavory background, do not
serve to enhance his credibility.

Nevertheless, Frank Tieri was ultimately convicted of racketeering and
conspiracy, undoubtedly due to the testimony of other witnesses at trial and
the failure of the defense to call a single witness in Tieri's behalf. Tieri
died only three months after his conviction in March, 1981 at age 77.
Tieri's poor health was cited throughout the trial by his counsel as preventing him from coherently conversing with Tieri and, therefore, interfered
with the preparation of an adequate defense. A conviction cannot stand
when death has deprived an offender the opportunity to appeal his conviction. As a result, Tieri's indictment was formally dismissed and the conviction vacated in May 1981.

The *Tieri* case was only the beginning of a massive prosecution effort
against organized crime. Other informants came forward, and electronic

eavesdropping of conversations saw some alleged organized crime figures literally convict themselves.

The Mob Trials of the 1980s and 1990s

The 1980s and 1990s will be remembered as a period when the U.S. Justice Department took new initiative and began prosecutions of a large number of reputed organized crime figures in federal courts around the country. The alleged leaders of 16 of the 24 "Mafia" groups, identified by the government, were indicted by 1986. Nearly 5,000 federal organized crime indictments were issued by grand juries in 1985 alone.[78] By 1988, the FBI reported that 19 bosses, 13 underbosses, and 43 "captains" had been convicted.[79]

This dramatic increase in prosecutions was not due to new laws, but simply was the result of devoting more existing resources to the problem. Many of these prosecutions took place in New York City and relied on the investigative efforts of a reorganized New York State Organized Crime Task Force. On the national level, there were changes as well. In President Reagan's first four years in office, his Attorney General authorized more than 700 federal wiretaps, better than twice the number during Carter's presidency.[80] In a similar way, prosecutors began to make use of the 15-year-old racketeering law (RICO), which provides for extended sentences and large fines and forfeitures for convicted offenders. In addition, undercover agents and government informants were being employed more often in organized crime investigations.

The significance of this investigation and prosecution effort is difficult to capture without illustration. The leaders of many Cosa Nostra groups were convicted and sentenced to long terms, including John Gotti in New York, Nicky Scarfo in Philadelphia, and Gennaro Angiulo in Boston, among many others.[81] Table 5.2 lists the outcome of most of the significant trials after the *Tieri* trial.

Five facts become apparent as one reviews the positions, offenses, and sentences of the principals in these cases. First, it is clear that many of these organized crime cases were significant. Many involved racketeering convictions that entailed the infiltration of legitimate or illegitimate businesses through bribery and extortion. The sentences imposed on the principals in these cases were severe. The average sentence was more than 25 years per offender. It is apparent from the ages of the principals involved in these cases that many are senior citizens. The average age of these offenders was more than 62. Given an average sentence of 25 years, even accounting for parole eligibility, it is likely that an entirely new leadership will emerge among many Italian-American organized crime groups. Perhaps the continued existence of some of these established groups is now in jeopardy, as new groups attempt to take over given the weakened position of some of these groups.

Table 5.2
Major Organized Crime Trials and Outcomes, 1985-1994

Year	Name	Age	Alleged Role	Offense	Outcome
1985	Gennaro Langella	47	Underboss of Colombo group in New York City	Perjury, obstruction of justice	10 years prison $15,000 fine
1986	Matthew Ianniello Benjamin Cohen (and six others)	65 66	No mention of organized crime in indictment	Skimming from NYC bars, restaurants	6 years 5 years
1986	Michael Franzese (and four others)	35	Son of "captain" in Colombo group	Racketeering & tax conspiracy	10 years, plus $15 million fine, forfeit
1986	Gennaro Anguilo (and four others)	67	Underboss of New England (Patriarca) group	Racketeering, gambling, loan-sharking, murder	45 years prison, $120,000 fine
1986	Anthony Spilotro (and eight others)	47	Overseer of Las Vegas operations for Chicago group	Conspiracy, racketeering in Las Vegas burglary ring	Mistrial (found murdered 2 days before retrial)
1986	Paul Castellano Anthony Gaggi Ronald Ustica Henry Borelli	72 60 41 37	Leader and members of Gambino crime group in New York	Car theft conspiracy and murder (Ustica and Borelli)	Castellano killed during trial, Gaggi, 5 years; others, life in prison
1986	Matthew Ianniello Benjamin Cohen (and four others)	65 66	"Captain" and associates in Genovese group	Racketeering, fraud, extortion in garbage collection	Acquitted
1986	Anthony, Joseph, and Vincent Colombo	41 39 35	Members of Colombo group in New York City	Racketeering, conspiracy, narcotics	14 years prison, 5 years prison, 5 years prison
1986	Santo Trafficante	71	Leader of Florida group	Racketeering, gambling	Mistrial
1986	Joseph Bonanno	81	Retired boss of Bonanno group	Contempt for refusal to testify	14 months jail
1986	Carmine and Alphonse Persico, Gennaro Langella (and seven others)	53 33 47	Head of Colombo crime group and associates in New York City	Labor & construction racketeering, extortion	39 years prison, 12 years prison, 65 years prison
1986	Paul Vario	73	Counselor in NYC Lucchese group	Extortion at JFK Airport	6 years prison, $25,000 fine
1986	Chang An-lo (and seven others)	30s	Leader and members of the United Bamboo Chinese gang in New York	Narcotics distribution, murder	25 years prison

Table 5.2, *continued*

Year	Name	Age	Alleged Role	Offense	Outcome
1987	Paul Castellano Anthony Salerno Anthony Corrallo Gennaro Langella Philip Rastelli (and four others)	72 75 73 48 69	"Commission" trial of leaders of Gambino, Genovese, Lucchese, Colombo, Bonanno groups in	Racketeering, conspiracy, loan-sharking, labor bribery, extortion in construction	Castellano murdered during trial, other leaders each received 100 years in prison
1987	Philip Rastelli (and seven others)	69	Leader of Bonanno group in New York	Labor racketeering in moving industry	12 years prison
1987	Ilario Zannino	67	Underboss in New England group	Gambling, loansharking	30 years prison
1987	John Gotti Armand and Aniello Dellacroce (and six others)	46 38 71	Leader of Gambino crime group and associates	Gambling, loansharking hijacking, murder	Gotti acquitted, Armand disappeared, Aniello died before trial
1987	Gaetano Badalementi, Salvatore Catalano (and 14 others)	64 46	"Pizza Connection" Turkey-Sicily-Brazil-New York drug importation via pizzerias	Narcotics distribution, conspiracy	Each received 45 years prison and $1.1 million fine
1987	Nicodemo Scarfo	58	Boss of Philadelphia group	Extortion from developers, narcotics distribution	14 years prison, acquitted
1988	Carlos Lehder	38	A Medellin Cartel leader	Drug smuggling, conspiracy	2 consecutive life terms, plus 135 years prison
1989	Loren Piccarreto	38	Head of Rochester, NY crime group	Gambling and extortion	7 years prison
1989	Nicodemo Scarfo (and seven others)	59	Boss of Philadelphia group	Murder	Life in prison (overturned on appeal, due to prosecutorial misconduct)
1989	Nicodemo Scarfo Philip Leonetti (and 13 others)	59 36	Boss of Philadelphia group	Racketeering, murder, extortion, narcotics, gambling	55 years prison, 45 years prison
1990	John Gotti	49	Boss of Gambino crime family in New York	Assault	Acquitted
1990	Rayful Edmond III	25	Head of Washington, D.C. cocaine ring	Drug trafficking	3 life terms
1990	Matthew Ianniello	70	Captain in Genovese group	Racketeering, extortion	5 years prison

Table 5.2, *continued*

Year	Name	Age	Alleged Role	Offense	Outcome
1990	Charles Porter Louis Raucci	58 61	Underboss and member of Pittsburgh group	Racketeering, narcotics, tax violations	28 years prison
1991	Raymond Patriarca, Jr.	47	Leader of New England group	Racketeering	8 years prison
1991	Nicholas Bianco	59	Boss of Patriarca (New England) group	Racketeering	11 years prison
1992	Joseph Russo (and four others)	58	Counselor in New England group	Kidnapping, extortion, murder	16 years prison
1992	Victor Orena	58	Acting boss of Colombo family	Racketeering, murder, loansharking, conspiracy	Life in prison
1992	Thomas Pitera	37	Soldier in Bonanno group	Six drug-related murders	Life in prison
1992	John Gotti	51	Boss of Gambino group in New York	Five murders, including that of Paul Castellano	Life in prison
1993	Michael Tacetta Michael Perna	46 50	Head of Lucchese group in New Jersey	Racketeering and murder conspiracy	30 years prison
1993	Thomas Gambino	64	Captain in Gambino group	Racketeering gambling, loansharking	5 years prison
1993	Johnny Eng	36	Head of Flying Dragons in New York's Chinatown	Racketeering, heroin trafficking	24 years prison, $3.5 million fine
1993	Salvatore Lombardi (and six others)	54	Captain in Genovese group in New Jersey	Racketeering, extortion, gambling	22 years prison, $175,000 fines
1993	John Riggi	69	Boss of New Jersey crime group	Murder conspiracy	7 years prison, begins after cur- rent sentence
1993	Gregory Scarpa, Sr.	65	Captain in Colombo crime group in New York	Murder conspiracy	10 years prison (Scarpa was terminally ill)
1994	John and Joseph Gambino	53 47	Members of Gambino crime group	Racketeering, narcotics trafficking	15 years prison
1994	Joseph Lovett	44	Former chapter leader of Pagans motorcycle gang	Trafficking in methamphetamines	27 years prison
1994	Salvatore Avellino, Jr.	58	Associate of Lucchese group on Long Island	Racketeering and murder conspiracy	10 years prison plus 21 years probation
1994	Leonard Falzone	59	Enforcer in Buffalo crime group	Racketeering and loansharking	5 years prison

Second, it can be seen that although most of the cases took place in New York City, many other parts of the country have been affected as well. Convictions affecting organized crime operations in New England, New Jersey, Chicago, Las Vegas, Pittsburgh, Philadelphia, and Washington, D.C. attest to the national scope of the prosecution effort.

Third, the prosecution focus remains on organized crime of Italian-Americans. The overwhelming majority of cases were of alleged "Mafia" groups, although conviction of members of the "United Bamboo" Chinese gang, the leader of the "Flying Dragons," a leader of the Pagans motorcycle gangs and a Washington, D.C. cocaine ring leader for narcotics distribution is a hopeful sign of the recognition of serious organized crime among non-Italians.

Fourth, the debate over the existence of a "Mafia" was finally rendered moot in a 1986 trial, when the defendants in the "Commission" trial (i.e., the alleged "bosses" of the New York City crime "families") conceded that the "Mafia exists and has members." Furthermore, the defense claimed "there is a commission" that is mentioned in wiretapped conversations of the defendants. Testimony from Sicilian informer Tommaso Buscetta corroborated this claim. He stated that he was told by Joseph Bonanno in 1957 that "it was very advisable" to set up a commission in Sicily "to resolve disputes" among criminal groups.[82] If this testimony is true, it appears that any organization of criminal groups in Sicily was modeled after that in America, rather than the common belief (discussed earlier in this chapter) that a 'Mafia' organization was imported to America from Sicily. In his autobiography, Joseph Bonanno claims to have set up such a commission in America, but he refused to testify in the "commission" trial and was jailed for contempt.

Similar to both Valachi's and Fratianno's testimony in 1963 and 1980, the role of the commission, according to the defendants in the "commission" trial, is only to approve new members and to avoid conflicts between the groups. The prosecution argued, however, that four of the defendants participated in "the ruling council of La Cosa Nostra, or the 'Mafia' which directed criminal activity."[83] The defendants maintained that "Just because someone is a Mafia member, it doesn't mean that he has committed the crimes in this case." The distinction the defense attempted to make was that the Mafia was a loose social and business association of individuals with similar backgrounds, but without a criminal purpose, that could be likened to a plumber's, or businessmen's, professional association which has as a purpose the *avoidance* of conflict.[84] The purpose of the defense's admissions in the "commission" trial was to challenge the government "to prove that it has actually engaged in the crimes of which it has been accused."[85] The charges included bid-rigging of concrete prices, extortion, and (in the case of one defendant) murder. The charges were ultimately proven, and the defendants were each sentenced to 100 years in prison.

A fifth outcome of the mob trials was the fact that several resulted in acquittals and mistrials. It has been argued by some that the government's heavy reliance on former criminals as paid government witnesses is a questionable practice. Juries may not be willing to convict a defendant when the case is based largely on the testimony of a criminal-turned informant.[86] The issues posed by the use of paid government informers are assessed in Chapter 8.

Although it is difficult to assess the long-term result of these successful organized crime prosecutions, several immediate impacts have already been felt: increased violence, more sophisticated criminal operations, and a possible shift in the primary activities of organized crime groups.

As has been seen already in the shooting of Paul Castellano, the threatened incapacitation of a crime leader through imprisonment can lead to murder. It has been argued that successful prosecution of organized crime leaders will bring to power younger, more aggressive leaders who will use violence more freely to protect their interests and avoid prosecution.[87] The car-bombing murder of Frank DeCiccio in New York City soon after Castellano's death was seen as a retaliatory act by some police officials. It can be expected that more violence will occur in the struggle for leadership of organized crime groups and the effort to avoid prosecution by "protecting" illicit enterprises and "eliminating" suspected informants.

A second result of successful prosecutions will be a shift in organized crime activities. Interviews with law enforcement officials reveal that organized criminals may be shifting to "safer" activities that are better protected from street-level investigations. Increasing organized crime involvement in credit card and airline ticket counterfeiting, and in illicit toxic waste disposal, have been cited as examples of this trend.[88] As a result, the infiltration of legitimate business may prove to be an area of greater interest to organized crime, rather than the more visible activities necessary in catering to the vices of narcotics, gambling, and loansharking.

Third, organized crime will have to become more sophisticated in its operation to maintain acceptable levels of success. As sociologist Mary McIntosh has suggested, the "technology" or sophistication of organized criminal activity responds to law enforcement effectiveness. Once law enforcement strategy becomes more effective, as the mob trials indicate, "we can expect the criminal technology to reach rapidly the same level of efficiency in order to maintain acceptable levels of success."[89] This sophistication may take the form of greater dealings in the *financing* of criminal activities than in the *operation* of criminal enterprises. Gambling and narcotics sales have been claimed to be the two largest sources of organized crime revenue. It is possible that traditional racketeers, who wish to remain in the gambling and narcotics business, will back off from operating these higher-risk enterprises and be content to finance other illicit entrepreneurs for a percentage of the profits. Illegal profits can then be laundered through legally owned businesses, such as restaurants and nightclubs. In order to accomplish this, there may be greater efforts among organized criminals in the future to infiltrate legitimate businesses to obtain access to money for financing and to have the means to launder illicitly obtained cash. Labor union funds and the construction industry have been favorite targets in the past.

As a result, the successful prosecution of organized crime leaders in recent years may be a mixed blessing. Although it may disrupt operations for a short period, it will also bring to power younger, and more violent leaders, shift organized crime activities to "safer," but more complex, scams and possibly encourage further organized crime infiltration into legitimate business to finance illicit business and to launder illegally obtained profits. Chapter 12 will examine approaches, other than prosecution, to combatting organized crime directed at long-term prevention.

References to Chapter 5

[1]   Dwight C. Smith, Jr., *The Mafia Mystique* (Lanham, MD: University Press of America, 1990), p. 28.

[2]   Joseph L. Albini, *The American Mafia: Genesis of a Legend* (New York: Irvington, 1971), pp. 159-167; Humbert S. Nelli, *The Business of Crime:Italians and Syndicate Crime in the United States* (Chicago: University of Chicago Press, 1981), ch.2; Smith, *The Mafia Mystique*, pp. 27-44.

[3]   Albini, *The American Mafia*, ch.5; Nelli, *The Business of Crime*, ch.3; Smith, *The Mafia Mystique*, p. 32.

[4]   Thomas M. Pitkin and Francesco Cordasco, *The Black Hand: A Chapter in Ethnic Crime* (Totowa, NJ: Littlefield Adams, 1977), pp. 22-30.

[5]   Smith, *The Mafia Mystique*, p. 32.

[6]   Albini, *The American Mafia*, p. 125; some of the sources he cites are in Italian, except Luigi Barzini, Jr., "The Real Mafia," *Harper's Magazine* (June, 1954); Douglas Sladen, *Sicily* (New York: E.P. Dutton, 1907); Alexander Nelson Hood, *Sicilian Studies* (New York: Dodd, Mead and Co., 1916); Bolton King and Thomas Okey, *Italy Today* (London: James Nisber and Co., 1901); Robert Neville, "The Mafia is Deadlier," *The New York Times Magazine*, (January 12, 1964); Gavin Maxwell, *Ten Pains of Death* (New York: E.P. Dutton, 1960); William Agnew Paton, *Picturesque Sicily* (New York: Harper and Brothers, 1900); Michele Pantaleone, *The Mafia and Politics* (New York: Coward-McCann, 1966).

[7]   Albini, *The American Mafia*, p. 133.

[8]   Ibid., p. 135.

[9]   Henner Hess, *Mafia and Mafiosi: The Structure of Power* (Lexington: D.C. Heath, 1973), p. 155.

[10]   Ibid., p. 170.

[11]   Ibid., p. 127.

[12]   Henner Hess, "The Traditional Sicilian Mafia: Organized Crime and Repressive Crime," in R. Kelly, ed., *Organized Crime: A Global Perspective* (Totowa, NJ: Rowan and Littlefield, 1986), p. 123.

[13]   Anton Blok, *The Mafia of a Sicilian Village, 1860-1960* (New York: Harper & Row, 1974), p. 10-11.

[14]   Ibid., p. 92.

[15]   Gaia Servadio, *Mafioso: A History of the Mafia from Its Origins to the Present Day* (New York: Dell, 1978), p. 3.

[16]   Servadio, *Mafioso*, pp. 19-20.

[17]   See also Barzini, "The Real Mafia."

[18]   Servadio, *Mafioso*, p. 268.

[19]   Pino Arlacchi, *Mafia Business: The Mafia Ethic and the Spirit of Capitalism* (London: Verso, 1986), p. 4.

[20]   Ibid., p. 26.

[21]   James Walston, "See Naples and Die: Organized Crime in Campania," in R. Kelly, ed. *Organized Crime: A Global Perspective* (Totowa, NJ: Rowan and Littlefield, 1986), p. 139.

[22]   Ibid, pp. 153, 143.

[23]   Ibid., p. 137.

[24]   E.J. Dionne, "Naples Gang War: And Now the Courtroom Scene," *The New York Times*, (April 16, 1985), p. 2.

[25]   Arnold H. Lubasch, "Mafia Member Testifies on Sicily 'Commission'," *The New York Times*, (November 1, 1985), p. B3.

[26]   Franco Ferrarotti, "The Sicilian Mafia: 1860-1977," *Italian Journal*, v. 5 (1989), pp. 17-28.

[27]   Raimondo Catanzaro, *Men of Respect: A Social history of the Sicilian Mafia* (New York: The Free Press, 1992), p. 18.

[28]   Ralph Blumenthal, *Last Days of the Sicilians: The FBI Assault on the Pizza Connection* (New York: Times Books, 1988); Shana Alexander, *The Pizza Connection: Lawyers, Money, Drugs, Mafia* (New York: Weidenfeld and Nicolson, 1988); Peter Stoler, "The Sicilian Connection," *Time*, (October 15, 1984), pp. 42-51.

[29]   Claire Sterling, *Octopus: The Long Reach of the International Sicilian Mafia* (New York: W.W. Norton, 1990).

[30]   Sterling, *Octopus*, p. 289.

[31]   " Italian Court Sentences 97 After Four-Year Trial," *Organized Crime Digest*, (March 9, 1994), p. 8.

[32]   Pino Arlacchi, *Men of Dishonor: Inside the Sicilian Mafia* (New York: William Morrow, 1993), p. 21.

[33]   Ibid., p. 35.

[34]   Anthony Attanasio, Sr., "The Sicilian Mafia Enters the 21st Century," *Organized Crime Digest*, (August 11, 1993), p. 1.

[35]   John Landesco, *Organized Crime in Chicago*, Part III of the Illinois Crime Survey, 1929 (Chicago: University of Chicago Press, 1968), p. 277.

[36]   Ibid., p. 278; Laurence Bergeen, *Capone: The Man and the Era* (New York: Simon and Schuster, 1994).

[37] F. Browning and J. Gerassi, *The American Way of Crime* (New York: G.P. Putnam & Sons, 1980); John Morgan, *Prince of Crime* (New York: Stein and Day, 1985).

[38] Virgil Peterson, *The Mob: 200 Years of Organized Crime in New York* (Ottawa, IL: Green Hill, 1983); J. Joselit, *Our Gang: Jewish Crime and the New York Jewish Community, 1900-1940* (Bloomington, IN: Indiana University Press, 1983); George Wolf with Joseph DiMona, *Frank Costello* (New York: Bantam, 1975).

[39] Peterson, *The Mob*.

[40] Timothy Jacobs, *The Gangsters* (New York: Mallard Press, 1990); Sid Feder and Joachim Joesten, *The Luciano Story* (New York: Award Books, 1972).

[41] See Richard Monaco and Lionel Bascom, *Rubouts: Mob Murders in America* (New York: Avon Books, 1991).

[42] Eliot Ness with Oscar Fraley, *The Untouchables* (New York: Pocket Books, 1957).

[43] U.S. Senate Special Committee to Investigate Organized Crime in Interstate Commerce, *Third Interim Report* (Washington, DC: U.S. Government Printing Office, 1951), p. 2.

[44] William H. Moore, *The Kefauver Committee and the Politics of Crime, 1950-1952* (Columbia: University of Missouri Press, 1974), p. 134.

[45] Moore, *The Kefauver Committee*, pp. 237-238.

[46] Ibid., p. 241.

[47] Joseph L. Albini, *The American Mafia: Genesis of a Legend* (New York: Irvington, 1971), p. 210.

[48] Daniel Bell, "Crime as an American Way of Life," *The Antioch Review*, v. 13 (June, 1953), 131.

[49] Burton B. Turkus and Sid Feder, *Murder, Inc.* (New York: Manor Books, 1951).

[50] Bell, "Crime as an American Way of Life," p. 144; see also Francis A.J. Ianni, *Black Mafia: Ethnic Succession in Organized Crime* (New York: Simon and Schuster, 1974).

[51] Smith, *The Mafia Mystique*, pp. 162-163.

[52] Ibid., p. 171.

[53] New York State Joint Legislative Committee on Government Operations, *Interim Report on the Gangland meeting at Apalachin* Part III, Legislative Document No. 25., 1958, p. 101.

[54] Smith, *The Mafia Mystique*, p. 194.

[55] New York State Temporary Commission of Investigation, *The Apalachin Meeting* (New York: State Investigations Commission, 1963), p. 20.

[56] *United States v. Buffalino et al.*, 285 F.2d 408 (2d Cir. 1960).

[57] Peter Maas, *The Valachi Papers* (New York: Bantam, 1969), p. 1.

[58] U.S. Senate Committee on Government Operations Permanent Subcommittee on Investigations, *Organized Crime and Illicit Traffic in narcotics: Hearings Part I* 88th Congress, 1st session (Washington, DC: U.S. Government Printing office, 1963), p. 180.

[59] Turkus and Feder, *Murder, Inc.*, p. 201.

[60] Alan A. Block, "History and the Study of organized Crime," *Urban Life*, v. 6 (1978), pp. 455-474; Humbert S. Nelli, *The Business of Crime*, pp. 179-218.

61   President's Commission on Law Enforcement and Administration of Justice, *Task Force Report: Organized Crime* (Washington, DC: U.S. Government Printing office, 1967); Donald R. Cressey, *Theft of the Nation* (New York: Harper & Row, 1969).

62   U.S. Senate, *Organized Crime and Illicit Traffic in Narcotics*, p. 80.

63   Ibid., pp. 116, 194.

64   Smith, *The Mafia Mystique*, pp. 217-242.

65   Ibid., p. 234.

66   Gordon Hawkins, "God and the Mafia," *The Public Interest*, v. 14 (1969), pp. 50-51.

67   *United States v. Tieri, Trial Transcript*, 80 S.D.N.Y. Cr. 381, pp. 2181-2183.

68   Ibid., pp. 2304-2305.

69   It should be noted that, prior to trial, defense counsel, Jay Goldberg, sought to have the prosecutor disqualified from this case. A letter Ackerman submitted to the U.S. Parole Commission asking for Fratianno's early release from prison, claimed that Fratianno's testimony led to the conviction of four persons in an earlier case involving fraud at the Westchester Premier Theatre. Goldberg pointed out that no one was convicted at the trial in which Fratianno testified. The presiding Judge, Thomas Griesa, denied this motion to disqualify the prosecutor, however.

70   *United States v. Tieri, Trial Transcript*, pp. 863, 870.

71   U.S. Senate Committee on Governmental Affairs Permanent Subcommittee on Investigations, *Organized Crime and the Use of Violence: Hearings Part I* 86th Congress, 2nd session (Washington, DC: U.S. Government Printing Office, 1980), pp. 114-116.

72   U.S. Senate, *Organized Crime and Illicit Traffic in Narcotics*, pp. 386-387.

73   U.S. Senate, *Organized Crime and the Use of Violence*, pp. 90, 19.

74   U.S. Senate, *Organized Crime and Illicit Traffic in Narcotics*, pp. 270-271.

75   *United States v. Tieri, Trial Transcript*, pp. 875-878.

76   U.S. Senate, *Organized Crime and the Use of Violence*, p. 88.

77   Ovid Demaris, *The Last Mafioso* (New York: Bantam, 1981), pp. 20-22.

78   Stewart Powell, Steven Emerson, Kelly Orr, Dan Collins, and Barbara Quick, "Busting the Mob," *U.S. News & World Report*, (February 3, 1986), pp. 24-31.

79   James B. Jacobs, *Busting the Mob: United States v. Cosa Nostra* (New York: New York University Press, 1994), p. 4.

80   Ibid., p. 25.

81   John H. Davis, *Mafia Dynasty: The Rise and Fall of the Gambino Crime Family* (New York: Harper-Collins, 1993; Donald Cox, *Mafia Wipeout: How the Feds Put Away and Entire Mob Family* (New York:SPI Books, 1992); Frank Friel and John Gunther, *Breaking the Mob* (New York: Warner Books, 1992); Gerard O'Neill and Dick Lehr, *The Underboss: The Rise and Fall of a Mafia Family* (New York: St. Martin's Press, 1989); John Cummings and Ernest Volkman, *Goombata: The Improbable Rise and Fall of John Gotti and His Gang* (Boston: Litlle, Brown, 1990).

82   Arnold H. Lubash, "Mafia Member testifies on Sicily 'Commission'," *The New York Times*, (November 1, 1985), p. B3.

83 Arnold H. Lubash, "Persico Asks Jury Not to be Duped by Mafia Label," *The New York Times*, (September 19, 1986), pp. 1, 24; Ronald Smothers, "Tapes Played at Mob Trial Focus on Money and Power," *The New York Times*, (January 26, 1986), p. 20.

84 Ed Magnuson, "Hitting the Mafia," *Time*, (September 29, 1986), pp. 14-22.

85 Michael Oreskes, "Commission Trial Illustrates Changes in Attitude on Mafia," *The New York Times*, (September 20, 1986), pp. B29-30.

86 Alan M. Dershowitz, "Gotti Case Shows Flaws of Buying Witnesses," *The Buffalo News* (March 20, 1987), p. C3.

87 Annelise G. Anderson, *The Business of Organized Crime* (Stanford, CA: Hoover Institution press, 1979), p. 144.

88 Powell et al., "Busting the Mob," p. 26.

89 Mary McIntosh, *The Organisation of Crime* (London: Macmillan, 1975).

Chapter 6

Presidential Investigations of Organized Crime, 1967 and 1987

The true history of the President's Commission on Organized Crime is a saga of missed opportunity.
10 members of the 18-member President's Commission in 1987

In the last 30 years there have been two Presidential Commissions that have focused specifically on organized crime. The Task Force on Organized Crime of the President's Commission on Law Enforcement and Administration of Justice reported to President Johnson in 1967, and the President's Commission on Organized Crime reported to President Reagan in 1986 (although the final report was not released until 1987).

Both these investigations took approximately two years to complete, relying on hearings, testimony, and research staff to conduct their analyses. This chapter compares the observations and conclusions of these two Commissions in their assessment of:

1. the proper definition of organized crime,
2. the primary activities of organized crime groups,
3. their role in public and private corruption,
4. national efforts to prevent organized crime, and
5. recommendations for the future.

Such an analysis is useful in assessing changes in the government's understanding and response to organized crime during the last three decades.

The Government's Perception of Organized Crime

The Task Force on Organized Crime (TFR) concluded in 1967 that organized crime was a "society." In particular, the "core of organized crime in the United States consists of 24 groups" exclusively of Italian origin and totaling 5,000 members. The term "Mafia" was not mentioned in the text of the report, although it was mentioned in a footnote as the name of this "nation-wide crime syndicate."[1] It was claimed that the 24 groups of this syndicate work with and control other rackets groups of other ethnic derivations.

This information was credited to the Kefauver and McClellan Senate Committee investigations of the 1950s and 1960s, which brought national attention to organized crime. Based on the testimony of criminal-turned-informant Joseph Valachi in 1963, which said he had never heard of a "Mafia" but, rather, the "Cosa Nostra," the TFR concluded that this Italian-based syndicate had changed its name from the Mafia to La Cosa Nostra.

The Report went on to detail the structure of each organized crime group, or "family," relying heavily on the testimony of Joseph Valachi four years earlier. The now familiar vernacular of "Commission," "boss," "underboss," and "soldier" were all detailed in this report. Although it was admitted that knowledge of organized crime at that time was comparable to "the knowledge of Standard Oil which could be gleaned from gasoline station attendants," the Task Force was not deterred from publishing elaborate charts and schematic diagrams of how these groups of the Cosa Nostra were supposedly organized in the United States.[2]

President Reagan's Commission on Organized Crime published seven volumes of hearings and four reports during its more than two years of existence. Although the Commission disbanded and submitted its final report to the President on April 1, 1986, the final report was not published and made available to the public until April, 1987. Nevertheless, the Reagan Commission did its best to attract public attention. It held public hearings in a number of large cities at which primarily law enforcement officials testified about organized crime. The Commission's four ultimate reports included the subjects of money laundering, labor racketeering, drug use and trafficking, and a final report.

It is clear that the definition of organized crime offered by the Reagan Commission was broader than that given 20 years earlier. In its hearings on organized crime of Asian origin, the Commission concluded,

> Since the early 1960s, when Joseph Valachi provided dramatic testimony concerning activities of La Cosa Nostra (LCN), many people (including representatives from leading law enforcement agencies) have gained the impression that organized crime in the United States is dominated by, or consists almost totally of the LCN "families" whose members are of Italian origin.[3]

The Commission observed, however, that ". . . it is misleading to describe the more prominent Asian groups as "emerging groups" inasmuch as they engage in much illicit activity, corruption, and violence to protect their activities."[4]

This view of organized crime as involving much more than Italian-Americans is a significant departure from the focus of the 1967 report. This emphasis was further evidenced in other parts of the 1986 Commission investigation. At the conclusion of the hearings on cocaine distribution, for example, the Commission declared,

> The testimony in this record portrays a state of war . . . a situation in which large, sophisticated organizations, based abroad but with agents and collaborators within our borders, have launched a massive, well-armed and well-financed invasion of our country by sea and air, resulting in thousands of our citizens being killed or disabled.[5]

Similarly, the hearings on heroin distribution had a multi-ethnic perspective. The Commission concluded that "..more and more groups of different ethnic origins are becoming substantially involved in heroin importation and distribution networks."[6] The Commission's report on drugs concluded, "America's cocaine supply at present originates exclusively from South America."[7] It also claimed that in 1984, "Mexican traffickers provided a 32 percent share of the heroin consumed in the United States."[8] Finally, the Commission noted in the hearings on gambling that "Not only the traditional organized crime groups, but also numerous emerging groups, participate in the lucrative gambling market."[9] In its final report, the Commission outlined the operations of organized crime among Italian-American groups, outlaw motorcycle gangs, prison gangs, Chinese, Vietnamese, Japanese, Cuban, Columbian, Irish, Russian, and Canadian criminal groups.[10]

It can be seen, therefore, that a great deal of emphasis was placed on organized criminal activity, apart from the traditional focus on Italian-American organized crime. This emphasis distinguishes the 1986 Commission investigation from the 1967 Task Force report.

Activities of Organized Crime Groups

The 1967 Task Force was emphatic in its claim that "law enforcement officers agree almost unanimously that gambling is the largest source of revenue" for organized crime.[11] The report provided estimated figures of this revenue, but admitted the figures may not be accurate.

The TFR claimed that loansharking "is the second largest source of revenue for organized crime" and is funded by gambling profits.[12] No reliable estimates of its magnitude were available. Interestingly, only two paragraphs in the entire TFR were devoted to narcotics. It was found that narcotics are "imported by organized crime" and sold by independent pushers. Heroin was the only drug mentioned by name in the report. It was also concluded that prostitution and bootlegging "play a small and declining role in organized crime operations" and little attention was given these in the report.[13]

The TFR discussed the infiltration of legitimate business and how organized criminals invest illegal profits to establish a "legal source of funds." It was mentioned twice that organized criminals pay no taxes on these funds, but the "cumulative effect" of this problem "cannot be measured."[14]

One additional form of organized criminal behavior addressed by the Task Force was labor racketeering, a discussion that consisted of only three paragraphs. The infiltration of labor unions was seen as a way to "enhance other illegal activities," such as "stealing from union funds and extorting money by threats of possible labor strife."[15]

It is apparent that the 1967 presidential investigation of organized crime focused heavily on gambling and loansharking, especially as conducted by groups of Italian-Americans. Much less attention was given to narcotics trafficking or labor racketeering.

The conclusions of the 1986 President's Commission ranked the prevalence of the activities of organized crime quite differently from that offered in 1967. Also, the nature of the activities addressed were somewhat different.

The report on narcotics, for example, concluded that "This Commission has found drug trafficking to be the most widespread and lucrative organized crime activity in the United States."[16] Furthermore, it accounts "for nearly 40 percent of this country's organized crime activity," and it generates an "annual income estimated to be as high as $110 billion."[17] This is a marked departure from the conclusions of the 1967 TFR which found gambling to be the largest and most lucrative organized crime activity.

The report on labor-management racketeering brought much more attention to the problem of labor racketeering than was given in the 1967 report. The Commission noted that although, "the majority of unions and

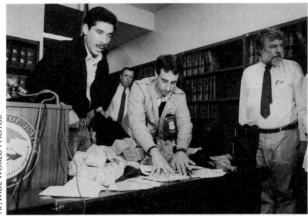

Federal agents display U.S. currency seized when 16 persons were charged with allegedly operating a money-laundering network in New York and New Jersey, at a news conference at the New York office of Brooklyn U.S. Attorney Andrew Maloney on May 12, 1989. Maloney said the money represented profits of the Cali cocaine cartel, and was the largest drug money laundering network to be broken in the Northeast.

businesses have not been tainted by organized crime," there are severe problems in those organizations where organized crime exists.[18]

Money laundering also received much more attention in the 1986 report than in the report 20 years earlier. Although no estimates were given of the amount of money laundered, it was concluded that police agencies recognize that "narcotics traffickers, who must conceal billions of dollars in cash from detection by the government, create by far the greatest demand for money laundering schemes."[19]

Finally, the Commission's hearings on gambling involved testimony regarding casino skimming, basketball betting, and boxing. No separate report on gambling was issued, however.

Political and Commercial Corruption

The 1967 Task Force Report found that "all available data indicate that organized crime flourishes only where it has corrupted local officials."[20] This was because "neutralizing local law enforcement is central to organized crime's operations." A degree of immunity from prosecution is required to insure the continuance of the criminal enterprise. Although the TFR found "no large city is completely controlled by organized crime," it observed, nonetheless, "in many there is a considerable degree of corruption."[21]

The major problem faced by the Task Force was that it was "impossible to determine" the extent of the corruption of public officials in the United States. This lack of information was aggravated by the fact the many of those providing information to the Task Force were, themselves, public officials (i.e., police or politicians).

The 1986 President's Commission on Organized Crime found there has been a failure of banks to cooperate adequately with the intent of the Bank Secrecy Act in reporting large cash transactions, suggesting the possibility of commercial corruption in not questioning the source of large cash deposits. Such cooperation was seen as necessary to fight laundering of illegally obtained cash. The clear connection between labor-racketeering and corruption was also spelled out by the Commission.

> By manipulating the supply and costs of labor, organized crime
> can raise its competitor's costs, force legitimate businesses to deal
> with mob-run companies, and enforce price-fixing, bid-rigging,
> and other anti-competitive practices throughout an industry.[22]

The Commission went on to recommend increased penalties and law enforcement efforts against narcotics, claiming such a policy "will not undermine organized crime policy."[23] They noted, however, that there is evidence to the contrary indicating that by making narcotics a higher-risk market, it results in fewer, more sophisticated organizations that increase the price of the product and the violence associated with it.

The Commission's hearings found that gambling continues to be most conducive to corruption, due to the wide perception that it is a nonserious activity.

> Unlike illegal drugs, for example, which are in large part controlled by some form of organized crime and which are universally condemned, gambling is not an activity which is thought to be a harmful practice in and of itself, notwithstanding organized crime's persistent involvement. Much of what we saw and heard in the three days of hearings lends credence to the view that gambling, legal or illegal, is considered to be a relatively harmless pursuit, with no serious negative effects on society or the individual.[24]

Corruption was seen by the 1986 Commission as a more concrete issue with more definable limits, than in the 1967 report which found it was "impossible to determine its extent." The 1986 Commission was also more specific as to the causes of corruption. Nevertheless, the 1986 Commission, like the 1967 investigation, was dominated by information provided by public officials themselves. This probably worked against obtaining a reliable estimate of the true extent of official corruption related to organized crime.

National Efforts to Control Organized Crime

The TFR blamed the pervasiveness of organized crime on "belated recognition" of the problem. It was not until the publicity generated by the Kefauver Committee in 1950, Apalachin incident in 1957, and McClellan Committee hearings in the early 1960s that organized crime received much public or official attention (see Chapter 5 for a discussion of these events).

In 1954, the Department of Justice formed the Organized Crime and Racketeering Section to focus specifically on organized crime prosecutions, although by the early 1960s IRS tax investigations still netted the bulk of convictions related to organized crime. The TFR notes that the discovery of illicit federal wiretaps and electronic surveillance in 1965 "slowed the momentum" of the prosecutive effort against organized crime.[25]

Of the 71 cities surveyed by the Task Force it was found that 17 of the 19 cities with admitted organized crime problems had specialized organized crime units within their police departments. It was discovered that few special prosecutors were assigned to organized crime cases, and that few programs to gather intelligence existed.

The TFR concluded that public and private crime commissions are among "the most effective vehicles for providing public information" about organized crime. They were found to be particularly helpful in "exposing organized crime and corruption and arousing public interest."[26]

Unlike the 1967 report, which proposed many new tools to combat organized crime, the 1986 Commission generally found existing tools to be adequate, but were simply not seen as the answer in preventing organized crime over the long term. With regard to narcotics, for example, the Commission found that interdiction "is at best a random and occasional threat" as long as cocaine continues "in its current flood, unabated at its source." Furthermore, it was found that source country eradication will not succeed "unless it is comprehensive, long-term, and visibly supported by a national commitment" in the United States to stamp out demand.[27]

Prosecution was not seen as an effective solution for labor-racketeering either. It was concluded that these rackets are "not easily deterred by prosecutive efforts that merely 'count bodies' as a measure of success."[28]

> The data compiled by the Commission confirm that the government's emphasis on the "big four" international labor unions has been both justifiable and fruitful, but has not ended the control racketeers exercise over the unions.[29]

The current prosecutive effort was found to be "fragmented, and lacks adequate coordination" among government agencies. A greater emphasis on civil remedies was encouraged "to bankrupt individual mobsters and to discourage union officers, employees, and public officials from accommodating organized crime."[30] Unfortunately, the Commission undertook no evaluation of federal prosecution efforts, due to a lack of cooperation by the Justice Department. This failure to carry out one of its primary objectives led to dissension among many of the commissioners and to criticism of the Commission's work.[31]

Recommendations for the Future

The TFR cited in 1967 many existing shortfalls of efforts to combat organized crime, which were used as basis for recommendations for change. The most significant recommendations can be grouped into five categories.

First, the Task Force found that there are "difficulties in obtaining proof" in organized crime investigations. There were instances of noncooperation in victimless crimes and the reluctance of informants "to testify publicly."[32] The TFR recommended, among other suggestions, a witness protection program, a federal wiretapping law, and a provision for special grand juries to be enacted by Congress. These recommendations were later to become law in 1968 and 1970.

Second, the TFR found a "lack of resources" in the fight against organized crime. Staffing problems, arrests for minor offenses, and poor pay for prosecutors were all cited as examples. As the TFR concluded, an effective investigation and prosecution effort may not be fruitful "without years of intelligence gathering." The push for agencies to pile up numbers of arrests and convictions "may divert investigative energy to meaningless low-level gambling arrests that have little effect on the criminal organizations."[33] It was recommended that state Attorneys General and police departments in large cities establish specialized organized crime units.

Third, there was an apparent "lack of coordination" among investigators of organized crime. It was found that agencies "do not cooperate with each other in preparing cases, and they do not exchange information with each other." The threat of police corruption in organized crime cases results in officers and agencies who "do not trust each other." In addition, jurisdictional problems, and the failure to develop strategic intelligence were cited as continuing problems. Once strategic intelligence information was developed, it "would enable agencies to predict what directions organized crime might take, which industries it might try to penetrate, and how it might infiltrate." The need for special prosecutors, federal technical assistance, and a federal computerized information system for organized crime were suggested. It was noted, however, that "comprehensive strategic planning" will not be possible "even with an expanded intelligence effort," until "relevant disciplines, such as economics, political science, sociology, and operations research, begin to study organized crime intensively."[34]

Fourth, The TFR criticized the "failure to use available sanctions" in organized crime cases. Gambling was cited as a specific example. It was recommended that extended prisons terms for felonies committed as part of a continuing enterprise be established. This subsequently became law through the Racketeer Influenced and Corrupt Organizations section of the Organized Crime Control Act in 1970.

Fifth, the TFR cited that "lack of public and political commitment" in the fight against organized crime. Without public pressure, politicians "have little incentive" to be serious in efforts against organized crime. Permanent investigating commissions with subpoena power were recommended for the states, as were citizens crime commissions, and better investigative reporting on organized crime that emphasizes its costs to the public.

The 1967 TFR concluded with four consultant's papers. Donald Cressey outlined the structure of organized crime in the United States, as first described by Joseph Valachi in 1963. John Gardiner conducted a case study of political corruption in a small city. G. Robert Blakey wrote a paper that set forth the elements of the eventual federal wiretapping law and parts of the Organized Crime Control Act of 1970. Finally, Thomas Schelling attempted to explain the existence of organized crime as a study in economics.

The 1986 President's Commission made recommendations for each of its identified problem areas: drugs, labor racketeering, money laundering, and gambling. The report on drugs made 13 recommendations arguing that drug policy "must emphasize more strongly efforts to reduce the demand for drugs."[35] It was recommended that the cost of drug enforcement be subsidized by seizure and forfeiture of traffickers' assets, and that the United Nations should sponsor a model "International Controlled Substances Act" to assist in eradicating narcotics distribution at its source.

With regard to labor-management racketeering it was found that the 1970 Racketeer Influenced and Corrupt Organization (RICO) provisions "and union decertification laws have been underutilized."[36] Prosecutive efforts to remove racketeer influence over unions and legitimate businesses were seen as "largely ineffective."

> This situation does not stem simply from too few laws or unavail-
> able remedies. It arises from a lack of political will, a lack of
> fixed responsibility, and a lack of a national plan of attack.[37]

The need for a national strategy to combat labor racketeering was recognized, as was better organization of prosecution efforts. It was suggested that anti-trust offenses become eligible for electronic surveillance under Title III. Similarly, Title III wiretap authority was recommended for money-laundering offenses, as was improved cooperation of financial institutions in enforcing the Bank Secrecy Act.

There was less consensus about strategies to fight gambling. There appeared to be disagreement over the priority that gambling enforcement should have in a strategy to reduce organized crime.

> The extent to which illegal gambling should be targeted, either
> as unacceptable per se or as a revenue source for other . . . orga-
> nized criminal activities, and the priority to be given to any
> such targeting, is one of the more challenging subjects facing
> policy makers and law enforcement officials in the near future.[38]

Similar to the 1967 investigation, the 1986 Commission recommended several new laws, but many of these were suggestions that the states adopt laws that already exist on the federal level, such as wiretapping, witness immunity, special grand juries, and broad racketeering laws.[39] As noted earlier, however, the impact of these existing laws on the federal level was not examined.

The 1986 Commission report concluded with several appendices. First was a summary of five case studies of "mob connected lawyers." This was followed by an economic model proposed by Wharton Econometric Forecasting Associates for estimating the income of organized crime. Third, there was a survey of prosecutors regarding their access and use of various tools to combat organized crime. Finally, there was a paper by G. Robert Blakey that summarizes how organized crime is defined in statutes and case law.

Table 6.1 outlines the major differences between the 1967 and 1987 Presidential investigations of organized crime. As discussed above, the more recent Commission investigation is more expansive in its perception of the scope of organized crime and, if the Commissions are both correct in their conclusions, there has been a significant shift in organized crime activities in the last two decades.

Table 6.1
**Comparison of Findings and Recommendations
of the Two Presidential Investigations of Organized Crime**

Subject	Task Force Report, 1967	President's Commission, 1987
Crime Groups	Nearly exclusive focus on Italian-Sicilian groups.	Specific recognition of organized crime among at least 10 other ethnic, national, and geographic groups.
Narcotics	Only two paragraphs on narcotics in the report. Heroin the only drug mentioned by name.	Five days of hearings on cocaine and heroin, and a 500-page interim report on the drugs-organized crime link, recognizing the problems of interdiction and source country eradication, and the need to reduce demand.
Labor Racketeering	Only three paragraphs devoted to labor racketeering in report.	Two days of hearings and a 400-page interim report and appendix on labor racketeering encouraging civil remedies and a less-fragmented prosecution approach.
Money Laundering	No specific mention of money laundering in the report.	One day of hearings and a 90-page report on money laundering, focusing on the collusion of some banks with organized crime.
Gambling	Gambling seen as largest source of organized crime revenue.	Uncertain of the attention that should be devoted to gambling, and narcotics found to be largest source of revenue.
Penalties	Emphasis on criminal penalties to reduce organized crime involvement in drugs and other crimes.	Recognized that civil remedies and reduced demand may be more effective in reducing organized crime activities.
New Laws	Many proposals for new laws, including wiretapping, witness immunity and protection, and RICO, which have since become law.	Recognized that existing laws have been underutilized. Fewer proposals for new laws, except for state versions of federal laws and better inter-agency law enforcement cooperation.

Summary of Similarities

Three interesting similarities can be noted in the two Presidential investigations of organized crime. First, both Commissions recognized the pivotal role of money in funding organized criminal activity. In 1967, it was argued that "It is the accumulation of money, not the individual transactions themselves . . . that has a great and threatening impact on America."[40] Twenty years later, it was concluded that "Without means to launder money, thereby making cash generated by a criminal enterprise appear to come from a legitimate source, organized crime could not flourish as it now does."[41] Therefore, it is the generation and accumulation of income that lies at the heart of organized crime. This would argue strongly for greater reliance on civil remedies in organized crime prosecutions.

Both Presidential investigations suggested more severe drug penalties on the grounds that they will affect drug trafficking. The basis for this belief is debatable, as noted earlier, and the experience of the last 30 years does not make it clear that long sentences for drug traffickers will reduce their incidence. It appears that still more attention must be given to civil penalties, and to efforts to reduce demand. Without reduced demand, the market for illicit drugs will never disappear.

Third, both investigations cited similar problems on more than one occasion. Both mentioned a lack of investigative resources, a lack of coordination among agencies, a failure to share information, a failure to make use of existing sanctions, and a lack of political or public conviction to fight organized crime. There is a continuing problem among law enforcement agencies in their unwillingness to cooperate in criminal investigations. Organized crime activity often takes place across several jurisdictions, and yet local, county, state, and federal enforcement agencies appear unable to cooperate in most instances in the fight against organized crime. In many ways, the inefficiency of the law enforcement response assists the maintenance of criminal enterprises in keeping the risk of detection low.

This inefficiency of law enforcement efforts was a major component of the political controversy that surrounded the release of the 1986 Commission report. The Commission consisted of 18 members, yet 10 of them filed a joint supplemental report claiming that the Commission did not do "an adequate job in assessing the effectiveness of the [law enforcement] response to organized crime."[42] Likewise, these commissioners believed that the Commission's efforts were also not adequate in assessing the criminality of "other ethnic groups," and the Commission itself was poorly organized in that final drafts of Commission reports "were not even shown to Commission members before publication."[43] As a consultant to the Commission concluded, "The Commission will not be remembered for what it did. It will be remembered for the job that it didn't do."[44]

Nevertheless, similarities in the findings and recommendations of the two Commissions provide a framework for the criminal justice response to organized crime. Subsequent chapters on investigation, prosecution, defense, and sentencing will assess the extent to which these recommendations have been adopted in practice.

References to Chapter 6

1   President's Commission on Law Enforcement and Administration of Justice, *Task Force Report: Organized Crime* (Washington, DC: U.S. Government Printing Office, 1967), pp. 1, 6.

2   Ibid., p. 33.

3   President's Commission on Organized Crime, *Organized Crime of Asian Origin* record of hearing III, October, 1984 (Washington, DC: U.S. Government Printing Office, 1984), p. v.

4   Ibid., p. 407.

5   President's Commission on Organized Crime, *Organized Crime and Cocaine Trafficking* Record of Hearing IV, November, 1984 (Washington, DC: U.S. Government Printing Office, 1984), p. 477.

6   President's Commission on Organized Crime, *Organized Crime and Heroin Trafficking* Record of Hearing V, February, 1985 (Washington, DC: U.S. Government Printing Office, 1985), p. 389.

7   President's Commission on Organized Crime, *America's Habit: Drug Abuse, Drug trafficking and organized Crime* Interim Report, March, 1986 (Washington, DC: U.S. Government Printing Office, 1986), p. 73.

8   Ibid., p. 109.

9   President's Commission on Organized Crime, *Organized Crime and Gambling* Record of Hearing VII, June, 1985 (Washington, DC: U.S. Government Printing Office, 1985), p. vi.

10   President's Commission on Organized Crime, *The Impact: Organized Crime Today* April, 1986 (Washington, DC: U.S. Government Printing Office, 1987), pp. 58-128.

11   *Task Force Report*, p. 2.

12   Ibid., p. 3.

13   Ibid., p. 4.

14   Ibid., p. 5

15   Ibid.

16   *America's Habit*, pp. 2-3.

17   Ibid., p. 71.

18   President's Commission on Organized Crime, *The Edge: Organized Crime, Business, Labor Unions* Interim Report, March, 1986 (Washington, DC: U.S. Government Printing Office, 1986), p. 2; President's Commission on Organized Crime, *Organized Crime and Labor-Management Racketeering in the United States* Record of hearing VI, April, 1985 (Washington, DC: U.S. Government Printing Office, 1985), p. vi.

[19]   President's Commission on Organized Crime, *The Cash Connection: Organized Crime, Financial Institutions, and Money Laundering* Interim Report (Washington, DC: U.S. Government Printing office, 1984), p. 7.

[20]   *Task Force Report*, p. 6.

[21]   Ibid.

[22]   *The Edge*, p. 1.

[23]   *America's Habit*, p. 464.

[24]   *Organized Crime and Gambling*, p. 637.

[25]   *Task Force Report*, pp. 11-12.

[26]   Ibid., p. 14.

[27]   *Organized Crime and Cocaine Trafficking*, p. 477.

[28]   *The Edge*, p. 6.

[29]   Ibid., pp. 245.

[30]   Ibid., pp. 5-6.

[31]   Philip Shenon, "Crime Panel Issues Its Final Report," *The New York Times*, (April, 2, 1986), pp. 1, B8; "Writing the Book on the Mob," *The New York Times*, (April 5, 1986), p. 26.

[32]   *Task Force Report*, p. 14.

[33]   Ibid., p. 15.

[34]   Ibid., p. 15.

[35]   *America's Habit*, p. 463.

[36]   *The Edge*, p. 5.

[37]   Ibid., p. 307.

[38]   *Organized Crime and Gambling*, p. 637.

[39]   *The Impact: Organized Crime Today*, pp. 129-170.

[40]   *Task Force Report*, p. 2.

[41]   *The Cash Connection*, p. 3.

[42]   *The Impact: Organized Crime Today*, p. 176.

[43]   Ibid., p. 173.

[44]   G. Robert Blakey, cited in Philip Shenon, "U.S. Crime Panel: Discord to the End," *The New York Times*, (April 4, 1986), p. 16.

Chapter 7

Nontraditional Organized Crime

> They live off the alleged or real personal misfortunes of those with much more talent than they have.
>
> Frank Sinatra

The phrase "nontraditional organized crime" has become synonymous with "non-Italian" organized crime. Unfortunately, books and investigations deal with non-Italian organized crime in the same one-dimensional fashion they approached Mafia-linked crime. That is to say, the use of ethnicity as a descriptor of criminal activity is extremely limited, fails to explain the existence of the activity itself, and often comes perilously close to ethnic stereotyping. As noted in Chapter 1, "Italian" is no more a descriptor of organized crime in New York, for example, than "African-American" describes armed robbery, or "Caucasian" describes embezzlement there. In each case, overbroad generalizations are made, and a variety of criminal activity committed by others is overlooked. This chapter (and book) aims to correct these past mistakes.

Using Ethnicity to Explain Organized Crime?

Rather than describing organized crime in terms of the nature of the *groups* that engage in it, it is more useful to describe the nature of the *organized crime activity* itself, and how and why various groups specialize in certain activities (or fail to specialize). In this way, we can see organized crime as the result of exploitation of criminal opportunities, rather than as a problem of particular ethnic groups.

The Ethnicity Trap

When the President's Commission on Organized Crime attempted to characterize "Organized Crime Today," it fell into the "ethnicity trap."

Instead of focusing on the causes and prevention of criminal opportunities and the crimes themselves, it identified 11 different groups: nine by ethnicity, one by location (prison gangs), and one by means of transportation (motorcycle gangs). This typology lacks both clarity and logic.

The ethnic groups included in the President's Commission report included Italian, Mexican, Chinese, Vietnamese, Japanese, Cuban, Colombian, Irish, Russian, and Canadian. This is xenophobic in several important respects. First, our two bordering neighbors, Mexico and Canada, are identified, and the other ethnic groups represent most of the recent immigration waves of the twentieth century. Only the Irish and Italian groups are nineteenth century immigrants. It is interesting that no British, French, German or other European groups were identified. Are we to assume there are no people involved in organized crime from Europe? The point is that a list of ethnic groups, focusing primarily on our nearest neighbors and newest immigrants, is an extremely constricted view of organized crime.

In its discussion of prison gangs, the President's Commission identified four specific gangs of this type: Mexican, Aryan Brotherhood, Black Guerillas, and the Texas Syndicate. Once again, we are faced with a querulous mix of ethnicity, racism, race, and geographic location as descriptors of organized crime groups. This offers little guidance to the investigator, policymaker, scholar, or student who attempts to understand the problem of organized crime. A more organized and systematic approach is needed.

A Typology of Traditional and Nontraditional Organized Crime

This chapter presents nontraditional organized crime in a manner consistent with the typology presented in Chapter 1: provision of illicit services, provision of illicit goods, and the infiltration of legitimate business. Using these three categories of organized crime activity, different kinds of organized crime groups can be examined to see how they specialize in certain activities (or do not) and work by themselves (or in conjunction with other groups). This presentation should enable the reader to see the interrelationships among different types of organized *crimes* and the types of *criminals* who engage in them.

Groups Specializing in the Provision of Illicit Services

The provision of illicit services involves gambling, loansharking, and sex, as detailed in Chapter 2. These are among the oldest vices, and organized crime groups have engaged in these activities for many years. As this section will demonstrate, notoriety of certain organized crime groups does not always provide a good indicator of their illegal activities.

Gambling and Loansharking

The roots of the gambling-organized crime link in the United States, as shown in Chapter 2, lies primarily on the prohibition of most forms of gambling on one hand, and the prohibition of alcoholic beverages on the other. These legal changes spurred the organization of illicit entrepreneurs to provide liquor and gambling opportunities to a customer base that remained after these prohibitions were passed.

During the 1920s and 1930s bootleggers of illegal alcohol became intertwined with providers of illegal gaming. As historian Mark Haller explains, bootleggers and gambling entrepreneurs originally "co-existed," but bootleggers ultimately infiltrated the illegal gambling industry for three reasons: they were younger, more violent, and sought "coordination of the nightlife and commercialized entertainment of a city."[1] Therefore, bootleggers, who existed due to prohibition, eventually became involved in illegal gambling, as another profitable way to serve their customers. It was this predictable expansion of the illegal bootlegging market that began the notorious associations among Al Capone, Sam Giancana, Lucky Luciano, Bugsy Siegel, and others with illegal gambling.

In contemporary America, illegal gambling continues virtually everywhere. Given the fact that Cosa Nostra groups have been identified in only 25 or so cities in the United States, there is a great deal of room for other groups to cater to the existing demand. A study by Potter and Gaines of rural organized crime in eastern Kentucky found some interesting similarities with the urban, "Cosa Nostra" version. First, the vices in highest demand formed the basis for the illicit services provided. In Kentucky, this was primarily marijuana, alcohol (there are some dry counties there), sex, and gambling. Most of the syndicates there were run by people who were related to one another, and corruption of government officials was extensive.[2] In fact, the familial nature of the groups is reminiscent of the Cosa Nostra, although their structure is more fluid.

African-American criminal groups have operated illegal lotteries for many years. Even with the passage of state-

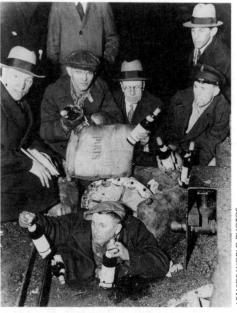

A pile of coal failed to conceal about $300,000 worth of liquor from Prohibition agents when they boarded the coal steamer *Maurice Tracy* in New York Harbor on April 8, 1932. The agents shoveled coal for about one hour before they discovered 3,000 bags of bottled beverages. Here they are inspecting the capture.

AP/WIDE WORLD PHOTOS

sponsored lotteries in most states, illegal lotteries continue to flourish because they have no minimum bet, credit is available, and the odds are better. In addition, a number of African-American groups have been found to work the illegal gambling market in conjunction with other groups. For example, several African-American groups throughout New Jersey have been found to receive financing, layoff bets, or split proceeds with New York City and Philadelphia families of the Cosa Nostra.[3] In Francis Ianni's pioneering study titled *Black Mafia*, he found no "Mafia" or other structure that linked together black organized crime operations.[4] Nevertheless, large African-American organized crime groups have endured in recent years, such as Nicky Barnes in New York and El Rukns in Chicago; gangs that have matched the power and influence of any existing group.[5] Most of these large, independent groups have dealt primarily in drugs, while gambling in urban settings has often been conducted in conjunction with Cosa Nostra groups.

The Yakuza in Japan have been known to be involved in the vices, and especially in gambling and loansharking. The Yakuza include at least seven distinct groups with a long history in Japan. Their presence in the United States was limited to Hawaii and California, but they have spread to Canada and eastern U.S. cities in recent years.[6] They are most interesting in the fact that membership is openly flaunted, and the Yakuza consider themselves legitimate businessmen. A primary activity of Yakuza is extortion, and their structure and other activities are explained more fully below.

Prostitution and Pornography

Chicago was identified by the President's Commission on Organized Crime as "one of the few cities" where prostitution is "controlled" by the Cosa Nostra.[7] In most cities, however, prostitution is a mixed bag. In one international scheme, a Chinese Tong flew young Asian women from Taiwan to Guatemala, and drove them to Mexico. Mexican smugglers then sneaked them into the United States. Madame Shih ran brothels in seven American cities, charging $20 at the door and $50 to $80 more for the prostitutes' services. The Madame and a Chinese film director ultimately were found to be behind the scheme.[8] Such a complex, international, and multi-ethnic scheme illustrates how organized crime groups are adapting to changes in criminal opportunities, the law, and enforcement strategies.

Prostitution has also been the result of Chinese gangs smuggling illegal immigrants into the United States. Large fees are charged, and the only way many women can hope to repay the debt is through prostitution.[9] This method of racketeering and extortion by Chinese gangs is discussed in the next section.

Russian mafia groups run prostitution enterprises in Russia, but it is not clear that prostitution is an enterprise they are pursuing actively in the United States.[10] Stolen property appears to be the focus of Russian crime groups, as explained below.

Groups Specializing in the Provision of Illicit Goods

The provision of illicit goods includes drug trafficking and dealing in stolen property. Drug trafficking has become the international organized crime of choice in the 1990s. Stolen property is most often organized in nations where a weak economy and weak government structure combine to provide an underground market for goods. The cases below describe the multi-ethnic and multi-national nature of many of these criminal organizations.

Drugs

Interviews with 130 law enforcement officials from 34 different federal, state, and local agencies revealed that an estimated 80 percent of all cocaine is Colombian in origin.[11] Coca leaf production, which provides the source for cocaine manufacturing, comes from Peru, Bolivia, and Colombia. Regardless of where its cultivated, however, "nearly all of the cocaine which enters the United States comes out of Colombia."[12] The two major drug organizations in Colombia are the Medellin cartel and the Cali cartel. These organizations use thousands of employees to process, ship, smuggle, and distribute cocaine around the world. According to the U.S. Drug Enforcement Administration, Colombian drug traffickers "have succeeded in monopolizing cocaine manufacturing and distribution throughout the world."[13]

These cartels have enjoyed a great deal of success for two primary reasons: (1) Colombia is a poor nation with a weak government, and (2) they protect themselves from their own employees. First, Colombia is an otherwise impoverished nation with an unstable government. The incredible wealth amassed by the manufacture of cocaine is unmatched anywhere in the country. This makes corruption rather easy, and the mobilization of the public against drug traffickers almost impossible.

Second, cartel members who live in the United States are not conspicuous. They do not live in large houses, drive fancy cars, or otherwise call attention to themselves. They are equipped with false identification, the cartel provides an attorney if arrested, and the attorney works for the best interests of the cartel (rather than for the defendant).[14] To prevent arrested members from becoming informants, cartel employees are told to invest their profits back in Colombia; and investments are lost if the employee betrays the organization. Less subtle is outright threat of violence against the member and his family, if they cooperate with police. These methods of insulation from detection have led U.S. prosecutors to rely heavily on apprehension through money laundering *after* the drugs have been sold. Following the money trail has been easier than following the drug trail. Money laundering is discussed further in Chapter 9.

Jamaican gangs, known as "posses," are involved both in narcotics and firearms trafficking. Crack cocaine is their primary product, made by mixing powdered cocaine with baking soda or ammonia and water. When it is dried, it is broken into small "rocks" and sold inexpensively. These gangs are very violent and have as their only common thread their origin in the island of Jamaica. Interviews with law enforcement officials found "little gang loyalty" among the posses, and the members change gang affiliation "with little consequence."[15] Several significant cases have been made against Jamaican posses, most involving crack cocaine or weapons violations. Cases in Baltimore, Ohio, Brooklyn, and Kansas City are examples.[16] In the Kansas City case, for instance, the Jamaicans introduced "crack" to Kansas City and were involved in its distribution there. More than 65 Jamaicans were convicted, more than 100 crackhouses raided, and over 200 guns seized.[17]

Other Afro-lineal groups include Nigerians and African-Americans. Some Nigerians have been found to be involved with bank fraud, as well as heroin smuggling into the United States. Nigerians obtain their heroin primarily from Southeast Asia and a mule (usually a woman or child) receives instructions and swallows the drugs, which are sealed in condoms and smuggled into the United States.[18] Some African-Americans have been found to be involved in narcotics trafficking both as importers and distributors within U.S. cities.[19]

The term "narco-terrorism" has been sometimes used in connection with drugs and organized crime. The phrase conjures up notions of drug manufacturers who are also terrorists. This does not appear to be the case. Instead, the term more aptly describes the terrorist-type tactics used by drug organizations to intimidate governments, such as the Medellin cartel in Colombia. As head of the Medellin cartel, Pablo Escobar had a private army of an estimated 1,000 men. His propensity to kill rivals, friends, politicians, and police, earned him the label of "narco-terrorist." He was said to be responsible for some 400 murders. He was killed by police in a raid in 1993; a death possibly encouraged by his many enemies both within and outside the drug world.[20] Narco-terrorism also describes the interactions between drug traffickers with revolutionary organizations against an incumbent regime, such have been found in some South American and Asian nations.[21]

According to reports from the Australian Federal Police, Chinese triads have a virtual monopoly over drug importation and distribution within Australia.[22] Nine separate gangs operate there, most of them out of the Chinatown districts of Sydney and Melbourne. The police have reported that these Chinese gangs have linked with Italian and Lebanese groups, and that Vietnamese refugees are used as low-level couriers. Nevertheless, it is believed that the triads comprise a total of 2,000 members, or one percent of the Chinese living in Australia.[23]

One investigator spent more than two years visiting 13 countries, and interviewing law enforcement officials about Chinese organized crime. He was told that in place of "large, cohesive, and centrally controlled Triad societies," there now exist a "multiplicity of small fluid criminal gangs," originating in Hong Kong and dealing primarily in heroin.[24] He found the need for international law enforcement cooperation, tied to multinational intolerance of the Triad activities in the drug trade. If this does not occur, he concluded, the Triads will become "as powerful a force for evil as ever the Italian Mafia has been in the past."[25]

Triads are secret groups that were first organized in the 1600s to overthrow the Manchu dynasty. Now the Triads are right-wing nationalists. Membership is prohibited in mainland China, exposing one to a possible death sentence. They are also outlawed in Hong Kong, but this is where Triad societies' "world headquarters" exists.[26] Tongs are more like the mafiosi in Sicily who act "as power brokers mediating individual and group conflicts within the community."[27] Tongs are not entirely criminal organizations, as they perform legitimate functions in the Chinese community, such as business and benevolent associations, and many of their members hold real jobs and are unconnected with the crimes committed by "core" members. The first reports of Triad street gangs in the United States was in San Francisco in the 1850s, corresponding to the first wave of Chinese immigration. A study of Chinese Triads and Tongs in New York City, that involved analysis of police reports and interviews with gang members, found no evidence of an "international structure" of these gangs, which appear local in origin and influence, primarily operating in Chinatown districts of large cities.[28] Nevertheless, large Chinese Triads have been reported to be functioning in the United States and Canada with estimates ranging in number from seven to 12 Triads, totaling more than 1,000 members.[29]

The Tongs have been in the United States for 150 years, and they have "neither infiltrated the larger American society nor victimized people who are not Chinese."[30] When compared to Italian-American organized crime, the role of the Tongs in American crime has been described as "relatively marginal." It has been noted that both language and cultural barriers serve to confine Chinese organized crime to limited areas, and for these reasons, Chinese criminals . . . have little desire to expand their activities to a society that is so alien to them." And even if they wanted to, those same language and cultural differences would inhibit the corrupt relationships with government agencies necessary to protect criminal enterprises.[31]

Although Chinese groups have a history of involvement in gambling and extortion, it is heroin trafficking from Southeast Asia that constitutes their primary criminal activity. As Hong Kong and China merge in 1997, it will be important to observe how Hong Kong criminal groups react to escape the more punitive Chinese government. It has been predicted that up to 25 percent of Hong Kong's 5.6 million residents will leave for other shores before 1997.[32] This may have already occurred to some extent, as the successful Mafia-linked prosecutions of the last decade weakened their control over drug distribution in certain cities, making it easier for the Chinese groups to traffick in heroin and cocaine in the United States.[33] As one detective has observed, the Chinese groups have "the potential of making the Mafia in America look like a fraternity of wimps."[34]

Two of the largest Chinese groups are the United Bamboo and the Fuk Ching. United Bamboo was the target of a two-year multi-agency investigation. It ended in the arrest of 20 gang members in the United States and Hong Kong. The gang was charged with smuggling 137 pounds of heroin (street value $137 million) from Burma, through China, to Hong Kong, to San Francisco, to New York City and Newark, New Jersey, and also to Washington, D.C.[35] Fuk Ching is involved in alien smuggling (described under "extortion" in this chapter), as well as heroin and gun trafficking.

The President's Commission on Organized Crime found the Bruno-Scarfo Cosa Nostra group in Philadelphia to be more "heavily involved than other families in the trafficking of methamphetamines."[36] The extent to which Sicilian members of Cosa Nostra are present in the United States is "unclear," although they are believed to be concentrated in the northeastern United States. Interestingly, authorities do not agree about the precise relationship between American and Sicilian Cosa Nostra groups. Some believe there is a formal agreement between them, while others believe it varies with different criminal enterprises.[37] The latter position appears to be the most accurate, given the evidence presented in actual cases. In the "pizza connection" trial, for example, it was found that Sicilian Cosa Nostra members supplied heroin to people in the American Bonanno Cosa Nostra group.[38] In a six-month trial in 1994, five defendants, some linked to the Bonanno crime group in New York, were convicted for their role in buying heroin from Chinese smugglers and selling it to a Puerto Rican gang.[39] In a similar way, 18 tons of canned "meat" were seized in Russia and opened. They were found to contain 1,100 kilograms of cocaine. The shipment had been sent from Colombia to Finland, and moved to Russia by train. The scheme was linked to organized crime interests in Russia, Colombia, and Israel.[40]

Drug trafficking through Poland, the Czech Republic, Hungary, Bulgaria, and Romania also has increased sharply in the last few years. Although most of the drugs are destined for western Europe and the United States, central and eastern European countries are being used to disguise the origin of the narcotics and because their government and law enforcement structures have weakened since the end of the Communist era.[41] All these cases show inter-ethnic cooperation in organized crime continues to exist where the market and profits make it necessary.

An interesting example of a multi-national drug case is *United States v. Vasquez-Velaso*. The defendant, Javier Vasquez-Velaso, was convicted at trial of racketeering and murder. Along with three co-defendants, Vasquez-Velaso were part of the "Guadalajara Narcotics Cartel" that distributed large amounts of drugs from Mexico to the United States.[42]

In the meantime, the U.S. Drug Enforcement Administration was having some success against the drug cartel, resulting in millions of dollars in drug losses and cash seizures. As a result, the cartel engaged in retaliatory actions against DEA agents in Mexico. This included the killing of DEA agent Enrique Camarena, informants, and others mistakenly believed to be associated with the DEA.

These murders took place in Mexico, and raise an important issue about the ability of the U.S. government to enforce its laws against those who violate them outside of its borders. Vasquez-Velaso was not charged with the killing of Camarena, although his associates were. Instead, he was charged with murder and racketeering for participating in the beating deaths of two persons in Mexico mistakenly believed to be DEA agents.

Vasquez-Velaso argued that he could not be charged with crimes not committed in the United States. The U.S. Court of Appeals held that it looks to "congressional intent" when deciding on extraterritorial application in a given case. In addition, it does not violate two important principles of international law:

1. *Objective Territorial Principle*—jurisdiction is asserted over acts performed outside the United States that produce detrimental effects within the United States, and

2. *Protective Principle*—jurisdiction is asserted over foreigners for an act committed outside the United States that may impinge on the territorial integrity, security, or political independence of the United States.[43]

The Court held that extraterritorial application of the law in this case was not unreasonable, and it also corresponded with the principles of international law. This is because "drug smuggling is a serious and universally condemned offense, no conflict is likely to be created by extraterritorial regulation of drug traffickers."[44] Similarly, the Court repeated its holding from an earlier case involving an accessory to the murder of DEA Agent Camarena.

> We held that because drug trafficking by its nature involves foreign countries and because DEA agents often work overseas, the murder of a DEA agent in retaliation for drug enforcement activities is a crime against the United States regardless of where it occurs.[45]

Therefore, the U.S. Court of Appeals found "Congress would have intended" extraterritoriality in cases like this one. Even though Vasquez-Velaso did not murder a DEA agent, the Court declared, "the record clearly supports the government contention that [the two victims] were murdered in retaliation for the DEA's activities in Mexico."[46]

The issue of extraterritoriality is likely to arise again in the future as organized crime becomes global in scope. Consider the case of the indictments brought against 18 people in Dallas for international drug smuggling. Nigerian heroin smugglers recruited non-Nigerian Dallas residents to smuggle heroin into the United States. According to the indictment, the Nigerian recruiters provided airline tickets and expense money for the couriers, in addition to a salary of $5,000 to $10,000 per trip. The first courier would be sent to Thailand, the heroin source, and would take the heroin from there to an intermediate non-source nation (such as the Philippines, Kenya, Poland, or western Europe) and deliver it to a second courier there. The second courier would conceal the heroin in a suitcase, or strap it to his or her body, and smuggle it into the United States. The strategy was designed to deceive U.S. authorities who would not suspect the courier who had not been to the source country, and the suspicious courier who had been there would possess no drugs.[47] Such a scheme capitalizes on multiethnic cooperation among criminals, as well as points to the need for international cooperation and surveillance by law enforcement agencies.

AP/WIDE WORLD PHOTOS

FBI agents sort through packages of cocaine and cash that were seized from the Philadelphia-based cell of the Cali cocaine cartel in 1992. Seventy-six people were charged with operating the international drug trafficking ring, which brought $750 million worth of drugs into the Philadelphia area from 1989 to 1992.

The "internationalization" of organized crime activities is typified by the narcotics trafficking described above. The immense problems posed by manufacture, transportation, shipping, smuggling, and distribution have resulted in "marriages of convenience" where criminal groups work together, albeit suspiciously, to make a mutual profit. An example of this phenomenon is the alliance between some Sicilian mafia groups and the Medellin cartel in Colombia.[48] The shooting death of Pablo Escobar during a police raid on his home in 1993 has done little to slow the flow of cocaine from Colombia.[49] In his absence, the Cali cartel has gained control of the bulk of cocaine manufacturing and distribution in Colombia. The Cali cartel may have learned from the murderous ways of Escobar in that they are less prone to violence, and more skilled at bribery and corruption.[50] Therefore, organized crime groups come to live off one another in carrying out international criminal schemes, and also learn from one another's mistakes.

Stolen Property

A study of organized crime in Poland found no criminal syndicates involving illicit goods and services. Instead, a "black market" has created groups that misappropriate state property and provide scarce goods that are in demand.[51] The dissolution of the Soviet Union appears to have had the same result: organization and exploitation of the "shadow economy."[52] It has been found, for example, that organized crime has flourished in the "manipulation of the voucher system," whereby state property is allocated to citizens.[53] Likewise, the political changes throughout central and eastern Europe have produced new opportunities for organized crime, most associated with the precipitous drop in the standard of living. Growing unemployment, high inflation, and scarcity of goods have led to "more and more people . . . turning to the black market and to crime as a means of supplementing their income."[54] The subterranean economy has formed the wellspring of many organized crime groups over the years, including the Bahamas after it became politically independent of Great Britain.[55]

The true extent of Russian organized crime in the United States is still not well documented.[56] It is known, however, that Soviet Jews emigrated to the United States and elsewhere when the Soviet Union liberalized its Jewish emigration policy in the mid-1970s. It is estimated that as many as 100,000 former Soviets came to the United States with more than 40,000 settling in Brighton Beach, Brooklyn. It is also alleged that criminals from Soviet jails were included in this wave of immigration.[57]

A significant case involving Russian organized crime entailed motor fuel tax fraud in New Jersey. The scam involved a number of Russian immigrants who bought no. 2 fuel oil, sold it as diesel, charged the customer taxes, but never paid them to the government. It was a complicated scheme involving dummy corporations, which hoped to "lose" the taxes in a paper trail of buyers, sellers, oil refineries, and distributors.[58] An important aspect of this case was that the Russians knew they had to pay "tribute" to Cosa Nostra families in the area they were operating, and did so. In fact, a member of the Colombo crime family in New York, and a dual U.S.-Israeli citizen, were charged with the murder of Russian Michael Markowitz, who was convicted in the gasoline tax scam, and who later became a government informant.[59] This "loosely-knit" group of Russian immigrants also have been found to be engaged in money laundering, fraud, murder, and trafficking in radioactive materials.[60]

It has been discovered that nuclear materials have been "missing" from the former Soviet Union and eastern European nations. That material is then being offered for sale illegally in western Europe, primarily in Germany. Thus far, there have been no cases of weapons-grade uranium or plutonium for sale.[61]

In Toronto, luxury car thefts have been blamed on Russian organized crime connected to Brighton Beach in Brooklyn. Sought after automobiles, especially large Buicks and Cadillacs, can be shipped legally from Canada to Russia for less than $1,000. They can be sold in Russia for $40,000. The Royal Canadian Mounted Police established a unit in Toronto in 1993 to combat the so-called Russian mafia.[62]

The President's Commission on Organized Crime found "firearms trafficking" to be common in Cosa Nostra groups in the north central United States, although Jamaican posses appear to be most active in gun-running. Guns are either bought illegally or stolen, and then smuggled back to Kingston, Jamaica where they are sold to local gangs at inflated prices.[63] The demand for guns by organized crime groups sometimes leads them to suppliers not affiliated with their own group. One "independent" illegal trafficker was said to have sold weapons to both members of the Genovese crime family in New York, as well as to Chinese gangs in Manhattan.[64]

APWIDE WORLD PHOTOS

Two Hell's Angels stand handcuffed, faces to the wall, after their arrest during a narcotics raid in southern California. "Berdoo" refers to the San Bernardino, California, branch of the Angels to which they belong. Once content to invade small towns and taverns, picking fights, today's Hell's Angels, according to police and their informants, is a motorcycle mob that handles millions of dollars in narcotics, executes snitches, and secures favors for themselves by trading guns and explosives to police.

Outlaw motorcycle clubs vary widely in the extent to which they engage in criminal activity. Members of the Hell's Angels, the Outlaws, Pagans, Bandidos, and Satan's Choice have been documented committing a wide array of crimes.[65] Drug trafficking is the most common, along with robbery and extortion. Like the Chinese Tongs, the motorcycle gangs are comprised of many noncriminals, making it difficult to distinguish criminal members from the others. For example, the Toronto chapter of Satan's Choice were found to operate a drug lab that manufactured methamphetamines, "Canadian Blue," that were exported to the U.S.-based Outlaws motorcycle club. It was found that "mixed in with the narcotics dealers . . . were labourers and tradesmen, such as an electrician, a plumber, and a truck driver, along with a stock-market executive."[66] A sociologist who rode with the Rebels motorcycle club reported that they "are outlaws, but they are not professional criminals." They broke laws, but "rarely for profit." He found them to be criminal opportunists who committed misdemeanors, assaults, weapons offenses, drug possession, and other crimes, but they did not organize their criminal activity.[67] This variation both among and within motorcycle gangs makes it difficult to generalize about them beyond specific cases.

Groups Specializing in the Infiltration of Legitimate Business

The President's Commission on Organized Crime concluded that "labor racketeering and infiltration of the construction trades" are "primary" activities of Cosa Nostra groups in the northeast United States.[68] Forgery and arson for profit were found to be "prominent" among Cosa Nostra groups in the southern and western regions of the United States. Also, the New Orleans Cosa Nostra group was found to generate "most of its income" through the infiltration of legitimate business.[69] The extent to which nontraditional groups are involved in these, and other, kinds of criminal infiltration is described below.

Racketeering

Peter Reuter conducted a study of the garbage collection industry in the New York City area. He found that the companies in this area were "dominated by males of Italian origin," and that numerous firms were family enterprises. Interesting, he found that "ethnic homogeneity" is characteristic in the carting industry, although the ethnicity varies. In Chicago, most firms are run by those of Dutch origin. In Los Angeles, the Armenians and Jews dominate, and in San Francisco, the Italians appear to dominate.[70] Reuter found this ethnic homogeneity not to be accidental or conspiratorial. Instead, it is due to the fact that most of these firms are small and cannot afford to have a truck fail or employee not show up for work in order to conduct that day's business. Therefore, there is a need for carters to cooperate with each other to provide backup if one member experiences problems. Reuter also argues that the "low repute of the industry" left it to new immigrant groups with traditions of entrepreneurship.[71] Criminal conspiracies emerged largely in allocating customers among the carters in violation of anti-trust laws. In this way, the carters establish monopolies and large profits from not bidding against each other in open competition. Interestingly, Reuter found it was the *reputation* of being a racketeer (i.e., being "connected" to a larger criminal organization) that was more important than being an actual member of a conspiracy. The label of racketeer involvement "provides a reputational barrier to entry" into the market, where other potential carting competitors do not enter the market due to fear of retaliation by racketeers.[72]

Reuter admits that it is "difficult to determine" how the industry in general operates with regard to monopolistic customer allocation agreements or the involvement of racketeers outside the New York City area. As he notes, in most areas of the country "there are neither Mafia families nor any other comparable racketeering group." He suggests that an analysis of the customer market and prices charged for carting in different jurisdictions can provide clues regarding overcharging and potential conspiratorial arrangements.[73]

Racketeering appears to be a multi-ethnic enterprise in recent years. Cosa Nostra groups have been found to supply and service illegal video gambling machines that Chinese gangs have forced on bars and nightclubs.[74] The Irish, Russian, Chinese, Japanese, and groups from other ethnic background have engaged in racketeering. Such racketeering usually involves extortion, and the tactics employed mirror those first used in the country where the group originated.

Paul Clare's study of racketeering in Northern Ireland found paramilitary organizations and those based on political ideology to be the most common. He found no evidence of drug trafficking by these groups, but he found instances where illicit proceeds were used to purchase a legal business. He asserts that the Irish Republican Army Worker's Party owns three bars in California allegedly bought with funds taken in bank robberies in Ireland.[75]

Since the demise of the Soviet Union, Russian organized crime groups have been engaged in racketeering activities there. Businessmen have been found to hire gangsters for protection from other criminals. Also, a report in Russia claims that 75 percent of Russia's private businesses pay 10 to 20 percent of their earnings as a "street tax" to organized crime groups.[76] The extent of these racketeering and extortion tactics by Russian groups within the United States has not been clearly established, although Russia's Interior Ministry has identified nearly 200 Russian crime groups that are active internationally. Credit card scams, forgery and insurance fraud, and even contract killings linked to these groups have been reported in both the United States and Russia. As Joseph Serio has remarked, "When groups from the former Soviet Union further improve their organizational skills, the challenge to American law enforcement will be staggering."[77]

Extortion

Interviews with more than 600 Chinese-owned and operated businesses in New York City found more than 70 percent were approached by gang members for some type of extortion, most often demands for money.[78]

Most of these businesses (55 percent) made the payments and, although threats were common, violence was rare (less than four times per year). Interestingly, Tongs have emerged as "power brokers" or "middlemen" between the businesses and the gangs. The problem, of course, is that "merchants who resort to tong protection for a fee may find themselves in new partnerships."[79]

> From a purely economic calculus, merchants appear to be con-
> tent to deal with a powerful tong or gang boss rather than face
> the chaos of shakedowns from every street hoodlum. Thus, in a
> sense, there are as many "voluntary victims" as "involuntary
> victims" in a commercial environment where the lines of
> demarcation between the legal and illegal are blurred.[80]

The intergang murders that have occurred in the Chinese community appear to originate with "territorial conflicts" where gangs compete for extortion targets or "market share."[81]

The smuggling of aliens has also become an enterprise for some Chinese gangs, most notably the Fuk Ching. In one case, this group smuggled to New York City hundreds of illegal immigrants from mainland China, charging $23,000 each. The illegal aliens had the option of working as indentured servants (i.e., mules, enforcers, prostitutes) or becoming part of the Fuk Ching gang to pay off their debts. This insured the continuity of the illegal enterprise.[82] There are more than 50,000 Chinese aliens smuggled by criminal groups into the United States each year since 1990, according to one estimate.[83]

Vietnamese gangs arose in California during the early 1980s, after the arrival of thousands of Vietnamese refugees in the United States. These gangs are highly localized in nature, but they engage in common activities. Several of these gangs seek "donations" from legitimate Vietnamese businesses in the United States with promises of using it to help free Vietnam. These "requests" are sometimes accompanied with threats of being labeled a "procommunist." Such a label is tantamount to being called a traitor to one's homeland. These extortionate methods are used to support further criminal activity.

An examination of a Vietnamese gang in New York City found "the gang's weekly extortion rounds were the backbone of their entire operation . . . by continuously reasserting its presence, the gang was making it clear to area merchants who was boss on Canal Street."[84] The difference between this collection of "street tax" by the Vietnamese gang mirrors that of traditional Italian-American groups operating in different neighborhoods of the same city.

Robberies known as "home invasions" were started by Vietnamese gangs, where they would terrorize their victims for hours while they searched a home for valuables. Thus far, most crime by Vietnamese gangs have been against other Vietnamese.[85] It remains to be seen whether this will continue to be the case.

Traditional organized crime groups have been found to turn to nontraditional groups for "subcontracting" purposes. Cecil Kirby, a Canadian biker, was contracted by an alleged mafia group to commit murder.[86] Similarly, Clarence Smith, a member of the Outlaws motorcycle club was convicted for the murder of a witness who had testified against a nephew of Carlos Marcello, the alleged boss of the Cosa Nostra group in New Orleans.[87]

The generic term for organized crime groups in Japan is "boryokudan," which means "violent ones." The criminals call themselves "yakuza," which stands for "8,9,3." This is the worst possible hand in a popular Japanese card game (hanafuda), so the term is taken to mean a "loser."[88] Yakuza commonly have ornate tattoos and dress distinctively. If a member has committed a transgression in the eyes of his "boss," he may atone for it by cutting off the last joint of his little finger. This may be repeated for other transgressions on other fingers.[89] Unlike organized crime groups in the United States, gangs in Japan are usually open about their Yakuza affiliation. They consider themselves part of a "mutual aid society." As a result, membership in Yakuza groups is much larger than that of the American Mafia, which attempts to remain invisible.[90]

There are at least seven major Yakuza gangs. Membership involves an initiation and sworn oath of loyalty, much like that of traditional Italian organized crime groups. The structure of the gang is also much like that of a Cosa Nostra family, although it is somewhat more structured. Extortion is a primary activity of Yakuza groups. Sometimes they purchase stock in a targeted corporation, disrupting corporate meetings, and extort payment for "peace."[91] Police in Japan are limited in combatting the Yakuza because undercover police work and electronic surveillance are not permitted in Japan. Also, informants are unpopular and are not used in Japan.[92] Therefore, prosecutions usually result only after a witness voluntarily comes forward. This is rare.

Summary

Organized crime committed by both "traditional" and nontraditional" groups can be characterized by a typology of criminal activity. Although the size and organization of these groups vary, their methods of creating and exploiting criminal opportunities are remarkably consistent. All these groups engage in a definable scope of activity, most groups engage in more than one type of illicit enterprise, inter-ethnic cooperation is not uncommon, and the globalization of organized crime is upon us. The study of organized crime groups of diverse origins is important, as the director of the FBI has recognized:

we cannot allow the same kinds of mistakes to be made today in Russia, Europe and the U.S. that were made in responding to the threat of gangsterism that swept through the United States in the 20s and 30s. The failure of American law enforcement, including the FBI, to take effective measures against developing organized crime groups then, and subsequently through the 40s and 50s, permitted the development of a powerful, well-entrenched, American organized crime syndicate, which . . . has required over 35 years of concerted law enforcement effort and the expenditure of incredible resources to address . . . It still has not been overcome.[93]

Many nontraditional groups are in their early stages in the United States. Early efforts to understand their native underpinnings, language, culture, and method of operation will go a long way to preventing their existence as entrenched organized crime groups in the future.

As the President's Commission on Organized Crime concluded after its hearings on organized crime of Asian origin, "these groups have frequently exhibited the same characteristics as La Cosa Nostra families: significant involvement in illegal activities such as narcotics, gambling, and prostitution; efforts to corrupt police authorities . . . and the willingness to use violence" for purposes of intimidation.[94] Nevertheless the "ethnic insularity" of Asian groups in particular have made them difficult to understand and infiltrate. In order to effectively combat these groups, and the other groups described in this chapter, "law enforcement officers will need to explore methods to overcome barriers of language, culture, and tradition even more formidable than those on which La Cosa Nostra has long depended for its success."[95]

Read the case study below. Using the concepts from this chapter, answer the questions that follow, explaining your rationale.

The Case of Video Slot Machines

This structure of this gang is very fluid. Old gangs dissolve and are quickly replaced by new groups. Several of these groups distribute illegal video gambling machines to selected neighborhoods throughout the city. One individual has distributed more than 20 "Cherry Master" video slot machines to businesses, selected by their ownership, that include bars, nightclubs, and massage parlors. These groups cannot place their machines in other neighborhoods, because they are controlled by different gangs who would demand a split of the profits, as well as protection money.

Businesses that refuse these gambling machines are threatened, or damage is inflicted. Money is also extorted from these businesses for "protection" from damage or disruption. Business owners in the neighborhoods affected pay the extortion because it protects them from harassment, and they do not believe that the police, if called, can do anything about it.

Questions:

1. Given the facts above, can you guess which organized crime group is being described?

2. If gambling and extortion are used by a large number of organized crime groups to produce illegal income, what solutions would you recommend?

References to Chapter 7

[1] Mark H. Haller, "The Changing Structure of American Gambling in the Twentieth Century," *Journal of Social Issues*, v. 35 (1979), p. 110.

[2] Gary W. Potter and Larry K. Gaines, "Country Comfort: Vice and Corruption in Rural Settings," *Journal of Contemporary Criminal Justice*, v. 8 (February, 1992), pp. 36-61.

[3] New Jersey State Commission of Investigation, *Afro-Lineal Organized Crime* (Trenton: State Commission of Investigation, 1991), pp. 6-7.

[4] Francis A.J. Ianni, *Black Mafia: Ethnic Succession in Organized Crime* (New York: Simon and Schuster, 1974).

[5] Rufus Schatzberg, "African American Organized Crime," in R.J. Kelly, K. Chin and R. Schatzberg, eds. *Handbook of Organized Crime in the United States* (Westport, CT: Greenwood Press, 1994), pp. 189-212.

[6] David E. Kaplan and Alec Dubro, *Yakuza* (New York: Addison Wesley, 1986); "Japanese Recession Leaves Yakuza Little to Squeeze," *Organized Crime Digest*, v. 15 (March 23, 1994), p. 7; "Seven Large Chinese Triads Active in U.S. and Canada," *Organized Crime Digest*, (June 24, 1992), p. 1.

[7] President's Commission on Organized Crime, *The Impact: Organized Crime Today* (Washington, DC: U.S. Government Printing office, 1987), p. 46.

[8] "The New Face of Organized Crime," p. 37.

[9] 'Chinese Smuggling," *USA Today*, (September 1, 1993), p. 3.

[10] Brian Duffy and Jeff Trimble, "The Looting of Russia," *U.S. News & World Report*, (March 7, 1994), pp. 36-47.

[11] U.S. Comptroller General, *Non-Traditional Organized Crime* (Washington, DC: U.S. General Accounting Office, 1989), p. 12.

[12] Steven P. Tori, ed., *Narcotics in the 90s* proceedings of at conference (Pittsburgh: Middle Atlantic-Great Lakes Organized Crime Law Enforcement Network, 1994), p. 1.

[13] Ibid., p. 11; see Guy Gugliotta and Jeff Leen, *Kings of Cocaine* (New York: Harper & Row, 1990).

[14] Ibid., pp. 19-20.

[15] U.S. Comptroller General, "Nontraditional Organized Crime," p. 22.

[16] U.S. Department of Justice Immigration and Naturalization Service Investigations Division, *The INS Approach to Jamaican Posses* (Washington, DC: Immigration and Naturalization Service, 1988).

[17] Ibid., pp. 16-17.

[18] New Jersey State Commission of Investigation, *Afro-Lineal Organized Crime* (Trenton: State Commission of Investigation, 1991), p. 23.

[19] Ibid., pp. 2-16.

[20] Russell Watson et al., 'Death on the Spot," *Newsweek*, (December 23, 1993), p. 16; William Gately and Yvette Fernandez, *Dead Ringer: An Insider's Account of the Mob's Colombian Connection* (New York: Donald I. Fine, 1994).

[21] Peter A. Lupsha, "The Role of Drugs and Drug Trafficking in the Invisible Wars," in R.H. Ward and H.E. Smith, eds. *International Terrorism: Operational Issues* Chicago: University of Illinois Office of International Criminal Justice, 1988, pp. 177-190.

[22] Carl Robinson, "The Day of the Triads: Hong Kong's Gangs Move in on Australia," *Newsweek*, (November 7, 1988), p. 72.

[23] Ibid.

[24] Fenton Bresler, *The Chinese Mafia* (New York: Stein and Day, 1981), p. 53.

[25] Ibid., p. 218.

[26] Martin Booth, *The Triads: The Chinese Criminal Fraternity* (London: Grafton, 1991), p. xi.

[27] Ko-lin Chin, Robert J. Kelly, and Jeffrey Fagan, "Chinese Organized Crime in America," in R.J. Kelly, K. Chin, and R. Schatzberg, eds. *Handbook of Organized Crime in the United States* (Westport, CT: Greenwood, 1994), p. 215.

28 Ko-lin Chin, *Chinese Subculture and Criminality: Non-Traditional Crime Groups in America* (Westport, CT: Greenwood Press, 1990).

29 'Seven Large Chinese Triads Active in U.S. and Canada,' *Organized Crime Digest*, v. 13 (June 24, 1992), pp. 1-10; Michael D. Whittingham, "Asian Crime in Canada: A Contemporary Overview," *CJ International*, (February-March, 1992), pp. 3-4.

30 Ko-lin Chin et al., "Chinese Organized Crime in America," p. 236.

31 Ibid., p. 236.

32 U.S. Comptroller General, "Nontraditional Organized Crime," p. 34.

33 Peter Kerr, "Chinese Now Dominate New York Heroin Trade," *The New York Times*, (August 9, 1987), p. 1.

34 James Brady of Arlington, Virginia's gang task force, cited in Gerald L. Posner, *Warlords of Crime: Chinese Secret Societies—The New Mafia* (New York: Penguin, 1990), p. 261.

35 "Nontraditional Organized Crime," pp. 35-36.

36 President's Commission on Organized Crime, *The Impact: Organized Crime Today* (Washington, DC: U.S. Government Printing Office, 1987), p. 45.

37 Ibid., p. 56.

38 Peter Stoler, "The Sicilian Connection," *Time*, (October 15, 1984), p. 42.

39 William Kleinknecht, "Mob-Linked Man Walks in Drug Trial," *New York Daily News*, (May 10, 1994), p. 8

40 Juan Gonzalez, "Bust Just Tip of Iceberg," *New York Daily News*, (April 27, 1994), p. 9; see also Barbara Ross and Juan Gonzalez, "Multi-Ethnic Group Invades Drug Biz," *New York Daily News*, (April 27, 1994), p. 20.

41 Raymond Bonner, "Poland Becomes a Major Conduit for Drug Traffic," *The New York Times*, (December 30, 1993), p. 3.

42 *United States v. Vasquez-Velaso*, 15 F.3d 833 (9th Cir. 1994).

43 at 840.

44 *United States v. Vasquez-Velaso* at 841.

45 at 840-1; *United States v. Lopez-Alvarez*, 970 F.2d 583 (9th Cir.) *cert. denied* 113 S. Ct 504 (1992).

46 at 842.

47 'Worldwide Nigerian Heroin Smuggling Ring Smashed,' *Organized Crime Digest*, (May 27, 1992), p. 3; "New Breed of Smugglers," *USA Today*, (September 23, 1991), p. 3.

48 William Gately and Yvette Fernandez, *Dead Ringer: An Insider's Account of the Mob's Colombian Connection* (New York: Donald I. Fine, 1994).

49 Russell Watson et al., "Death on the Spot," *Newsweek*, (December 13, 1993), p. 16.

50 Ibid., p. 19.

51 Dick Ward, "Organized Crime, Corruption Add to Law Enforcement Problems," *CJ International*, v. 7 (January-February, 1991), p. 1; A.E. Marek, "Organized Crime in Poland," in R.J. Kelly, ed. *Organized Crime: A Global Perspective* (Totowa, NJ: Rowan & Littlefield, 1986), pp. 159-171.

52 Alexander S. Nikiforov, "A Response to Joseph Serio's 'The Soviet Union: Disorganization and Organized Crime'," *Criminal Organizations*, v. 8 (Spring, 1994), pp. 10-12.

53 Louise I. Shelley, "Post-Soviet Organized Crime: Implications for the Development of the Soviet Successor States and Foreign Countries," *Criminal Organizations*, v. 9 (Summer, 1994), pp. 14-22.

54 Matti Joutsen, "The Growth of Organized Crime in Central and Eastern Europe," in J. Albanese, ed. *Contemporary Issues in Organized Crime* (Monsey, NY: Willow Tree Press, 1995), p. 201.

55 Alan A. Block, *Masters of Paradise: Organized Crime and the Internal Revenue Service in The Bahamas* (New Brunswick, NJ: Transaction Publishers, 1991).

56 James O. Finckenauer, "Russian Organized Crime in America," in R.J. Kelly, K. Chin and R. Schatzberg, eds. *Handbook of Organized Crime in the United States* (Westport, CT: Greenwood Press, 1994), pp. 245-267.

57 Traci Anne Attanasio, "How Russian Organized Crime Took Root in the U.S.," *Organized Crime Digest* v. 15 (October 12, 1994), p. 71; Nathan M. Adams, "Menace of the Russian Mafia," *Reader's Digest*, (August, 1992), pp. 33-40; Richard I. Friedman, "Brighton beach Goodfella," *Vanity Fair*, (January, 1993), pp. 26-41.

58 Ibid., pp. 261-262.

59 Manuel Perez-Rivas, "Mob Ties Cited as 2 Indicted in Slaying," *New York Newsday*, (December 22, 1993), p. 31.

60 Louis Freeh, "Russian Organized Crime Groups Spread in U.S.," *Organized Crime Digest*, v. 15 (June 22, 1994), p. 1; Brian Duffy and Jeff Trimble, "The Looting of Russia," *U.S. News & World Report*, (March 7, 1994), p. 46.

61 Ibid., pp. 5-6; Seymour Hersh, "Hijack the State," *Atlantic Monthly*, (June, 1994).

62 "Russian Emigres are Canada's Newest Organized Crime Threat," *Organized Crime Digest*, v. 15 (May 11, 1994), p. 1.

63 Jack Seamonds, "The New Face of Organized Crime," *U.S. News & World Report*, (January 18, 1988), pp. 29-37.

64 Scott Ladd, "Armed with Law," *New York Newsday*, (March 15, 1994), p. 15; Jack Seamonds, "Ethnic Gangs and Organized Crime," *U.S. News & World Report*, (January 18, 1988), p. 35.

65 President's Commission on Organized Crime, *The Impact: Organized Crime Today* (Washington, DC: U.S. Government Printing Office, 1987), pp. 58-73.

66 Daniel R. Wolf, *The Rebels: A Brotherhood of Outlaw Bikers* (Toronto: University of Toronto Press, 1991), p. 268.

67 Ibid.

68 President's Commission on Organized Crime, *The Impact: Organized Crime Today* (Washington, DC: U.S. Government Printing Office, 1987), p. 45.

69 Ibid., p. 46.

70 Peter Reuter, "The Cartage Industry in New York," in Michael Tonry and Albert J. Reiss, Jr., eds. *Beyond the Law: Crime in Complex Organizations* (Chicago: University of Chicago Press, 1993), p. 154.

71 Ibid., p. 155.

72   Ibid., p. 179.

73   Ibid., p. 198.

74   William Kleinknecht, "Ethnic Mix is Crime Recipe," *New York Daily News*, (December 14, 1993), p. 3.

75   Paul K. Clare, *Racketeering in Northern Ireland: A New Version of the Patriot Game* (Chicago: University of Illinois Office of International Criminal Justice, 1989), pp. 1-53.

76   Cited in Jonathan Karl, "Mob-Rule, Russian Style," *New York Post*, (March 15, 1994), p. 12.

77   Cited in "Jet-Setting Russian Gangsters Pose Trans-Atlantic Challenge," *Organized Crime Digest*, v. 15 (February 23, 1994), pp. 1-4.

78   Ko-lin Chin, Jeffrey Fagan, and Robert Kelly, *Gangs and Social Order in Chinatown* (Washington, DC: National Institute of Justice, Unpublished final report, 1994).

79   Ibid., p. 4.

80   Ibid.

81   Ibid., p. 5.

82   U.S. Comptroller General, "Nontraditional Organized Crime," p. 36; see also Maria Puente, "Ransom Scheme Uncovered," *USA Today*, (April 7, 1994), p. 3.

83   Roy Godson and William J. Olson, *International Organized Crime: Emerging Threat to U.S. Security* (Washington, DC: National Strategy Information Center, 1993), p. iii.

84   T.J. English, *Born to Kill: America's Most Notorious Vietnamese Gang* (New York: William Morrow, 1995), pp. 234-235.

85   "Nontraditional Organized Crime," p. 46.

86   Cecil Kirby and Thomas C. Renner, *Mafia Assassin* (Toronto: Methuen, 1986).

87   *The Impact: Organized Crime Today*, pp. 68-69.

88   U.S. Department of Justice Federal Bureau of Investigation Criminal Investigative Division, *Oriental Organized Crime* (Washington, DC: Federal Bureau of Investigation, 1985), p. 29.

89   Ibid., p. 30.

90   David E. Kaplan and Alec Dubro, *Yakuza* (New York: Addison Wesley, 1986), p. 141.

91   David E. Kaplan and Alec Dubro, *Yakuza* (New York: Addison Wesley, 1986), pp. 179-181.

92   "Oriental Organized Crime," p. 35.

93   Louis Freeh, "Russian Organized Crime Group Spreads in U.S., Europe," *Organized Crime Digest*, v. 15 (June 8, 1994), pp. 3-4.

94   President's Commission on Organized Crime, *Organized Crime of Asian Origin*, Hearings Part III (Washington, DC: U.S. Government Printing Office, 1984), p. 401.

95   Ibid., p. 402.

Chapter 8

Investigative Tools

It's about time law enforcement got as organized as
organized crime.
Rudolph Guiliani (1984)

Investigators of Organized Crime

Federal investigations of organized crime are usually conducted
through the U.S. Department of Justice. The Department of Justice is located in Washington, D.C., but it is represented across the country by 94 U.S.
Attorneys located in every federal judicial district. Each U.S. Attorney is
assisted by a staff of assistants of up to 160 lawyers in the largest metropoli-
tan areas to about 10 in less populated areas. Unfortunately, few of these
offices have specialized units that deal specifically with organized crime.

There existed federal organized crime strike forces in 14 U.S. cities,
with suboffices in 12 other cities. But the total of 122 Strike Force attorneys
nationwide were reassigned and made assistant U.S. attorneys by Attorney
General Dick Thornburgh in 1990.[1] His rationale was to give the U.S. Attorney in each district greater control over organized crime prosecutions in his
or her jurisdiction, although the former Strike Force attorneys were still to
work organized crime cases. There was an outcry in Congress when the
Strike Forces were abolished, arguing their independence was needed given
the higher turnover of U.S. Attorneys as appointed officials.[2] Many experienced Strike Force prosecutors resigned after this reassignment, including
11 of the 15 prosecutors in the Brooklyn office. Now that virtually all of the
cases-in-progress from that period have been adjudicated, the next few
years will reveal whether the demise of the Strike Forces has any effect on
organized crime prosecutions in the United States.[3]

Federal agencies that participated with the strike forces included the
Bureau of Alcohol, Tobacco, and Firearms [ATF], Customs Service, Internal Revenue Service [IRS], and U.S. Secret Service [all of these agencies

167

are in the Department of Treasury], the Drug Enforcement Administration [DEA], Immigration and Naturalization Service, U.S. Marshals Service, and FBI [all in the Department of Justice], the Department of Labor, the U.S. Postal Service, and the Securities and Exchange Commission. The strike forces obtained about 83 percent of their cases from the investigations of only four agencies: the ATF, DEA, FBI, and IRS.[4]

Federal prosecutions of organized crime cases usually develop in the following manner: once one of these law enforcement agencies has a reasonable belief about the existence of organized illegal activity in its jurisdiction, a case initiation report is prepared by an assistant U.S. Attorney. This report is forwarded to the Department of Justice Criminal Division's Organized Crime and Racketeering Section [OCRS]. Once the investigation is completed, a prosecutive memorandum is written. The memorandum is reviewed by the U.S. Attorney and OCRS for approval. After approval is obtained, the attorney in charge of the case will present the evidence to a grand jury. If the citizens of the grand jury concur in a finding of probable cause of illegality, they will issue an indictment to formally accuse the suspect of a crime. The indictment will ultimately be followed by a plea of guilt or a trial to determine guilt or innocence.

The enforcement of state laws against organized crime is not standardized. Some states have established specialized enforcement units to investigate solely organized crime cases, while others have no distinct organized crime enforcement unit. In most states, local or state police obtain evidence of organized crime activity through surveillance or informants, and it is referred to the county prosecutor or state attorney general's office for a decision to prosecute or to conduct further investigation.

Investigative Techniques and Intelligence Gathering

Unlike traditional policework, where a crime is committed, someone calls the police, and the police begin a search for the offender, organized crime requires a more sophisticated approach. That is to say, conventional policing is primarily reactive: police generally *respond* to crimes *after* they have been committed. The investigation of organized crimes, however, must place more emphasis on proactive approaches. Because many organized crimes of infiltration or conspiracy are not reported by the victim, investigations must often be initiated based only on reasonable suspicion of criminality or on informants' tips. Most investigations of organized crime activity, therefore, require long, and often tedious, searches through financial records, interviews, and surveillance activities. Only in this way can sufficient evidence be gathered to establish probable cause for arrest and indictment.

Because of the unique nature of some types of organized crime, investigators must follow special rules. An example is obscenity cases. In Indiana, police seized thousands of books and films from Fort Wayne Books based on a finding of probable cause. The U.S. Supreme Court held that such a pretrial seizure violated the First Amendment because there had been no judicial determination that the materials seized were, in fact, obscene. Therefore, the materials *believed* to be obscene by police must be found to be obscene beyond a reasonable doubt at trial (or by plea) before police may seize the remaining stock.[5] The Court argued that prior cases "firmly hold that mere probable cause to believe a legal violation has transpired is not adequate to remove books or films from circulation."[6]

Determining probable cause can be difficult in organized crime cases due to the number of people involved in many operations, and the often diffused nature of the activity being investigated. Judges review a police officer's determination of probable cause by assessing whether there is a "fair probability that contraband or evidence of a crime will be found."[7] A review of that decision on appeal "is to uphold the warrant as long as there is a substantial basis for a fair probability that evidence will be found."[8] For example, a warrant issued to Pittsburgh Police to search a commercial building for illegal video poker machines was challenged in court. It was argued it did not contain probable cause and was overly broad, both violations of the Fourth Amendment of the U.S. Constitution. The U.S. Court of Appeals recognized that the supporting affidavit submitted by the police "must be read in its entirety and in a common sense and nontechnical manner."[9] Even though the warrant did not contain direct evidence of criminal wrongdoing, direct evidence is not required. "Instead, probable cause can be, and often is, inferred by 'considering the type of crime, the nature of the items sought, the suspect's opportunity for concealment and normal inferences about where a criminal might hide stolen property'."[10] Indirect evidence, such as prior arrests and convictions for similar crimes, "is not only permissible, but is often helpful."[11]

A search warrant must also be specific in its statement of probable cause, in order to protect a person's lawful privacy of personal property and effects. In searches for specific papers, for example, "it is certain that some innocuous documents will be at least cursorily perused in order to determine whether they are among those papers to be seized." But the Fourth Amendment does not prohibit a search "merely because it cannot be performed with surgical precision."[12] In one case, IRS agents searched a person's bank records for alleged failure to file currency transaction reports needed for large cash deposits (see "Bank Secrecy Act" in next chapter). All financial records were seized, and the defendant argued on appeal that the seizure exceeded the stated purpose of the search (i.e., evidence of five instances of criminal behavior involving financial transactions). The U.S. Court of Appeals held, however, seizure of "every piece of paper or documents relating to a business is proper when probable cause exists that the enterprise is permeated by fraud."[13] The court held in the IRS case that the language of the warrant must be "sufficiently specific," although the police are not required to list the items in "elaborate detail," and upheld the validity of the warrant.[14]

It can be seen from these examples that successful organized crime investigations require more training and perseverance than investigations of conventional street crimes. In some cases, evidence is sought not to build a case, but to gather *intelligence*. This information is organized and used in building subsequent cases later on.[15] For example, it does not make sense to arrest every drug sale in a city, if the suppliers and higher-level distributors remain untouched. Surveillance, interviews, informants, and searches can be used to establish the precise nature and scope of an enterprise, so it may be successfully defeated. The remainder of this chapter explains five major kinds of investigative tools that are used most often in organized crime cases.

Financial Analysis

An investigative technique commonly employed in organized crime investigations is financial analysis. The IRS uses certain methods of financial analysis in its tax investigations, especially where no records or books are kept. These methods are now used by investigators of other forms of organized crime and corruption.[16] There are essentially three types of methods for financial analysis: net worth method, expenditures method, and bank deposits method. All three are designed to determine the total wealth or expenditures made by someone to compare with his or her reported income. In the net worth method, any change in net worth is adjusted to allow for nontaxable receipts and for reported income, the balance being unreported income. The expenditures method measures funds by their flow during the year, rather than observing changes in net worth from the beginning to the end of the year. The bank deposits method involves an examination of receipts for bank deposits, cash purchases [money spent without going through banks], and money stored in other places [cash on hand].

For example, the University of Wisconsin notified the state Attorney General about an employee they suspected of embezzling funds from the University. The employee in question was in charge of collecting money from students for copying documents, amounting to over $100,000 per year. Investigators from the state Attorney General's corruption unit conducted a financial analysis of the employee's spending habits and found that she was spending far in excess of her earnings. When confronted with the facts, the employee confessed to a systematic embezzlement scheme conducted over a four-year period that netted $40,000 to $50,000. The corruption unit discovered that the University's poor accounting and auditing practices permitted this to occur.[17]

In a Buffalo case, tax records indicated a man earned $13,000 a year working for a dry cleaning company, but was believed to make more than $500,000 per year in narcotics trafficking. He bought a salon from a friend and used that as a front. He invented phony customers, made large cash purchases, and attempted to create a false paper trail that made the drug money appear legitimate.[18] Financial analysis that compared his legal income with his expenditures revealed a large gap of unaccounted for cash which he could not explain.

It should be kept in mind that many organized crime prosecutions have been made from IRS records of reported income in comparison to spending habits. Al Capone was caught in this manner. The IRS examined his bank accounts and spending habits in Miami and Chicago and found that he spent $7,000 for suits, $1,500 per week for hotel bills, $40,000 for his house on Palm Island, $39,000 worth of phone calls, and $20,000 worth of silverware, indicating an annual income of $165,000. He could not account for this income by any lawful means. Capone was ultimately tried and convicted for failing to pay taxes on $1 million of illegal income.[19] It can be seen, therefore, that financial records can be a fruitful technique for discovering organized criminal activity, such as the establishment of fictitious companies to launder funds, overpayment of employees or subcontractors to obtain kickbacks, and other fraudulent schemes.

Al Capone, attending a Chicago football game in 1931.

Electronic Surveillance

Title III of the Omnibus Crime Control Act authorized federal law enforcement officials to eavesdrop in the conversations of crime suspects provided they obtain a warrant.[20] The warrant must show that there is "probable cause" to link a specific person to a particular crime. Title III had two stated purposes: it was a weapon to fight organized crime, and it was designed to safeguard the privacy of oral communications. The actual offenses for which Title III permits the use of electronic surveillance arguably go beyond its stated purposes. It permits the use of wiretapping or electronic eavesdropping ("bugging") for most suspected federal offenses punishable by one year or more imprisonment.

The problem with Title III is that it never defines "organized crime." Case law provides little guidance as to when generic felonies become eligible for eavesdropping. In a Maryland case, for example, a conspiracy among three people to distribute cocaine was found *not* to constitute organized crime, and electronic interceptions of conversations were suppressed.[21] In an Ohio case, a conspiracy of three people to extort money from a bank occurred. The court concluded, "Extortion is a crime 'characteristic' of organized crime. That is all that is required." So eavesdropping was permitted.[22] But in a Massachusetts case, a scheme by two local government officials to extort a kickback from a contractor "did not create reasonable suspicion" of organized crime involvement, and a consensual interception was suppressed.[23] A common legal definition of organized crime, such as that described in this book, would go a long way in clarifying the precise acts for which electronic surveillance is appropriate in organized crime investigations.

A total of 32 states have adopted electronic surveillance laws similar to Title III for violations of state laws. States may not enact statutes more permissive than Title III, although they may restrict it more severely. Several states have done so. In Texas, for example, wiretapping is permitted only to investigate certain drug felonies (excluding marijuana possession). Illinois has a similar law.

Changes in technology since Title III created a need for changes in the scope of the law. If wire and oral communications are protected from warrantless interception, why are conversations over cellular or cordless telephones that are carried primarily over radio waves not protected? What expectation of privacy do you have in communicating by modem? Is your e-mail private?

Questions like these, together with some U.S. Supreme Court cases, required clarification of Title III. The result was the Electronic Communications Privacy Act (ECPA).[24] It created a third legal category called "electronic communications" to be added to "wire" and "oral" communications covered by Title III. ECPA protects electronic communications and also regulates pen registers and trap-and-trace devices not addressed by Title III. The Act also permits "roving wiretaps" that allow investigators to intercept transmissions from multiple phones or locations that sometimes are employed by criminal groups.

Prior to ECPA, surreptitious or intentional interceptions of mobile radio-telephone conversations, ham radio broadcasts, cordless telephone conversations, and pager messages were allowable.[25] Title III suggested that if a radio communication "is susceptible to being overheard by the general public, then the participants to the communication lack a reasonable expectation of privacy."[26] ECPA now protects most of these communications making nonconsensual interception by private persons a crime. Police can intercept them with an "ECPA order," which is a special warrant that can be obtained by a wider range of officials and can be used for a broader range of offenses than a Title III order.[27] Radio communications *not* protected by ECPA are those "transmitted by stations for the use of the general public," or those involving ships, aircraft, vehicles, citizen's band radio, and electronic bulletin boards.[28] Personal e-mail is protected, however, due to its private nature (as a form of mail) and the need for passwords to access it. Likewise, remote communications from terminals or modems to computers is protected for similar reasons.

Pagers have varying degrees of protection from interception under ECPA. Tone-only pagers can be intercepted without judicial approval of any kind. Those that display messages can be intercepted only with an ECPA order, because they are electronic communications with a greater "expectation of privacy" than tone-only pagers. Tone and voice pagers require a Title III warrant that protects these "conversations" from interception without probable cause.

Cellular phones are unique in that they operate in a group of "service areas" with low-power transmitters. When you call a cellular phone, a transmitter sends the signal through the air over a radio frequency to a cell location. It travels over telephone lines or microwave systems to a telephone switching station which transfers the call's frequency and switches it automatically as the person with the cellular phone moves from cell to cell. These calls can be intercepted with specially designed scanners. Under ECPA these calls are protected from warrantless interception, even though they are carried, in part, over radio waves. Nevertheless, cordless telephone conversations are not protected by Title III or ECPA. The cordless portion of these conversations "may be intercepted, and their contents used, without court authorization."[29]

ECPA expands Title III in others ways as well. Electronic communications that are scrambled or encrypted are protected from unauthorized interception because they are not "readily accessible."[30] Law enforcement agencies have developed decoding software they would like to see adopted by the telecommunications industry to intercept these conversations in criminal investigations, but a court order is required for eavesdropping.[31] In addition, "cloned" cellular phones have become a cottage industry for organized crime in recent years. A cloned phone has someone else's number programmed into it for billing purposes. This makes it extremely difficult for a tap or trace to be useful. Criminals use these phones for a few weeks, and then throw them away. The telecommunications industry is working to make it more difficult to clone or to use cloned cellular phones, but cases have already been discovered where drug dealers have used these clones because the calls cannot be traced to them.[32]

ECPA provides both civil and criminal penalties for *disclosure*, as well as for interception, of communications when a person has reason to know the information was obtained unlawfully.[33] Ten states have now incorporated ECPA standards into their state electronic surveillance statutes.[34]

Since the passage of Title III, the U.S. Supreme Court has made many rulings in cases involving electronic surveillance. The net result has been a continuing expansion of the scope of electronic eavesdropping. Some of these court decisions have made it possible to use wiretap or eavesdropping evidence in court even when:

1. the evidence involves people who are third parties not named in the warrant who are implicated in intercepted conversations,[35]

2. names of suspects are inadvertently omitted from wiretap warrants,[36]

3. those whose dwellings are entered for placement of a bug without explicit court authorization,[37] and

4. a warrant is not required to conduct pen register surveillance (i.e., recording the numbers dialed from a telephone) or electronic "beeper" surveillance (i.e., surveillance through a radio transmitter).[38]

Each of these interpretations of Title III involved separate U.S. Supreme Court cases, but the law regarding pen registers has since been changed. Trap-and-trace devices are the converse of pen registers: one records the telephone numbers of incoming calls, the other the telephone number of outgoing calls. ECPA changed the law regarding these devices in that they are now subject to court authorization called an "ECPA Order," although neither probable cause nor reasonable suspicion are required. Instead, the application must only certify "that the information likely to be obtained is relevant to an ongoing criminal investigation begin conducted by that agency."[39] These devices often have switches that allow conversations to be overheard (in addition to recording phone numbers) with the flip of a switch. This is a great temptation, when recording numbers requires no warrant, while intercepting conversations does. Under ECPA pen registers and trap-and-trace devices require court authorization when they are capable of converting to a monitoring device—even if the monitoring capability is disabled."[40]

ECPA adds a "good faith" defense for police officers who eavesdrop using a warrant later found to be invalid. This follows on the trend begun in the U.S. Supreme Court in 1984 in creating exceptions to the exclusionary rule.[41] Ironically, there is no such defense for private citizens. A civilian defendant's "mistaken good faith belief" that it was lawful to intercept a communication does *not* constitute a defense.[42] Private citizens who violate Title III or ECPA, or police who engage in warrantless eavesdropping, are subject to criminal penalties of up to five years imprisonment and civil penalties up to $10,000 per day.

Table 8.1 provides a summary of authorized electronic surveillance by state and federal law enforcement agencies since 1970. It can be seen that the number of taps installed has grown by more than 70 percent from 1970 to 1992. Telephone taps have remained the most popular, although interceptions of electronic communications have grown since the passage of the ECPA in 1987. Although cellular phones account for only 10 percent of all telephone numbers in use, approximately one-third of telephone taps are now for cellular phones.[43] Room bug installations are few, because of their limited range and the need for a covert entry to place the microphone. This is both difficult and dangerous for the police officer, although several of the important organized crime prosecutions of the last decade, including those of Paul Castellano and John Gotti, relied on room microphones.[44] In the case of Paul Castellano, a bug was placed in his kitchen, where he conducted business. In Gotti's case, they were placed in his social club, an apartment, and in hubcaps of cars on the street, so conversations could be intercepted while he took walks. In Buffalo, the luxury boat and car of Benjamin "Sonny" Nicoletti were bugged in a gambling investigation.[45]

Table 8.1
Court-Authorized Electronic Surveillance in the United States

Devices	1970	1980	1992
Number Installed	597	524	846
Telephone Wiretaps	90%	91%	75%
Room Microphones	4%	5%	4%
Electronic Communications	NA*	NA*	13%
Combination of Intercept Methods	4%	4%	7%
Number of Extensions/ Per Device	246 41%	201 38%	646 76%
Total Days in Use/ Days per Device	11,200 19 days	11,939 23 days	32,430 38 days

*Electronic communications not covered in Title III, only added after passage of Electronic Communications Privacy Act in 1987.

Compiled from: Administrative Office of the United States Courts, *Reports on Applications for Orders Authorizing or Approving the Intercept of Wire or Oral Communications.*

The proportion of intercept orders that entail extensions from the original 30-day approval period has nearly doubled, as has the total days per interception. Each extension must be approved by a judge, raising the question about the length of a "search" of one's words or electronic communications. An investigation of organized crime on the New York City waterfront involved eavesdropping at three locations. One office was bugged for seven months and the telephone inside tapped for four and one half months. A second office was bugged for three months and the phone there bugged for one month. A third telephone was tapped in another office for two months. The argument raised by the defendant at trial was that his privacy was violated due to the length and number of the intercepts, even though the wiretaps and room microphones were placed with court authorization. The court held that the complexity of the criminal activity under investigation, and the nature of the premises under surveillance, must be considered in making such a judgment. The intercepted conversations were admitted in court.[46]

Table 8.2 presents the suspected offenses for which court-authorized electronic surveillance was undertaken from 1970 to 1992. A significant shift in law enforcement priorities can be clearly seen. Gambling went from more than one-half of all intercepts in 1970 to only seven percent of all intercepts in 1992. Conversely, drug investigations involving electronic surveillance have more than tripled in 22 years. This is a reflection of shifting public perceptions of the seriousness of these offenses, as well as shifts in organized crime activity itself. Chapter 6 explained how the President's Crime Commission in 1967 found gambling to be the largest source of revenue for organized crime. It was replaced by illegal narcotics trafficking, as determined by the President's Commission on Organized Crime in 1987. Table 8.2 also shows how racketeering investigations involving electronic surveillance doubled from 1980 to 1992. A review of the list in Chapter 5 of significant organized crime convictions in the decade 1985-1994 reveals that many of these cases involved racketeering and narcotics charges.

Table 8.2
Suspected Crimes in Authorized Electronic Surveillance
(Percent of all authorized intercepts)

Major Offenses	1970	1980	1992
Gambling	55%	35%	7%
Drugs	21	50	69
Loansharking and Extortion	4	2	1
Racketeering	NA*	5	10
Homicide/Assault	3	2	4
All Others	17	6	9

*Racketeering not codified in law until 1970 as part of the Organized Crime Control Act.

Compiled from: Administrative Office of the United States Courts, *Reports on Applications for Orders Authorizing or Approving the Intercept of Wire or Oral Communications.*

Table 8.3
Results of Electronic Surveillance

Averages per Intercept	1970	1980	1992
Persons Intercepted	44	136	117
Intercepted Conversations	655	1,058	1,861
Percent Incriminating Conversations	45%	30%	19%
Cost per Tap	$5,524	$17,146	$46,492
Total Arrests/ Arrests Per Tap*	1,874 3.1	1,871 3.6	2,685 3.2
Total Convictions/ Convictions Per Tap*	NR**	259 0.5	607 .72

*It is difficult to determine with precision year-to-year changes in arrests and convictions resulting from electronic surveillance. This is because arrests and convictions can occur a year or two following the surveillance, as more evidence is gathered.

**Court-authorized electronic surveillance began in 1969, after the passage of Title III a year earlier. No convictions were reported for 1970.

Compiled from: Administrative Office of the United States Courts, *Reports on Applications for Orders Authorizing or Approving the Intercept of Wire or Oral Communications.*

Table 8.3 illustrates the results of electronic surveillance since 1970. It can be seen that more people are intercepted and many more conversations are overheard now than was the case 10 and 20 years ago. This may be due to increases in the size and complexity of organized crime activities. On the other hand, the percentage of these conversations that are incriminating has dropped markedly to 19 percent in 1992. This suggests that perhaps conspiracies are becoming "part-time" activity resulting in fewer crime-related conversations during a given period, or that the cases chosen for electronic surveillance are becoming less appropriate. Perhaps there also is a saturation point at which such surveillance ceases to be productive for investigative purposes. This is difficult to know without analysis of intercept characteristics in successful versus unsuccessful investigations. This has not yet been done.

Given broad court authority to employ electronic surveillance, a limiting factor to its more widespread use is its prohibitive cost. The average cost per tap is almost nine times higher than it was in 1970. Inflation has taken its toll over this period, but electronic surveillance is still one of the most expensive tools in the investigative repertoire. The cost is high largely due to the minimization requirement of Title III that mandates non-crime conversations be excluded from interception to the extent possible. This means a police officer must be present 24 hours a day to listen to the beginning of each conversation and to turn off the tape recorder if the conversation is not related to the eavesdropping warrant. Also, transcription of tapes, analysis of conversations and directions of the conspiracy, as well as follow-up physical surveillance, and other leads produced by the intercept, must be undertaken when conducting electronic surveillance. It is an intensive investigative tool that requires large amounts of dedicated time, given the 30-day approval period.

The cost and effectiveness of electronic surveillance remains a matter of debate. It has formed the basis for many significant organized crime convictions in recent years, but some have questioned its cost-benefit. A "substantial minority" of the National Wiretap Commission concluded that even though it "has resulted in the conviction of a very small number of upper echelon organized crime figures," in terms of cost, manpower, and convictions overall, it has been "generally unproductive."[47] Many significant convictions since that report may change this conclusion, although what is needed is an objective assessment of the cost-benefit of electronic surveillance versus other competing investigative tools. In an analysis of wiretap transcripts, and other material, Kip Schlegel found electronic surveillance to have problems because criminal conspiracies "often take an inordinate amount of time to complete." Also, their planning generally takes places across "a variety of locations," working against the utility of electronic eavesdropping. In addition, there are problems of interpretation (e.g., is a "hit" a robbery, a murder, a monetary loss?) and in validity (people often lie, brag, and mislead others in their conversations).[48]

The increasing utilization of electronic surveillance illustrates its growing acceptance as a law enforcement tool. Whether it works best in certain types of cases, locations, suspects, or in conjunction with other investigative tools, has not been objectively studied. When such an analysis is conducted, electronic surveillance may be more profitably carried out in terms of costs and convictions.

Informants

The use of informants in organized crime cases is common. It can be argued that use of confidential informants is the most cost-effective investigative tool in organized crime cases.

The typical informant is a criminal who chooses to cooperate with the police in exchange for a reduced charge, sentence, or immunity from prosecution. But this is not always the case. Some honest people simply wish to report wrongdoing.[49] Informants, whether they be criminal or not, wish anonymity. Courts have generally held that the government is entitled to keep secret an informant's identity who has provided information about a possible law violation.[50] This is called the "informer's privilege." The privilege is not absolute, however, and can be overcome if the defense can show it is relevant to the defendant's case.[51]

Information obtained from the informant is commonly used to investigate more serious criminality. For example, an arrested street drug dealer can be used to determine who the suppliers are in a given area. An illegal waste disposer can provide information about the organizers of the illicit enterprise. Such informants are extremely cost-effective because there is usually little expense involved, unless the informant is paid for the information or is placed in the witness protection program (discussed in Chapter 9). In addition, informers can provide information that would require months of undercover investigation to obtain.

In recent years there has been a well-documented stream of organized crime figures who have become informants. Such high-level criminals as Nicky Barnes, Jimmy Fratianno, Sammy Gravano, Mickey Featherstone, Anthony Casso, Anthony Accetturo, and Michael Franzese all became informants for the government and testified against their former cohorts in crime.[52] This has occurred for three reasons:

1. Extended sentences available under the racketeering and drug laws force criminals to consider prison as the "end of the line," rather than as merely a cost of doing business,

2. The Witness Protection Program (discussed in the next chapter) allows a potential informant a way to avoid the wrath of his co-conspirators if he testifies against them, and

3. A diminished sense of "honor among thieves" and loyalty to an organization or heritage than was the case in the past. Many criminals are simply in it for the money, and when caught, they look for the easiest way out, regardless of who might be "sacrificed" to accomplish it.

Different observers placed varying levels of weight on these three reasons, but certainly some combination of them has changed the stakes in creating criminal informants.[53]

The low cost of informants is offset to some degree by problems of reliability and credibility. As noted in Chapter 5, several of the mob trials of the 1980s resulted in acquittals due to juries not believing the testimony of government informants. As a journalist reported after one of these acquittals, "The last piece of evidence requested by the jury for re-examination was a chart introduced by the defense that showed the criminal backgrounds of seven prosecution witnesses. It listed 69 crimes, including murder, drug possession and sales, and kidnapping."[54] The concern here, of course, as Alan Dershowitz has pointed out, "A bought witness may tell the truth—but only if it suits his interest to do so."[55]

AP/WIDE WORLD PHOTOS

Salvatore "Sammy the Bull" Gravano, former underboss in the Gambino crime family, is sworn in at a hearing of the Senate Permanent Investigations subcommittee on Capitol Hill, April 1, 1993. The subcommittee was holding hearings on corruption in professional boxing.

This issue of the reliability of informants (in the mob trials many were forced to admit they had lied in the past) and credibility (will juries believe the testimony of admitted criminals?) are problems particularly when the witnesses have been, or are being, paid by the government. This situation appears, at least in some cases, to work against the credibility of the informant's testimony from the jury's perspective. For example, Sammy Gravano's testimony against former "boss" John Gotti was apparently believed by the jury, but his testimony against Pasquale Conte and other alleged crime figures in another trial, was not. Two hours after it began deliberations, the jury sent out a note that said, "We believe that Sammy Gravano's testimony is essential to the government's case. We have already debated his credibility, and have reached an impasse."[56]

One factor that works against the development of noncriminal informants is the fear that their identities will eventually become known. The occasional body of a cooperating witness found slain "gangland style" may have some deterrent effect, although such incidents are rare when they involve people outside the criminal organization itself.[57] The FBI thought the Freedom of Information Act would reduce the willingness of people to provide information or to become informants, due to a fear that their identity could ultimately become known. A review of the files of 7,000 FBI agents over 19 months documented only 19 instances of people refusing to provide information out of fear of discovery.[58] Noncriminals become informants, therefore, for other reasons. These reasons should be examined, so that noncriminals from business, government, and neighborhoods can be used more often to develop cases.

The generally low cost of informants, together with their ability to provide information more rapidly and with less risk than electronic surveillance or undercover investigations, insures that they will remain an important investigative source in organized crime cases. The merits and problems of witness immunity and the witness protection program, as they relate to government informants, are assessed in the next chapter.

Undercover Investigations

Undercover investigations are not used as much as commonly believed in organized crime cases due to the length of time required to gain acceptance and access to information about criminal organizations, and also the constant danger to the undercover officer if his or her identity was discovered. In recent years, there have been several extremely significant undercover agents whose work resulted in numerous convictions. The most well-known agent is Joe Pistone, who worked undercover as "Donnie Brasco" inside the Bonanno crime group in New York for six years. His work resulted in more than 100 convictions of organized crime figures.[59] Other undercover agents have also produced significant cases over the years.[60]

Sting operations involve more officers, but they are also long term, and expensive investigations. A scam involving the exchange of drugs for green cards for immigrants was ended after a two-year sting operation in New York State. Fifty-seven drug suspects and 39 illegal immigrants were arrested.[61] The FBI charged 76 people for dealing in stolen furs, cars, and other property valued at $17 million from a boutique they had set up in New Jersey.[62] Other stings elsewhere in New Jersey and Florida enjoyed similar success, although they usually involved at least a two-year investigation.[63]

A study has found that the agents selected for undercover assignments tend to be the "newly recruited and inexperienced members," and that supervision of these agents in the field "may be lax." Interviews with undercover agents have discovered that these agents are exposed to great danger without adequate briefing or preparation.[64] The effectiveness and consequences of undercover operatives have also not been evaluated.

> There is little information about how effective undercover investigations are, what they cost (economically, psychologically, or constitutionally), or why they fail. Similarly, the extent to which police departments use the strategy is unknown.[65]

The adjustment problems of undercover officers after completing their assignment has also not received enough attention from either police agencies or the public.[66] The FBI claims that its undercover agents were responsible for 680 convictions, $5.7 million in forfeitures, and $741.1 million in potential economic losses prevented in a single year. Although these figures were modified somewhat by a General Accounting Office audit, the benefits of undercover work have not yet been objectively evaluated against their costs in terms of time invested, risk, manpower, and their impact on the officer, the police agency, and on affected third parties.[67]

In the case of Joseph Pistone, he and his family had to move four times while he was testifying, he did not see his family for three months while undercover, and he resigned from the FBI without serving long enough to earn a pension due to threats against him.[68] He believes there is a $500,000 contract on his life, so his life undercover appears to have changed, rather than ended, as Pistone now hides from those he once investigated.

Citizens' Commissions

An often-overlooked investigatory resource for organized crime is citizens' commissions. These investigative commissions have been established from time to time throughout the history of the United States to examine the problems of crime in a specific locality. The Chicago Crime Commission and Pennsylvania Crime Commission are among the oldest and most productive of the citizens' crime commissions.[69] Over the years, these commissions have played a useful role in the investigation of organized crime.

> The New Mexico Special Prosecutions Division reported that when it first initiated operations, information and intelligence it received from the Governor's Organized Crime Commission was useful in choosing areas for further investigation and developing cases for prosecution.[70]

There are essentially three types of crime commissions:

1. Government funded, bi-partisan groups where investigators have police status but no arrest authority (e.g., Pennsylvania Crime Commission),

2. Funded by the private sector and has no law enforcement authority (e.g., Chicago Crime Commission),

3. Government-sponsored, temporary group to investigate a specific incident or phenomenon (e.g., Knapp Commission, President's Commission on Organized Crime).[71]

These commissions are useful in developing information and also in focusing public concern about organized crime. Due to the consensual nature of the vices, and the fact that many organized crime groups appear to kill within their group, the public is not as aroused on this issue as it should be. Commission hearings, reports, and publicity about specific incidents and trends in the community is a way to galvanize community feeling and reduce tolerance for organized crime activities in a locality.

The legal authority of citizens' commissions varies from state to state. In New Jersey, for example, the State Commission of Investigation may engage in electronic surveillance upon approval of the State Attorney General. Also, it has been found that witnesses feel freer to talk to these commissions because their main task is to gather information, rather than build specific cases.[72] As the National Association of Attorneys General has concluded:

> While it is true that most law enforcement agencies that do not
> have the benefit of a statewide grand jury or of electronic sur-
> veillance very much desire these tools, it also appears that anti-
> corruption efforts have been waged by states without them,
> using more traditional, less "easy" investigative tools.[73]

It is apparent, then, that the investigation of organized crime is not limited solely to the actions of law enforcement agencies, and that commissions that rely heavily on private citizens can be a useful adjunct to traditional law enforcement tools.

Commissions usually are not interested or empowered to make criminal cases. This enables them to take the "long view" and assess longer impacts of current trends. This distinguishes their role from traditional law enforcement. Of course, Commissions formed by the government can also be dissolved by the government. The Pennsylvania Crime Commission was allowed to expire in 1994, two months after it issued a report linking the State Attorney General to illegal video poker vendors.[74] The State Police are to assume the duties of the commission, although no funding was provided to carry them out. It appears as if the reason for the formation of a crime commission, i.e., a neutral, objective examination of a serious problem, has been forgotten in the case of Pennsylvania, in favor of political expediency.

Summary

The investigation of organized crimes involves strategies and techniques quite different from conventional crimes. Whereas traditional crimes of assault and theft involve force or stealth, organized crimes involve infiltration and conspiracy, which require the investigator to be as sophisticated as the offender. The techniques described in this chapter characterize the difference between organized crime investigations and those for other crimes. They involve more planning, organization, and are more time-intensive than traditional law enforcement tools. Each technique has been shown to have strengths and weaknesses, and they continue to be used in a variety of circumstances.

Critical Thinking Exercise

Using the information provided in this chapter, respond to the scenario below. Employ current legal principles to justify your response.

The Case of Standing Next to a Pay Phone

You are a police officer standing next to a prisoner at the lock-up. He is from Thailand and speaks little English. He communicates that he would like to make a telephone call. You agree, and stand next to him, pursuant to department policy.

You believe the prisoner may be implicating himself in further illegal activity on the telephone, so you turn on your pocket tape recorder and record his end of the telephone conversation without his knowledge. Although he spoke in Thai, you later bring the tape to a local college professor who speaks Thai. He transcribes the tape.

Your hunch was correct! The prisoner implicated himself in a crime while talking on the telephone.

Questions:

1. Is your tape recording admissible as evidence in court against the prisoner?

2. How would the case be different if the prisoner spoke on the telephone in English?

3. How would the case be different if you overheard the conversation without using a tape recorder?

References to Chapter 8

[1]   Michael P. Mayko, "Strike Force Retired," *Bridgeport Post-Telegram*, (December 31, 1989), p. C1.

[2]   Patrick J. Ryan, "A History of Organized Crime Control: Federal Strike Forces," in R.J. Kelly, K. Chin, and R. Schatzberg, eds. *Handbook of Organized Crime in the United States* (Westport, CT: Greenwood Press, 1994), pp. 333-358.

[3]   James B. Jacobs, *Busting the Mob: United States v. Cosa Nostra* (New York: New York University Press, 1994), p. 15.

[4]   U.S. Comptroller General, *Stronger Federal Effort Needed in Fight Against Organized Crime* (Washington, DC: U.S. General Accounting Office, 1981), p. 3.

[5] *Fort Wayne Books v. Indiana*, 109 S. Ct. 916 (1989).

[6] at 929; *New York v. PJ Video*, 106 S. Ct. 1610 (1986).

[7] *Jones v. United States*, 80 S. Ct. 725 (1960).

[8] *United States v. Conley*, 4 F.3d 1200 (3d. Cir. 1993) at 1205.

[9] at 1206.

[10] *United States v. Jackson*, 756 F.2d 504 (9th Cir. 1985).

[11] *United States v. Conley* at 1207.

[12] *United States v. Christine*, 687 F.2d 749 (3d Cir. 1982).

[13] *United States v. Offices Known as 50 States Distributing*, 708 F.2d 1374 (9th Cir. 1983).

[14] *United States v. Schmidt*, 947 F.2d 362 (9th Cir. 1991) at 373.

[15] Marilyn B. Peterson, "Intelligence and Analysis Within the Organized Crime Function," in R.J. Kelly, K. Chin, and R. Schatzberg, eds. *Handbook of Organized Crime in the United States* (Westport, CT: Greenwood Press, 1994), pp. 359-387.

[16] G. Robert Blakey, Ronald Goldstock, and Charles H. Rogovin, *Rackets Bureaus: Investigation and Prosecution of Organized Crime* (Washington, DC: U.S. Government Printing Office, 1978); Committee on the Office of the Attorney General, *Attorney Generals' Corruption Control Units* (Raleigh,NC: National Association of Attorneys General, 1978).

[17] *Attorney Generals' Corruption Control Units*, p. 10.

[18] Susan Schulman, "In Spending Drug Money, Dealers Risk Leaving Paper Trail for Police," *The Buffalo News*, (February 11, 1990), p. C1.

[19] See Laurence Bergreen, *Capone: The Man and the Era* (New York: Simon and Schuster, 1994); James D. Calder, "Al Capone and the Internal Revenue Service: State-Sanctioned Criminology of Organized Crime," *Crime, Law and Social Change*, v. 17 (1992), pp. 1-23.

[20] P.L. 90-351 Sec. 801(c) 82 Stat. 211-2 (1968).

[21] *Shingleton v. State*, 387 A.2d 1134 (1978).

[22] *Nabozny v. Marshall*, 781 F.2d 83 (1986) *cert. denied* 106 S. Ct. 2284.

[23] *Commonwealth v. Jorabek*, 424 N.E.2d 491 (1981).

[24] P.L. 99-508 Sec. 111(a) effective 1987.

[25] *United States v. Hoffa*, 436 F.2d 1246 (1970) cert. denied 91 S. Ct. 455; *United States v. Rose*, 669 F.2d 23 (1982) *cert. denied* 103 S. Ct. 63; *State v. Howard*, 679 P.2d 197 (1984); *Dorsey v. State*, 402 So.2d 1178 (1981).

[26] Clifford S. Fishman, *Wiretapping and Eavesdropping* (Cumulative Supplement) New York: Clark, Boardman, Callaghan (1994), p. 76.

[27] Ibid., p. 80.

[28] 18 U.S.C. Sec. 2511 (g)(ii).

[29] Ibid., p. 86.

[30] Sec. 2510(16)(A).

[31] Edmund L. Andrews, "U.S. Seeks Wiretap Software for Law Enforcement," *The New York Times*, (February 12, 1994), p. 1.

32   Richard Perez-Pena, "12 Charged in High-Tech Drug Deals," *The New York Times*, (November 23, 1993), p. B1.

33   Sec 2511(1)(c).

34   These states include: CO, FL, KS, MN, NY, NJ, OR, PA, WI, and UT. Clifford S. Fishman, *Wiretapping and Eavesdropping*, Cumulative Supplement (New York: Clark, Boardman, Callaghan, 1994), p. 33.

35   *United States v. Kahn*, 415 U.S. 143 (1974).

36   *United States v. Donovan*, 97 S. Ct. 658 (1977).

37   *Dalia v. United States*, 99 S. Ct. 1682 (1979).

38   *Smith v. Maryland*, 99 S. Ct. 2577 (1979) and *United States v. Knotts*, 103 S. Ct. 1081 (1983), *United States v. Karo*, 104 S. Ct. 3296 (1984).

39   Sec 3122(b)(2).

40   *People v. Bialostok*, 80 N.Y.2d 738 (1993).

41   *United States v. Leon*, 104 S. Ct. 3405 (1984).

42   *Williams v. Poulos*, 11 F.3d 271 (1st Cir. 1993).

43   "Lack of Privacy Can be Hindrance to Callers, Help to law Enforcement Officials," *The Buffalo News*, (June 26, 1994), p. 3.

44   Joseph F. O'Brien and Andris Kurins, *Boss of Bosses: The FBI and Paul castellano* (New York: Simon and Schuster, 1991; Howard Blum, *Gangland* (New York: Simon and Schuster, 1993; *The Gotti Tapes* (New York: Random House, 1992).

45   Dan Herbeck, "Wired for Sound," *Buffalo Magazine*, (September 29, 1991), p. 9.

46   *United States v. Clemente*, 482 F. Supp 102 (S.D.N.Y. 1979).

47   National Wiretap Commission, *Electronic Surveillance Report* (Washington, DC: U.S. Government Printing Office, 1976), p. 3.

48   Kip Schlegel, "Life Imitating Art: Interpreting Information from Electronic Surveillance," in M.J. Palmiotto, ed. *Critical Issues in Criminal Investigation* Second Edition (Cincinnati: Anderson Publishing Co., 1988), pp. 101-111.

49   Joseph Salerno and Stephen J. Rivele, *The Plumber* (New York: Knightsbridge, 1991).

50   *Lawmaster v. United States*, 114 S. Ct. 196 (1993).

51   *United States v. Foster*, 986 F.2d 541 (D.C. Cir. 1993).

52   Tim Shawcross, *The War Against the Mafia* (New York: Harper, 1995); Michael Franzese, *Quitting the Mob* (New York: Harper, 1993); John Pryor, "Heroin King-Turned-Informer Hopes He Can Strike deal," *The Buffalo News*, (March 20, 1983), p. 13; John P. Fried, "Ex-Mob Underboss Gets Lenient Term for Help as Witness," *The New York Times*, (September 27, 1994), p. 1; Jerry Capeci, "Lucchese Crime Boss Sings," *The Daily News*, (March 3, 1994), p. 8; Ovid Demaris, *The Last Mafioso* (New York: Bantam, 1982); T.J. English, *The Westies: The Irish Mob* (New York: St. Martin's, 1991); Selwyn Raab, "Mafia Defector Says He Lost His Faith," *The New York Times*, (March 2, 1994), p. B1.

53   James B. Jacobs, *Busting the Mob: United States v. Cosa Nostra* (New York: New York University Press, 1994), p. 12; Larry McShane, "Many in Mob Singing Like Canaries Lately," *The Buffalo News*, (April 6, 1994), p. 3.

[54] Leonard Buder, "Gotti is Acquitted in Conspiracy Case Involving the Mob," *The New York Times*, (March 14, 1987), p. 1.

[55] Alan M. Dershowitz, "Gotti Case Shows Flaws of Buying Witnesses," *The Buffalo News*, (March 20, 1987), p. C3.

[56] Pete Bowles, "Brooklyn Jurors Gore Sammy the Bull," *New York Newsday* (January 6, 1993), p. 32.

[57] Sarah Lyall, "Trash Hauler and Relative Killed on Long Island: Both Aided Investigators in Checking Mob Activities," *The New York Times*, (August 11, 1989), p. B1.

[58] Carl Stern, "FBI Informants," *The New York Times*, (February 10, 1982), p. 31.

[59] Joseph D. Pistone, *Donnie Brasco: My Undercover Life in the Mafia* (New York: Signet, 1989).

[60] Larry Wansley with Carlton Stowers, *FBI Undercover* (New York: Pocket, 1989); David McClintick, *Swordfish: A True Story of Ambition, Savagery and Betrayal* (New York: Pantheon, 1993).

[61] Seth Faison, "57 Dealers are Seized After Sting Across U.S.," *The New York Times* (December 1, 1993), p. B6.

[62] "Union City," *USA Today*, (September 27, 1990), p. 8.

[63] Jeanne DeQuine, "High-Tech Sting Zaps 93," *USA Today*, (December 7, 1988), p. 3; "Car Ring Sting," *USA Today*, (July 13, 1989), p. 3.

[64] George I. Miller, "Observations on Police Undercover Work," *Criminology*, v. 25 (1987), pp. 27-46; Michael F. Brown, "Criminal Informants," *Journal of Police Science and Administration*, v. 13 (1985), pp. 251-256.

[65] "Observations on Police Undercover Work," p. 44.

[66] Gary T. Marx, "Who Really Gets Stung?: Some Issues Raised by the New Police Undercover Work," *Crime & Delinquency*, v. 28 (April, 1982), pp. 165-193.

[67] U.S. Comptroller General, *Accomplishments of FBI Undercover Operations* (Washington, DC: U.S. General Accounting Office, 1984).

[68] Sam Meddis, "Hunted by the Mob, He's Still Plugging Book," *USA Today*, (January 17, 1989), p. 3.

[69] Virgil W. Peterson, "Citizens Crime Commissions," *Federal Probation Quarterly*, v. 17 (March, 1953), pp. 9-15; John Landesco, *Organized Crime in Chicago* Part III of the Illinois Crime Survey (Chicago: University of Chicago Press, 1929); Pennsylvania Crime Commission, *1990 Report* (Conshohocken, PA: Pennsylvania Crime Commission, 1991).

[70] *Attorney Generals' Corruption Control Units*, p. 59.

[71] Charles H. Rogovin and Frederick T. Martens, "The Role of Crime Commissions in Organized Crime Control," in R.J. Kelly, K. Chin, and R. Schatzberg, eds. *Handbook of Organized Crime in the United States* (Westport, CT: Greenwood Press, 1994), pp. 389-400.

[72] Knapp Commission, *Report on Police Corruption* (New York: George Braziller, 1973), p. 42.

[73] *Attorney Generals' Corruption Control Units*, p. 60.

[74] Jacob Clark, "Pennsylvania Loses its OC Watchdog: Crime Commission is Scuttled," *Law Enforcement News*, (June 30, 1994), p. 1.

Chapter 9

Prosecution Strategies

Nobody ever commits a crime without doing something stupid.

Oscar Wilde (1891)

Tools for the Prosecution

The last three decades have witnessed a dramatic increase in the scope, power, and use of investigative tools to aid in the prosecution of organized crime. In fact, a primary reason behind the Valachi hearings during the 1960s was to convince Congress of the need for legislation to make it easier to investigate and prosecute organized criminals. The reason why the Department of Justice had Valachi testify publicly in 1963 was made clear by Attorney General Robert Kennedy at the beginning of the hearings.

> One major purpose in my appearing here is to seek the help of Congress in the form of additional legislation—the authority to provide immunity to witnesses in racketeering investigations; and reform and revision of the wiretapping law.[1]

Kennedy also pointed to the need for public support. "We have yet to exploit properly our most powerful asset in the battle against the rackets: an aroused, informed, and insistent public.[2] These new laws were passed in 1968 and 1970, and it is not clear whether the public is yet sufficiently aroused about organized crime (see Chapter 12).

The first law to be enacted in response to Valachi's testimony (and its repetition in the 1967 President's Crime Commission Report) was Title III of the Omnibus Crime Control and Safe Streets Act of 1968. Title III provided law enforcement agencies with the power to wiretap in a wide variety of suspected criminal activities, including organized crime. The provisions of Title III are detailed in Chapter 8.

189

Two years later, the Organized Crime Control Act of 1970 was passed, establishing the power of "use" immunity from prosecution to compel witnesses to testify, special investigative grand juries, the witness protection program, and special sentencing provisions for organized criminals. Both these laws had vehement defenders and critics: the defenders pointing to the need for effective organized crime prosecutions, and the critics arguing the laws go too far and jeopardize innocent citizens.

According to the language of the Organized Crime Control Act,

> It is the purpose of this Act to seek the eradication of organized crime in the United States by strengthening the legal tools in the evidence-gathering process, by establishing new penal prohibitions, and by providing enhanced sanctions and new remedies to deal with the unlawful activities of those engaged in organized crime.[3]

The strengths and weaknesses of the provisions of this organized crime prosecution tool will be examined in this chapter.

The precise method by which cases are prosecuted is generating increasing attention, as governments seek to obtain maximum output from their agencies. The traditional model dictates that police investigate, and when they are finished, the case is turned over to the prosecutor's office for adjudication. This system has never worked very well, and is exacerbated by the separate government hierarchies to which police and prosecutors belong. The traditional model breeds distrust, suspicion, and poor work habits. Police feel they work hard and making "good" cases when they can. They become angry and frustrated when a number of their "good" cases are declined for prosecution or, if adjudicated, the police officers are treated poorly by the prosecution in court.

On the other hand, prosecutors often complain about the *lack* of "good" cases and what they consider to be shoddy police work. The result is each side blaming the other for the same problem. The failure to *communicate* at the *beginning* of an investigation, and also while the investigation is *in progress*, is at the root of most of this mutual interagency distrust. The historical problem of parallel government bureaucracies for police and prosecutors does not help the situation, but it does not prevent a solution. The establishment of police-prosecutor "teams" has been attempted in a number of jurisdictions and works extremely well. The reasons are obvious: investigative and prosecution priorities are agreed upon *before* the investigation begins, and police and prosecutors consult regularly with each other *during* the investigation about the types of evidence needed, use of informants, warrants and other investigative issues. By the time a case is close to the arrest stage, the prosecutor and police officer have been communicating daily for weeks or months, eliminating "surprises" in the courtroom later on. Examples of such police-prosecutor teams include the

Oriental Gang Unit in the New York City Police Department and the Mult-nomah County Organized Crime/Narcotics Task Force in Oregon.[4] The keys to the success of these programs include the fact that the police and prosecutor work in "physical proximity" and have "daily access" to each other. Investigators always work with the same prosecutors, and "vertical prosecution is the general rule."[5] Developing a sense of ownership over a case from the start also breeds a greater sense of responsibility for the out-come from all the parties involved. Indeed, there is much that can be done in realigning the historical working relationships between law enforcement and prosecution.[6]

Five important prosecution vehicles created since 1970 will be assessed below: the provision for use immunity of witnesses, the witness protection program, special grand juries, and the provision for extended penalties for crimes committed by continuing criminal enterprises. In addi-tion, the use of the Bank Secrecy Act in organized crime prosecutions will be examined.

Witness Immunity

The ability to provide witnesses with immunity was granted to federal law enforcement agencies in Title II of the Organized Crime Control Act of 1970. Witnesses to organized crime are often reluctant to testify about their knowledge either due to a reluctance or fear to become involved, or else due to an unwillingness to incriminate themselves. The Organized Crime Control Act of 1970 permits federal prosecutors to grant witnesses immunity from prosecution in exchange for testimony. The purpose, of course, is to make it easier to prosecute higher-echelon criminals through the testimony of less important figures.

The Act provides for *use immunity* which prohibits the use of evidence obtained through compelled testimony or any information directly or indi-rectly derived from such testimony. The only exception to this prohibition is prosecution for perjury or false statements given while under immunity.

Despite these safeguards, use immunity does not protect a witness from being prosecuted based on evidence obtained independently of the com-pelled testimony. Prior to 1970, only *transactional immunity* was permitted at the federal level. Transactional immunity prohibited *any* prosecution of a witness, whether or not the evidence was derived from the immunized testi-mony. As a result, use immunity is a more powerful prosecution tool than transactional immunity.

The allowance for independent evidence to be admitted in court through use immunity has caused concern among some observers that such an application of immunized testimony may violate the Fifth Amendment of the U.S. Constitution that states, in part, ". . . nor shall [a person] be compelled in any criminal cases to be a witness against himself." This is especially important in cases where testimony made under a federal grant of immunity exposes a person to prosecution under state laws. The U.S. Supreme Court dealt with this issue in *Malloy v. Hogan,* which held that the Fifth Amendment protection against self-incrimination is applicable to the states as a matter of due process for all citizens, guaranteed by the Fourteenth Amendment.[7] As a result, testimony given under a grant of immunity may not be used for criminal prosecution in another jurisdiction.

Nevertheless, use immunity has been criticized on other grounds as well. The extraction of forced testimony through the use of immunity has been questioned in the dissenting opinions of such U.S. Supreme Court cases as *Kastigar v. United States* and *Lefkowitz v. Cunningham.*[8] These criticisms include the fear that immunity may be provided by prosecutors as a mere "fishing expedition" to obtain information without any specific idea of the individuals or crimes suspected. Also, the use of independently derived evidence can be used against an immunized witness, and the burden to prove this independence from the compelled testimony is on the prosecutor. The problem remains that an overzealous prosecutor might use immunized testimony improperly in a subsequent case without any systematic oversight of his actions. As Block and Chambliss have pointed out, "one can easily imagine how difficult a time a defendant would have proving evidence was tainted."[9] Third, immunity provides no protection from civil suits for witnesses who incriminate themselves. Therefore, a person may be held liable for damages and compensation from an injured party, even though no criminal prosecution can result. Finally, the use of any testimony that is the result of "inducements" is suspect. Because immunized testimony is coerced, inasmuch as a defendant cannot refuse to testify after a grant of immunity without being held in contempt of court and imprisoned, such testimony is tainted, which makes it less convincing to judges or juries in criminal prosecutions. It can also lead to erroneous convictions of wrongfully accused defendants when false testimony made by an immunized witness is taken as fact by prosecutors, judges, or juries.

On the other hand, witness immunity has many defenders in the criminal justice system. It has been argued that for the conspiratorial crimes characteristic of organized crime, there are often few alternatives to obtaining evidence of a conspiracy from reluctant witnesses. As Robert Rhodes has observed, many prosecutors believe that immunity is a vital prosecution tool.

> Plea bargaining is not always an alternative; conspirators may simply refuse to talk when offered a reduction of their charges. That is almost always the case in organized-crime cases. Immunity forces testimony without forcing incriminating statements.[10]

It can also be argued that various procedural safeguards exist to insure that immunized testimony is not self-serving to the witness or that it is not false. First, the rules of criminal procedure, which include such provisions as cross-examination of witnesses at trial and the corroboration of certain types of evidence, serve as a check on the accuracy of immunized testimony. Second, the Organized Crime Control Act requires that the need for immunity be demonstrated to the U.S. Attorney General prior to it being granted, indicating that the testimony is "necessary to the public interest" and that the information cannot be obtained voluntarily from the individual. Third, the law permits perjury prosecutions in cases where the immunized witness is found to have lied.

It can be seen, therefore, that there are arguments both for and against the provision of use immunity. Unfortunately, no objective empirical evidence has been gathered to provide an indication of the relative costs (in terms of unprosecuted crimes and abuses of immunity) versus the benefits (convictions of upper-echelon organized crime figures). When such information is assembled, a more reliable judgment can be made of how witness immunity can be best used to balance the interests of the public and the interests of the witness.

Witness Protection Program

A second significant tool included in the Organized Crime Control Act was Title V, which authorized the U.S. Attorney General to provide security to government witnesses in organized crime cases. This authorization led to the establishment of the witness protection program.

A prosecuting attorney, who believes that a witness' life will be in danger due to testimony in an organized crime proceeding, can request admission of the witness to the witness protection program (WPP). This request is made to the Office of Enforcement Operations in the U.S. Justice Department, which determines whether the witness will be protected based on the recommendations of the FBI, the appropriate division of the Justice Department, and the U.S. Marshals Service. Once a witness is admitted to the program, a new identity is provided complete with new birth certificate and social security number. The witness is relocated to an area far from the target of his testimony, and he or she is provided a subsistence allowance and other help until the relocated witness can be self-supporting. These services and supervision are provided by the U.S. Marshals Service.

When the program first began, it was estimated that 25 to 50 witnesses would be relocated each year at a cost of less than $1 million. Since the program began in 1970, however, more than 4,400 witnesses and 8,000 family members have entered the program. The annual cost exceeds $25 million.[11] Clearly, the program has been utilized frequently in organized crime prosecutions.

The U.S. General Accounting Office [GAO] conducted an evaluation of the performance of the witness protection program, comparing its costs (as measured by relocations and crimes committed by witnesses while in the program) to its benefits (successful prosecutions of high-level organized criminals). The benefits of the program were evaluated by reviewing 220 cases that involved the testimony of protected witnesses. This sample of 220 included all the available cases involving witnesses admitted into the program during a single year. It was found that 75 percent of the defendants (965 of 1,283) that were subjects of the testimony of protect witnesses were found guilty, and 84 percent of these were sentenced to prison for a median term of 4.4 years. Of those defendants identified as "ringleaders," (N=150), 88 percent were convicted with a median sentence of 11.2 years. It was also discovered that nearly one-half of these cases involved narcotics (32%) or murder or murder conspiracy (13%) charges. The targets of these prosecutions were most often "various" organized criminal groups (43%), traditional organized crime groups (27%), or single criminal acts by an individual or group (15%). The remaining cases (15%) involved crimes by public officials, motorcycle gangs, union officials, prison gangs, or white collar professionals.

The relative importance of these prosecutions can be best judged when they are compared to federal prosecutions of organized crime cases that *do not* involve protected witnesses. The GAO found twice as many defendants are sentenced to two years or more in prison in cases involving protected witnesses than in other organized crime prosecutions.[12] In Canada, police continue to lobby for a witness protection program like that in the United States. They have a more modest, and less uniform program, there, and police officials believe it is a factor in preventing insiders from coming forward.[13]

The costs of the witness protection program involve both the cost of relocation and assistance provided to these witnesses, and also the possibility that protected witnesses may commit new crimes after being relocated. The GAO evaluation found that the typical protected witness entering the program had been arrested more than seven times. More than one-half of these arrests were for violent crimes. After admission to the program, the typical protected witness was arrested twice, and less than one-third of these arrests were for violent crimes. It appears, therefore, that protected witnesses engage in fewer crimes and fewer serious crimes after entering the program. As the GAO observed, however, these before-after comparisons are not necessarily genuine.

> The observation that protected witnesses were arrested more often and charged with more serious crimes before they entered the program when compared with postprogram arrests data may be almost entirely caused by differences in the pre- and post-program observation periods. For example, many witnesses had criminal histories of 10 years or more before they entered the program, while the average postprogram observation period for the witnesses sampled was only about 3.5 years.[14]

As a result, the before-after differences may simply be due to the fact that the follow-up of witnesses in the program was not long enough to compare fairly with their previous criminal behavior. If one looks only at the recidivism rate, however, it is possible to determine what percentage of protected witnesses are arrested for new crimes after their relocation.

The GAO examined the criminal activity of 365 protected witnesses admitted into the program. It was found that just over 21 percent were arrested within the next two years. Therefore, the benefits of the witness protection program in making possible significant organized crime prosecutions must be weighed against the more than $25 million annual cost of the program and the 21 percent recidivism rate of protected witnesses. One woman sued the federal government after her brother was killed, apparently by a witness relocated to her city.[15] Others have complained of shoddy treatment by the government, problems with their new identities, and their continued safety.[16] As the GAO concluded, "program benefits do not come without costs."[17] A reliable indication of the cost-benefit analysis of the witness protection program will be forthcoming only through a comparison of *similar* cases, including cases that employ protected witnesses with cases that do not.

In pragmatic terms, the high cost of the program has brought more attention in recent years to "graduating" protected witnesses from the program, once they are set up in a new community, new job, and new identity. A "significant problem" is how to "ease out" certain witnesses, "especially those who are older and who never held a legitimate job."[18] The large number of WPP informants that are career criminals makes this a daunting task. Job-training, and working for a living wage, are not easy activities for people who have no experience and whose youth has passed. It is likewise difficult not to "go home again" when that is the only place you've ever lived. As a result, the Witness Protection Program requires substantial motivation on the part of accepted witnesses to *completely* change their lives, a decision that is often difficult to carry out.

Special Grand Juries

Title I of the Organized Crime Control Act provided a third technique intended to increase the number and success of organized crime prosecutions. The provision for a "special grand jury" was designed to facilitate the investigation of organized crime across multiple jurisdictions.

According to the Act, special grand juries are to be called at least every 18 months in federal judicial districts of one million or more population. In addition, these grand juries can be called by special request of the prosecutor. The life of these grand juries may be extended up to 36 months.

Similar to traditional grand juries, the special grand juries hold secret proceedings where the prosecutor presents evidence to establish probable cause for indictment. Special grand juries have the added powers of issuing a public report at the end of the term that describes organized crime conditions or official corruption in the area, and they also can conduct continuing investigations along with police. It is due to these added functions that special grand juries are sometimes called "investigating grand juries."

Some states have since established investigating grand juries to deal with multi-county crimes in the same manner that special grand juries on the federal level are directed primarily at multi-state crimes. The President's Commission on Organized Crime believed that all states should establish legal authority for statewide grand juries.[19] Although some states already have laws authorizing a statewide grand jury, others face resistance from local district attorneys who do not wish to relinquish prosecutorial authority for crimes committed in their jurisdictions.

There has been much debate over the merits of special grand juries. Proponents argue that such broad investigative powers are necessary to prosecute organized crime successfully, whose crimes often span across several jurisdictions. Also, special grand juries may be better insulated from local political pressures, unlike county grand juries.

Critics of special grand juries, on the other hand, cite the grand jury's potential for use as harassment against groups based on their political leanings and the potential for their use to "invent" a case, rather than determining if one already exists. Both advocates and critics of special grand juries can cite case examples to demonstrate the productive use or, alternatively, the misuse of the broad powers of this prosecution tool.[20]

As a general rule, prosecutors are not required to present exculpatory evidence to a grand jury, and this has been criticized. Courts have held that "the function of a grand jury is investigative. Its proceedings are not adversary in nature, but rather consist of inquiries conducted by laymen without resort to the technicalities of trial procedure."[21] The failure to present evidence that "clearly negates the target's guilt" is abuse of a prosecutor's discretion.[22] In cases where a defendant alleges prosecutorial abuse of the grand jury, the court reviews the evidence brought to light by the defendant to see if it directly negates "any inference of guilt."[23] In a Virginia drug paraphernalia case, the defendant argued that the prosecutor's failure to present testimony regarding the significantly less carcinogenic attributes of Syrian or Oriental waterpipes constituted grand jury abuse by the prosecutor. The court found this information "hardly serves to exculpate" the defendant. The efficacy of the waterpipe in filtering tobacco smoke "bears little, if any, relationship to the question whether probable cause existed to believe that defendants were engaged in the manufacture, importation, distribution, or sale of drug paraphernalia."[24] Therefore, a claim of grand jury abuse must bear directly on the crime alleged and the suspect's responsibility for it.

Unfortunately, there has been no objective evaluation of the benefits (in terms of multi-jurisdiction organized crime prosecutions) versus the costs (in terms of harassment, unwarranted privacy invasions, and Fifth Amendment issues) of investigative grand juries. Until such an evaluation is conducted, the relative merit of special grand juries remains a matter of examining their operations in individual cases.

It is somewhat ironic, but it is interesting to note that the original purpose of grand juries was to protect citizens from arbitrary accusations by the government. Now, however, the reverse is true. Grand juries generally operate as a tool for the prosecution, rather than as a protective device for the accused. This has come about primarily through the lack of any representation of the accused before grand juries and the wide latitude given prosecutors in calling witnesses and in their use of evidence.[25] The grand jury was invented in England, where it has since been abolished. In the United States, preliminary hearings before a judge are often used to establish probable cause, in place of a grand jury. Nevertheless, investigative grand juries can function much like citizens commissions discussed in Chapter 8 with the added benefit of being able to prosecute those cases they discover.

Racketeering Influenced and Corrupt Organizations

A fourth important prosecution tool was included as part of the Organized Crime Control Act. Title IX of the Act, called "Racketeer Influenced and Corrupt Organizations" (RICO), makes it unlawful to acquire, operate, or receive income from an *enterprise* through a *pattern* of *racketeering activity*. This means that any individual or group (an "enterprise") who commits two or more indictable offenses ("racketeering") within a 10-year period (a "pattern") is subject to 20 years imprisonment, fines up to $25,000, forfeiture of any interest in the enterprise, as well as civil damages and dissolution of the enterprise itself.[26]

Although this statute was designed to combat organized crime infiltration of legitimate business, it has since been employed to prosecute criminal activities by a county sheriff's department, the Philadelphia traffic court, abortion protesters, a state tax bureau, the Tennessee governor's office, and the Louisiana Department of Agriculture. Clearly, the Use of RICO has been extended to encompass all forms of organized and white-collar crime.[27]

A U.S. Supreme Court case, *United States v. Turkette*, made it clear that the provisions of RICO encompass the crimes of *wholly illegitimate* enterprises, as well as crimes committed by otherwise legitimate businesses or government agencies.[28] As a result, *any* enterprise committing two or more felonies within a 10-year period (excluding any period of imprisonment) is subject to prosecution under RICO. The civil penalties allow for any injured party to recover threefold the damages sustained. Upon conviction the U.S. Attorney General can seize all property and assets of the illegal enterprise.

The application of RICO was extended further in *Sedima v. Imrex Co.*.[29] The case arose from a civil suit between two corporations, engaged in a joint venture. Sedima believed it was being cheated by Imrex through an over-billing scheme. It sued Imrex for mail and wire fraud (as the two predicate acts required to establish a "pattern" of racketeering activity under RICO). Sedima claimed injury of at least $175,000 from the over-billing and sought treble damages and attorney's fees.

The issues faced by the U.S. Supreme Court were two: (1) whether the predicate acts required for a RICO prosecution had to be *prior* (i.e., pre-existing) criminal convictions, and (2) whether simple monetary loss is sufficient to qualify as a "racketeering injury" to justify a RICO suit. In both cases, the Court favored broad application of RICO provisions.

It was held that prior criminal convictions are not required for a RICO suit. According to the Court, the "language of RICO gives no obvious indication that a civil action can proceed only after a criminal conviction." A five-justice majority held that "the word 'conviction' does not appear in any relevant portion of the statute," so predicate offenses need not be established prior to the suit filed under RICO.

> In sum, we can find no support in the statute's history, its language, or considerations of policy for a requirement that a private treble damages action under [RICO] can proceed only against a defendant who has already been criminally convicted. To the contrary, every indication is that no such requirement exists. Accordingly, the fact that Imrex and the individual defendants have not been convicted under RICO or the federal mail and wire fraud statutes does not bar Sedima's action.[30]

The Court also held that monetary loss is sufficient "racketeering injury" to qualify for prosecution under RICO. "Racketeering activity" under the law's provisions "consists of no more and no less than commission of a predicate act." The majority held, therefore, that "we are initially doubtful about the requirement of a 'racketeering injury' separate from the harm from the predicate acts." The majority reading of the statute "belies any such requirement."

This case continues the broad application of RICO to all forms of organized crime, whether committed by professional criminals or by corporations. According to the U.S. Supreme Court,

> This less restrictive reading is amply supported by our prior cases and the general principles surrounding this statute. RICO is to be read broadly. This is the lesson not only of Congress' self-consciously expansive language and overall approach, but also of its express admonition that RICO is to "be liberally construed to effectuate its remedial purposes."[31]

It can be seen that the Supreme Court relied heavily on the legislative history of the law to assess Congressional intent behind it.

A four-justice dissent argued that Congress did not intend that the RICO provisions apply to "garden-variety frauds," such as those in the *Sedima* case. They claimed that remedies under state law are adequate in such cases, and the severe penalties available under RICO encourage spurious suits.

> Litigants, lured by the prospect of treble damages and attorney's fees, have a strong incentive to invoke RICO's provisions whenever they can allege in good faith two instances of mail or wire fraud. Then the defendant, facing tremendous financial exposure in addition to the threat of being labelled a "racketeer," will have a strong interest in settling the dispute.[32]

Given the findings in the *Turkette* and *Sedima* cases, court interpretation of the RICO provisions is quite broad. Regardless of how one reads original congressional intent, the Court has found it to apply to both legitimate and illegal organizations without predicate convictions, and involving only monetary losses. Therefore, the scope of allowable prosecutions of organized crime under RICO is expansive, and it is the most potent weapon in the prosecutor's organized crime control repertoire.

State RICO laws, that apply to "patterns" of "racketeering activity" that violate state laws, have been passed in 24 states. The President's Commission on Organized Crime recommended that other states pass RICO laws as well for violations that do not involve federal laws, such as state beverage control or tax laws.[33] State-level RICO laws have been found to be little used thus far, much in the same was the federal RICO law was little used in its first 10 years of existence.[34]

Another racketeering statute available to federal prosecutors is the *Continuing Criminal Enterprise* (CCE) law which is limited to drug traffickers. CCE makes it a crime to engage in a conspiracy to commit at least three related violations of felony drug laws with five or more persons. To be convicted, the offender must be the organizer, manager, or supervisor of the continuing operation receiving substantial income or property from it. The law took effect in 1987, and provides for mandatory minimum sentences of 20 years for first violations, fines up to $2 million, and forfeiture of profits and any interest in the enterprise. In many ways, the CCE statute resembles a RICO law for drug law violations.

In 1990, for example, U.S. Attorneys nationwide investigated 2,704 suspects for RICO violations and another 440 for CCE violations. This constituted only three percent of all the suspects investigated that year, but these cases involved the most serious offenders and longest sentences upon conviction. Table 9.1 presents the flow of racketeering cases through U.S. Attorneys' offices in the United States.

Table 9.1
Investigation, Prosecution, and Conviction Outcomes

U.S. Attorneys 1990 Case Flow	Suspects Investigated	Defendants Charged	Offenders Convicted	Dismissed/ Acquitted
Racketeering (RICO)	2,704 (3% of total)	37% (of suspects)	81% (of defs.)	19% (of defs.)
Predicate Offenses	8,317 9%	27%	86%	14%
CCE	440 0.5%	29%	90%	10%
Other Drug Violations	31,071 32%	55%	85%	15%
All Other Offenses	53,228 56%	72%	79%	21%
Column Total	95,760	58,696	47,486	11,210

Complied from: Kenneth Carlson and Peter Finn, *Prosecuting Criminal Enterprises* (Washington, DC: Bureau of Justice Statistics, 1993).

The predicate offense category in Table 9.1 are those offenses that underlie the RICO charge, such as narcotics trafficking, extortion, or gambling. It can be seen that CCE prosecutions constitute, by far, the smallest category, but this is also the most narrow offense category listed. "Other drug" violations are all other federal drug laws, not including CCE violations. "All other offenses" include any other criminal matters handled by U.S. Attorney's Offices in 1990.

It can be seen that organized crime and drug offenses (i.e., RICO, predicate offenses, CCE, and other drug laws) constitute nearly one-half (44%) of all criminal cases handled by federal prosecutors. Almost three-quarters of these cases are alleged violations of federal drug laws.

There is significant fall-off between suspects investigated and defendants charged. Most of this is due to the nature of organized crime investigations. Cases often take a long time to develop, and many investigations end without result. The numbers can be somewhat misleading in that cases not resulting in formal charges are not necessarily dropped. In some cases RICO or CCE suspects are subsequently charged with other crimes. In a quarter of all cases, the suspect was referred for prosecution elsewhere, usually at the state level. The largest proportion of cases that did not result in formal charges were due to weak evidence, jurisdictional problems, and expiration of the statute of limitations.[35]

Once formally charged, defendants were convicted at a rate of 80 percent or better. In fact, the rate in organized crime-related cases is somewhat higher than the conviction rate in other federal cases. Most defendants plead guilty rather than go to trial, although plea rates were lowest in RICO (64%) and CCE cases (57%). More than 70 percent of defendants in other cases plead guilty.[36] Dismissal rates ranged from nine to 15 percent of organized crime-related cases. The rate was 18 percent for other offenses. Dismissals include nolle prosequi and deferred prosecutions. The acquittal rate ranged from one percent in CCE cases to a high of four percent in RICO cases. The average acquittal rate was three percent.[37]

It can be concluded that conviction rates are somewhat higher, and dismissal rates slightly lower, in federal organized crime cases than in other federal criminal prosecutions. Acquittal rates are lowest in CCE cases (one percent) and highest in RICO cases (four percent). The characteristics of the offenders convicted and the sentences they received are presented in Chapter 11.

Bank Secrecy Act

The Bank Secrecy Act was enacted in 1970 as a tool to make it difficult to "launder" illicitly obtained cash through legitimate channels. To accomplish this, the law established three primary requirements for banks and individuals.

The Act requires that banks must file a Currency Transaction Report (CTR) for every deposit, withdrawal, or exchange of funds more than $10,000. Second, a Currency or Monetary Instruments Report (CMIR) must be filed with the U.S. Customs Service if more than $10,000 in cash leaves or enters the United States. Third, a citizen holding bank accounts in foreign countries must declare them on his or her federal tax return. Violation of these provisions can result in criminal fines up to $500,000, as well as civil remedies by the Department of Treasury. The U.S. Treasury Department is responsible for enforcing these provisions through the Internal Revenue Service, Customs Service, Comptroller of the Currency, Federal Reserve System, Federal Deposit Insurance Corporation, Federal Home Loan Bank Board, National Credit Union Administration, and the Securities and Exchange Commission.

The U.S. General Accounting Office (GAO) conducted an examination of the effectiveness of this enforcement effort. The GAO found that the Treasury Department did not "play an active role" in administering the Bank Secrecy Act until 1985 when the Bank of Boston pled guilty to criminal violations of the Act. The number of civil reviews for compliance increased to 76 in that year, most resulting from "voluntary admission of possible noncompliance" by banks and other financial institutions. This is a dramatic increase in enforcement, as civil penalties totaling $800,000 from only seven financial institutions were imposed in the first 15 years of the Act, 1970 through 1984. In 1985 alone, 11 of the 76 reviews initiated by the Treasury Department resulted in civil fines totaling $5.1 million. By 1990, the IRS Criminal Investigation Division had conducted investigations that resulted in more than 1,000 convictions in only three years for crimes related to money laundering.[38] The Customs Service was similarly active in conducting investigations and making cases.

The GAO evaluation found that the potential of the Bank Secrecy Act to prevent laundering of illicit funds has not been realized. It found the Treasury Department "lacks current and specific information" about the way the various reporting agencies are handling their duties and, therefore, it cannot even determine "the number of financial institutions examined or the number of violations identified."[39] One problem is the growing volume of CTR's being filed. In 1992, nine million CTR's were filed reporting more than $417 billion in currency transactions.[40] Clearly, this intimidating volume of information works against it being used efficiently. Indeed, law enforcement agencies have been criticized for not exploiting CTR information. "The large volume of reports has made meaningful analysis difficult."[41]

The Financial Crime Enforcement Network (FinCEN) was established in 1990 in the Department of Treasury to support law enforcement agencies in identifying money laundering activity. With a staff of 200, FinCEN provides strategic analysis and disseminates financial data to federal, state, local, and foreign law enforcement agencies.[42] This agency should help traditional law enforcement agencies in keeping abreast of money laundering techniques and operations in their area.

The Bank Secrecy Act was subsequently amended to make it illegal to make multiple cash transactions just under the $10,000 in an effort to "wilfully" avoid the CTR requirement. The U.S. Supreme Court ruled in 1994 that people who have multiple cash transactions with banks under $10,000 each cannot be convicted of violating the Bank Secrecy Act "without proof that they knew such action is illegal."[43]

The potential of the Bank Secrecy Act to detect illicit fund transfers has not been reached. The ability of the Act to detect illegal movement of cash has been demonstrated in actual cases, however, where such detection was made a priority. For example, Maria Torres was stopped by Customs Officers at the Los Angeles Airport prior to boarding a plane for Vancouver, Canada. She was interviewed as part of a routine "outbound currency program" because she appeared to be "weighted down" with bulky clothes, and she was in a hurry. Torres told Customs she was carrying about $3,000. A search discovered over $146,000 in U.S. currency in the pockets of her jumpsuit, in her purse, and in a plastic bag she was carrying. She was convicted of failing to file a CMIR, fined $5,000, and given five years probation. The currency she was carrying was forfeited to the government.[44]

The ability of the Bank Secrecy Act to inhibit the laundering of illegally obtained cash in legitimate financial institutions led the President's Commission on Organized Crime to suggest that similar laws on the state level may provide information for state prosecutions as well. Such state laws, that now exist in about half the states, "reflect the critical need state law enforcement officials have for the information contained in the currency transaction reports." As the Commission noted, however, "this need can also be met by greater cooperation between state and federal officials."[45] State and local money laundering awareness and training have already begun.[46]

Critical Thinking Exercise

Using the information provided in this chapter, read the scenario below and respond to the questions that follow. Explain your rationale, given your knowledge of current law and policy.

The Case of Enough Evidence

You are a federal prosecutor faced with the case of a career criminal named "Clyde." Clyde is charged with loansharking and threatening people who fall behind on their payments. One of his neighbors, "Fifi," has information about Clyde selling stolen property which might help convict Clyde, but he is afraid to testify, given Clyde's reputation for threats. Fifi also has a checkered past with a few arrests for receiving stolen property. The only other evidence against Clyde is from Vinnie who he threatened for non-payment of a gambling debt, but Vinnie is a compulsive gambler with a prior record, he is nervous, and could skip town before trial.

Questions:

1. Do you have enough facts above to prove a RICO violation against Clyde?

2. If you had time to gather additional evidence, what would you look for?

3. If you were a juror, would you convict Clyde given the facts above?

Summary

The prosecution of organized crime cases has come a long way in the last decade or two. A large number of significant convictions were the result of successful use of the prosecution tools described in this chapter. The Witness Protection Program, RICO provisions, and the Bank Secrecy

Act have been especially important in prosecuting criminal *enterprises*, and not mere crime leaders, and in using information provided by *insiders* in a position to know. The Bank Secrecy Act attacks organized crime from the other direction: from the money back to the enterprise. Proper use of these prosecution strategies, together with an understanding of their strengths and weaknesses, bodes well for future efforts to contain organized crime in this manner.

References to Chapter 9

[1]   U.S. Senate Committee on Government Operations Permanent Subcommittee on Investigations, *Organized Crime and Illicit Traffic in Narcotics: Hearings Part I* 88th Congress, 1st session (Washington, DC: U.S. Government Printing Office, 1963), p. 15.

[2]   Ibid., p. 9.

[3]   Pub. Law 91-452; 84 Stat. 922.

[4]   John Buchanan, *Police Prosecutor Teams: Innovations in Several Jurisdictions* (Washington, DC: National Institute of Justice, 1989.

[5]   Ibid., p. 5.

[6]   Ronald Goldstock, "The Prosecutor as Problem Solver," in R.J. Kelly, K. Chin, and R. Schatzberg, eds. *Handbook of Organized Crime in the United States* (Westport, CT: Greenwood Press, 1994), pp. 431-450.

[7]   *Malloy v. Hogan*, 378 U.S. 1 (1964).

[8]   *Lefkowitz v. Cunningham*, 431 U.S. 801 (1977) and *Kastigar v. United States*, 92 S. Ct. 1653 (1972).

[9]   Alan A. Block and William J. Chambliss, *Organizing Crime* (New York: Elsevier North Holland, 1981), p. 205.

[10]   Robert P. Rhodes, *Organized Crime: Crime Control v. Civil Liberties* (New York: Random House, 1984), p. 194.

[11]   U.S. Comptroller General, *Witness Security Program: Prosecutive Results and Participant Arrest Data* (Washington, DC: U.S. General Accounting office, 1984).

[12]   Ibid., p. 20.

[13]   Peter Edwards, *Blood Brothers: How Canada's Most Powerful Mafia Family Runs Its Business* (Toronto: Key Porter Books, 1990), p. 170.

[14]   Ibid., p. 22.

[15]   "Suit Takes Fault with Federal Witness Protection Program," *Organized Crime Digest*, v. 15 (January 26, 1994), p. 1.

[16]   Jay Mathews, "One Witness' Experience Points Out Flaws in Protection Program," *The Buffalo News*, (August 23, 1990), p. 3; F. Montanino, "Protecting Organized Crime Witnesses in the United States," *International Journal of Comparative and Applied Criminal Justice*, v. 14 (Spring-Winter, 1990), pp. 123-132.

[17]   Ibid., p. 30.

[18] Robert J. Kelly, Rufus Schatzberg, and Ko-lin Chin, "Without Fear of Retribution: The Witness Protection Program," in R.J. Kelly, K. Chin, and R. Schatzberg, eds. *Handbook of Organized Crime in the United States* (Westport, CT: Greenwood Publishing, 1994), pp. 491-504.

[19] President's Commission on Organized Crime, *The Impact: Organized Crime Today* (Washington, DC: U.S. Government Printing Office, 1987), p. 163.

[20] "Judging the Grand Jury," *Time*, (February 7, 1992), pp. 59-60; Nathan Lewin, "The Misuse of Grand Juries," *The Nation*, (December 23, 1972), pp. 18-20; see *Organized Crime: Crime Control v. Civil Liberties*, ch. 4.

[21] *United States v. Ruyle*, 524 F.2d 1135 (6th Cir. 1975).

[22] *United States v. Olin Corp.*, 465 F. Supp 1127 (W.D.N.Y. 1979) and *United States v. Dorfman*, 532 F. Supp 118 (N.D. Ill 1981).

[23] *United States v. Dyer*, 750 F. Supp 1300 (E.D. Va. 1990).

[24] at 1301.

[25] Marvin E. Frankel and Gary P. Naftalis, *The Grand Jury: An Institution on Trial* (New York: Hill and Wang, 1977); Joel Stashenko, "Pending Appeal Makes a Case for Redefining Grand Jury's Role," *The Buffalo News*, (January 22, 1990), p. 3.

[26] Jeff Atkinson, "Racketeer Influenced and Corrupt Organizations, 18 U.S.C.: Broadest of Federal Criminal Statutes," *Journal of Criminal Law and Criminology*, v. 69 (March, 1978), pp. 1-18.

[27] John Poklemba and Peter Crusco, "Public Enterprises and RICO: The Aftermath of *United States v. Turkette*," *Criminal Law Bulletin*, v. 18 (May-June, 1982), pp. 197-203.

[28] *United States v. Turkette*, 101 S. Ct. 2524 (1980); Jan Neuenschwander, "RICO Extended to Apply to Wholly Illegitimate Enterprises," *Journal of Criminal Law and Criminology*, v. 72 (December, 1981), pp. 1426-1443.

[29] *Sedima v. Imrex*, 105 S. Ct. 3275 (1985).

[30] at 3284.

[31] at 3286.

[32] at 3294.

[33] President's Commission on Organized Crime, *The Impact: Organized Crime Today* (Washington, DC: U.S. Government Printing office, 1987), p. 135.

[34] Donald J. Rebovich, Kenneth R. Coyle, and John C. Schaaf, *Local Prosecution of Organized Crime: The Use of State RICO Statutes* (Washington, DC: National Institute of Justice, 1993).

[35] Kenneth Carlson and Peter Finn, *Prosecuting Criminal Enterprises* (Washington, DC: Bureau of Justice Statistics, 1993), p. 3.

[36] Ibid., p. 4.

[37] Ibid.

[38] U.S. Comptroller General, *Money Laundering: The U.S. Government is Responding to the Problem* (Washington, DC: U.S. General Accounting Office, 1991), p. 33.

[39]   U.S. Comptroller General, *Bank Secrecy Act: Treasury Can Improve Implementation of the Act* (Washington, DC: U.S. General Accounting Office, 1986), pp. 15-19.

[40]   U.S. Comptroller General, *Money Laundering: Characteristics of Currency Transactions Reports* (Washington, DC: U.S. General Accounting Office, 1993), p. 2.

[41]   U.S. Comptroller General, *Money Laundering: The Use of Bank Secrecy Act Reports by Law Enforcement Could be Increased* (Washington, DC: U.S. General Accounting Office, 1993), p. 1.

[42]   U.S. Comptroller General, *Money Laundering: Progress Report on Treasury's Financial Crimes Enforcement Network* (Washington, DC: U.S. Government Printing Office, 1993); U.S. Comptroller General, *Money Laundering: Treasury's Financial Crimes Enforcement Network* (Washington, DC: U.S. General Accounting Office, 1991).

[43]   *Ratzlaf v. United States*, 115 S. Ct. 1196 (1994).

[44]   Ibid.

[45]   *The Impact*, p. 169.

[46]   Clifford Karchmer and Douglas Ruch, *State and Local Money Laundering Control Strategies* (Washington, DC: National Institute of Justice, 1992); U.S. Comptroller General, *Money Laundering: State Efforts to Fight It are Increasing But More Federal Help is Needed* (Washington, DC: U.S. General Accounting Office, 1992).

Chapter 10

Organizing a
Criminal Defense

Justice is like a train that's
nearly always late.
Yevgeny Yevtushenko
(1963)

The legal defenses to organized crimes are somewhat more complex than are those for conventional crimes. Although the available defenses themselves do not change, the applicability of various defenses is an issue for some crimes more than for others. As a result, accusations of organized crimes are generally met with more organized and complex defenses. Several examples of defenses that come up almost exclusively in cases of organized crime will serve to illustrate the point: entrapment, duress, and other more offense-specific claims. The issue of "mob lawyers" will also be addressed as an issue of consequence for the defense in organized crime cases.

Entrapment

Entrapment is a defense that was made popular in the Abscam political corruption and DeLorean drug cases, where several defendants felt that they were "tricked" or "trapped" into committing crimes they did not wish to commit. Unfortunately, the courts have not always agreed with this position.[1]

The purpose of the entrapment defense is to prevent the government from manufacturing crime by setting "traps" for the unwary citizen. Also, the entrapment defense is aimed strictly at misconduct on the part of the government. That is, if a private citizen, not associated with the government, entraps another into committing an offense, the defense is not available.

The traditional (or "subjective") formulation of the defense of entrapment was established by the U.S. Supreme Court in 1932.[2] This case first recognized the defense of entrapment in the federal courts.

In this case, which occurred during prohibition, *Sorrells* was approached by an undercover police officer who had been in Sorrells' military unit during World War I. The two men got into a discussion of old times and, at several points in the conversation, the undercover police officer asked Sorrells if he could obtain some liquor for him (which was illegal at the time). The first two times the police officer asked for liquor, Sorrells said no. But after the third request, and not knowing his friend was now a police officer, Sorrells left and brought back some liquor.

Sorrells was arrested by the police officer and tried for possession and sale of liquor. Sorrells was convicted, and he appealed all the way to the U.S. Supreme Court. The Supreme Court reversed his conviction. The Court held that entrapment arises when "the criminal design originates with the officials of the government, and they implant in the mind of an innocent person the disposition to commit the alleged offense and induce its commission in order that they may prosecute."[3]

The Supreme Court held that the undercover officer's actions amounted to entrapment.

> Entrapment exists if the defendant was not predisposed to commit the crimes in question, and his intent originated with the officials of the government.

This 1932 finding in the *Sorrells* case is often called the *subjective formulation* of the entrapment defense, because it focuses on the defendant's frame of mind.

The government's role in committing a crime can range from trivial to very influential. The precise role necessary for entrapment has been the subject of many subsequent court decisions. The U.S. Supreme Court heard another entrapment case where two drug addicts were in a doctor's office for treatment of their addiction. One asked the defendant, Sherman, where he could obtain drugs. Sherman avoided the issue. They met for treatment at the same doctor's office three or four more times, however, and each time the same drug addict asked Sherman to get some drugs for him. Sherman finally acquiesced, and obtained the illegal drugs.[4]

As it turned out, the drug addict was an informer for police, and Sherman was arrested for selling drugs. Sherman raised the defense of entrapment at trial, but he was convicted and sentenced to 10 years imprisonment.

The U.S. Supreme Court decided to review Sherman's case, and it used the criteria for determining entrapment that was established in the *Sorrells* decision 26 years earlier. The Supreme Court looked at three criteria it felt important in considering the applicability of the entrapment defense. The fact that government agents "merely afford opportunities or facilities for the commission of the offense does not" constitute entrapment. Entrapment only occurs when the criminal conduct was "the product of *creative* activity" of law enforcement officials. The Court went on to say, "to determine whether entrapment has been established, a line must be drawn between a trap for the unwary innocent and the trap for the unwary criminal . . . On the one hand, at trial the accused may examine the conduct of the government agent; on the other hand, the accused will be subjected to an "appropriate and searching inquiry into his own conduct and predisposition" as bearing on his claim of innocence."[5]

The Supreme Court concluded that the police conduct in this case constitutes just what the entrapment defense is designed to prevent.

> The case at bar illustrates an evil which the defense of entrapment is designed to overcome. The government informer entices someone attempting to avoid narcotics not only into carrying out an illegal sale but also returning to the habit of use. Selecting the proper time, the informer then tells the government agent. The set-up is accepted by the agent without even a question as to the manner in which the informer encountered the seller. Thus the Government plays on the weaknesses of an innocent party and beguiles him into committing crimes which he otherwise would not have attempted. Law enforcement does not require such methods as this.

Four other justices on the Supreme Court concurred with the majority, but thought the decision ought to be arrived at using a different standard. These justices felt that,

> In holding out inducements [police] should act in such a manner as is likely to induce to the commission of the crime—*only* these persons and *not* others who would normally avoid crime and through self-struggle resist ordinary temptations. This test shifts attention from the record and predisposition of the particular defendant to the conduct of the police and the likelihood, objectively considered, that it would entrap only those ready and willing to commit crime.[6]

This standard is called the *objective formulation* of the entrapment defense. It can be stated as follows:

> Entrapment occurs when government agents induce or encourage another person to engage in criminal behavior by knowingly making false representations about the lawfulness of the conduct or by employing methods that create a substantial risk that such an offense will be committed by innocent [i.e., unpredisposed] persons.

As this objective formulation points out, the main difference is in the objective standard is that it shifts attention away from the prior record and predisposition of the defendant to the conduct of the police. Both the subjective and objective formulations address only the dangers of inducement to crime by innocent persons but, under the objective standard, the predisposition of the defendant is irrelevant.

The importance of the difference between the objective and subjective formulations of the defense is made clear in a subsequent case. An undercover police officer went to Russell's home, claiming he wanted to become involved in the manufacture of methamphetamine. The undercover officer offered to supply an essential ingredient of the illegal drug in return for half the total amount manufactured. The officer's actual aim, however, was to locate the manufacturing laboratory, so he demanded to see where the drug was actually made. Russell took the officer to the factory, and the officer eventually supplied him with the necessary ingredient to manufacture the drug. Russell and his associates were later arrested for the manufacture and sale of a controlled dangerous substance. Russell claimed that he was entrapped.[7]

The U.S. Supreme Court adhered to the subjective standard of its earlier decisions in *Sorrells* and *Sherman*. Furthermore, the Court rejected the argument that the constitutional requirement of due process mandated use of the objective standard. The result of the decision in *Russell* is that states are free to adopt either the subjective or objective formulation of the entrapment defense. The Court, therefore, upheld the conviction of Russell:

> It does not seem particularly desirable for the law to grant complete immunity from prosecution to one who himself planned to commit a crime, and then committed it, simply because government undercover agents subjected him to inducements which might have seduced a hypothetical individual who was not so predisposed.[8]

It is clear that this decision was reached according to the subjective standard due to its focus on the predisposition of the defendant, rather than on the conduct of the government agent. Three Justices dissented in this case, however, urging the adoption of the objective standard for entrapment. They felt that a reasonable application of the objective standard in this case would result in a finding of entrapment. The dissent argued that "the agent's undertaking to supply this ingredient to the respondent, thus making it possible for the government to prosecute him for manufacturing an illicit drug with it, was, I think, precisely the type of governmental conduct that the entrapment defense is meant to prevent."[9] It is easy to see from the Court's opinion in this case, as well as from the dissenting opinion, that use of the subjective or objective standard to establish entrapment can lead to very different conclusions based on the same set of facts.

In a recent case, the U.S. Supreme Court had an opportunity to re-evaluate the entrapment defense. Keith Jacobson ordered two magazines from a bookstore titled *Bare Boys*. The magazines contained photographs of nude pre-teen and teenage boys. Finding Jacobson's name on the bookstore mailing list, the Postal Service and the Customs Service sent mail to him using five different fictitious organizations and a bogus pen pal. The organizations claimed to represent those interested in sexual freedom and against censorship. The organizations were said to support lobbying efforts through sales of publications. Jacobson corresponded on occasion with these organizations, giving his views of censorship and the "hysteria" surrounding child pornography.

The correspondence to Jacobson was an attempt to see if he would violate the Child Protection Act of 1984 by receiving sexually explicit depictions of children through the mails.[10] After more than two years of receiving these mailings, Jacobson ordered a magazine depicting young boys engaged in sexual acts. He was arrested under the Child Protection Act, and a search of his house found no sexually oriented materials, except for the *Bare Boys* magazines and the government agencies' bogus mailings.

Jacobson was convicted at trial, although he claimed entrapment.[11] The appeal was heard by the U.S. Supreme Court, which recognized the government's burden under the federal government's subjective formulation. The prosecution must prove beyond a reasonable doubt that the defendant was disposed to commit the criminal act *prior* to first being approached by government agents.

The Court made several observations relevant to organized crime investigations. In the case of "sting" operations, for example, where a government-sponsored stolen property "fence" is set up, a defendant is provided an opportunity to commit a crime. The entrapment defense "is of little use because the ready commission of the criminal act amply demonstrates the defendant's predisposition."[12] Likewise, an agent who offers the opportunity to buy or sell drugs may make an immediate arrest under federal law, if the offer is accepted.

In the case of Jacobson, the Court conceded that if the government agents had simply offered him the opportunity to order child pornography by mail, and he promptly ordered it, the entrapment defense would not be applicable. But the facts in this case were different. By the time Jacobson violated the law, he had been the target of 26 months of repeated mailings. Jacobson's earlier order of the *Bare Boys* magazines cannot be used to show predisposition because they were legal at the time they were ordered, and Jacobson's uncontradicted testimony stated he did not know the magazines would depict minors until they arrived in the mail.

The U.S. Supreme Court has previously held that a person's sexual inclinations, tastes, and "fantasies . . . are his own and beyond the reach of the government."[13] It was held that in Jacobson's case the government "excited Jacobson's interest" in illegal sexually explicit materials and "exerted substantial pressure" to buy this material as part of a fight against censorship and infringement of individual privacy.[14]

The Court concluded in a five to four vote that "when the government's quest for conviction leads to the apprehension of an otherwise law-abiding citizen who, if left to his own devices, likely would have never run afoul of the law, the courts should intervene."[15] The U.S. Supreme Court intervened in this case and reversed Jacobson's conviction.

Under federal law, therefore, government agents "in their zeal to enforce the law . . . may not originate a criminal design," that entails creating the disposition to commit a criminal act in a person's mind, "and then induce commission of the crime so that the government may prosecute."[16] This is what the entrapment defense is designed to prevent.

The viability of a claim of entrapment is usually decided during pretrial motions before a judge; it is not decided by a jury. In order to invoke entrapment as a defense, the defendant must necessarily admit to engaging in the unlawful conduct. That is, if you claim you were entrapped, you are admitting that you did commit the crime. Despite the perspective of the federal courts, the objective standard has been adopted in the Model Penal Code, in the revised Federal criminal code, as well as in a number of states.[17]

Duress

A defense that often arises in cases of organized crime is duress. Generally, three conditions must be met for a successful claim of duress as a defense. A person must engage in a criminal act:

1. due to threat of serious bodily harm by another person,

2. the threat must be immediate without reasonable possibility for escape, and

3. in many jurisdictions, the defense is disallowed where a person intentionally or recklessly places himself in a situation subject to duress.

Therefore, if you join a gang of organized criminals who tell you to embezzle $1,000 from your employer, but you are caught, your attempt to claim a defense of duress (i.e., you were forced to do it against your will) would be denied in many states because you placed yourself in a situation subject to duress by joining the gang of criminals. The defense of duress is also called coercion or compulsion in some jurisdictions.

In a case in Carlsbad, California, Larry LaFleur claimed he was held at gunpoint by his co-felon Nick Holm and forced to shoot and kill their kidnapping victim. LaFleur argued the murder charge against him should be reduced to voluntary manslaughter because of the duress placed upon him by Holm.

The U.S. Court of Appeals commented that the defense of duress "is based on the rationale that a person, when confronted with two evils, should not be punished for engaging in the lesser of the evils."[18] The problem in LaFleur's case is that the two evils he was faced with (his own death and that of an innocent person) have the same degree of harm. The Court held that "consistent with the common law rule, a defendant should not be excused from taking the life of an innocent third person because of the threat of harm to himself."[19] There is no rule of "human jettison," nor does duress "legally mitigate murder to manslaughter." It should also be added that LaFleur recklessly placed himself in a situation subject to duress by engaging in a violent felony.

In a case involving two prison escapees who claimed there had been "various threats and beatings directed at them" inside the prison, the U.S. Supreme Court ruled that duress was not applicable because no "bonafide effort" was made by the defendants "to surrender or return to custody as soon as the claimed duress or necessity had lost its coercive force."[20] The defendants were at large for a month or more.

Therefore, criminal acts committed while under immediate, serious, and non-reckless duress are excused *only* while the coercive threats are in force, and the action taken results in less harm than the act avoided. Once the duress is ended, no further criminal conduct is excused under law.

Claims That Are Potential Defenses

Adequacy of Representation

Sometimes a defendant will allege that he or she acted improperly under "advice of counsel." Mistake in advice on the part of counsel is *not* a defense, however. It may be shown where it would disprove the requisite intent, but it is not an absolute defense in itself. As a result, a person who was told by his lawyer that a prostitution ring disguised as a "dating service" was legal would have no defense in a criminal case. The best the defendant could do would be to show that the crime was committed without "willfulness" or not "knowingly" if this was an element of the crime. In these cases, the degree of crime charged might be reduced (e.g., from first to second degree prostitution charges), if the jury believed the defendant's claim.

In a New York City case, Wong Chi Keung was convicted of conspiracy to distribute heroin. A lawyer who had represented her in an earlier case allegedly helped target her in the current case through his representation of a co-conspirator.[21] The court recognized that "prejudice is presumed" when a defendant can "establish that an actual conflict of interest adversely affects (her) lawyer's performance."[22] The court found that in Keung's case "no showing of either such a conflict or such an effect." This is because it was apparent that her attorney "had no role in selecting Wong as a target," and no confidences were disclosed to the lawyer.[23]

Absent a conflict of interest, it might be claimed that the attorney's performance "fell below an objective standard of reasonableness," and that "but for his deficient conduct the result of the trial would have been different."[24] In determining competency of counsel, the court examines the lawyer's performance of his or her task of representation. It is obviously difficult to find incompetency so great as to cause a different result in a case, and defendants rarely prevail on these grounds. In the *Keung* case, for example, the Court found her attorney "a skilled and persistent advocate" with "nothing to suggest a contrary result" in the outcome of the case.[25]

RICO Participation

A person is not liable for prosecution for racketeering under RICO, unless he or she has participated in the operation of management of the enterprise itself. Therefore, an accounting firm, which audited the books of an business enterprise and found them to be in order, did not "participate in management or operation" of the enterprise. As a result, it cannot be prosecuted under RICO for failing to inform the board of the business enterprise about its potential insolvency.[26]

Likewise, an attorney's sporadic involvement in a fraudulent scheme through the preparation of two letters, a partnership agreement, and assistance in a bankruptcy proceeding was "not sufficient" to meet the conduct or participation requirements for prosecution under RICO.[27]

Gambling While Intoxicated

Voluntary, self-induced intoxication is not a defense in criminal cases, although it is sometimes relevant when the intoxication and act occur under certain circumstances. In Atlantic City, a casino sued a patron to recover gambling losses he incurred at the casino.[28] He was a "high-roller," often betting $10,000 on a single hand of blackjack, and he would sometimes play five or more hands at the same time.

The nature of gambling is such that all gamblers will lose at least some of the time. Therefore, casinos "cause" people to lose money. The question in this case was the extent to which the casino is responsible to protect gamblers from financial loss if they gamble "while [their] mental facilities are impaired by alcohol." Any losses incurred while a casino patron is allowed to continue gambling while drunk "is proximately caused by the casino's negligence."[29] As a result, the patron would not be liable for losses under these circumstances. In criminal terms, however, any criminal conduct engaged in while voluntarily intoxicated would not be excused.

Extortion, Perjury, and Consequences

It is a defense to extortion that the defendant reasonably believed the charge to be true, and that his or her sole purpose was to compel or induce the victim to take reasonable action to make good a wrongful act. Therefore, an employer who demands that an employee, who stole $50, reimburse him or else he will turn him over to the police, has a defense to a charge of extortion.

It is also a defense to a charge of perjury to retract a false statement during the course of a proceeding before it substantially affects the proceeding *and* before it becomes manifest that its falsity would be exposed. Such a defense is designed to encourage witnesses to tell the truth, even in cases where they began telling lies during sworn testimony.

It is sometimes claimed that an offense committed was an "unintended consequence" and, therefore, a person should not be held accountable for it. A person is legally responsible for all unintended consequences, however, of any unlawful act.[30] Unintended consequence is only an allowable defense where the act (that caused the unintended result) was lawful. Therefore, a person who shoots at you, but misses and kills someone else, is criminally liable for that person's death, even though it was an "unintended consequence" of his or her action.

Amnesia

Occasionally, a defendant will claim that he "cannot remember" whether he committed a particular offense. Unfortunately, amnesia is not a defense in itself. If it is shown that, at the time of the act, the defendant did not understand the nature of the act and that it was wrong, an insanity defense may be appropriate. Amnesia, however, may only be considered in determining the penalty for a crime. Therefore, a judge can consider a valid claim of amnesia in sentencing, but it does not relieve the defendant of liability for the crime.

Mob Lawyers

The President's Commission on Organized Crime drew attention to what it called "mob-connected" lawyers. It was claimed these individuals "are not criminal lawyers. They are lawyer-criminals."[31] Although "few in number," the Commission believed they used their status to undermine the justice system. Five case studies of mob-connected lawyers were presented in the Commission's report to show precisely how these attorneys represented the interests of organized crime groups, rather than legal interests.

Martin Light was an attorney in New York, who now is serving a 15-year sentence for heroin possession. In testimony before the Commission, he said he represented a "crew" within a Cosa Nostra group. He stated that if a member of the crew was arrested and did not call him, Light would go to federal court and "see who he got as a lawyer. If he got [a] Legal Aid [attorney], that would be a tip-off that he might be cooperating." He said the penalty for a member who cooperated with the government was "death."[32]

Kevin Rankin was a lawyer for the Philadelphia Cosa Nostra group. He secured and utilized perjured affidavits and testimony on behalf of family members charged with crimes. He also paid a corrections officer to perjure himself.[33] Rankin was ultimately convicted for his role as a participant in an organized crime narcotics conspiracy. He was sentenced to 54 years in prison.

An interesting case is that of Frank Ragano who spent 30 years representing alleged organized crime figures such as Santo Trafficante of Florida, Carlos Marcello of New Orleans, and Jimmy Hoffa of the Teamster's Union.[34] In a recent book, he tells of how he was seduced by the power and influence of these individuals, and why he ultimately decided to leave that circle of clients. He told this story after the deaths of Trafficante in 1987 and Marcello in 1993. Ragano revealed that in his early association with Trafficante and Marcello, they "seemed incapable" of violence. Instead they appeared interested only in gambling enterprises, real estate deals, and "semi-legitimate" deals with politicians.[35] Ragano says that an elderly Trafficante told him about his role in the assassination of President John F. Kennedy.[36]

In terms of his role as a "mob lawyer," Ragano confesses that "my gravest error as a lawyer was merging a professional life with a personal life. Ambition and aspiration for wealth, prestige, and recognition clouded my judgment . . . Representing Santo and Jimmy was a shortcut to success—too much of a shortcut."[37] He admitted that he "crossed the professional line" when he became intimate friends with his infamous clients. He "gradually began to think like them and to rationalize their aberrant behavior. Their enemies became my enemies; their friends, my friends; their values, my values; their interests, my interests."[38] Ironically, an IRS audit of his tax records was ordered soon after his successful defense of Trafficante in 1986. Ultimately, he was sentenced to a year in prison.

The President's Commission concluded that the reasons for this unethical and illegal activity on the part of mob-connected attorneys includes friendship, drug addiction, greed, and excitement.[39] Remedies for the problem are less clear.

Under forfeiture laws the proceeds of organized crime-related activity may be forfeited to the government. Lawyers argue that if the fees paid to them by organized crime-linked defendants can be forfeited under this provision, attorneys will avoid representing this kind of client.[40] This impacts upon a defendant's right to counsel and due process. If defense attorneys are required to ask their clients about the source of their legal fees, it would set a poor precedent for "high profile" defendants. Should their physicians, accountants, and pastors be required to ask the same question? This does not appear to be workable or desirable.

Finally, there is "no uniform or coordinated procedure" for federal, state, and local jurisdictions to exchange information regarding disciplinary problems with attorneys. Attorneys disciplined in one state, therefore, "are not automatically scrutinized in other states where they may also be licensed to practice."[41] There is also "no formal arrangement" where state bar disciplinary committees are notified of disciplinary actions or convictions against attorneys in federal court within or outside their state.[42] Although the problem appears to be small, the issue of mob-connected lawyers will likely become larger without greater efforts toward apprehension and disciplinary actions against those who violate the law or the rules of professional responsibility.

Summary

As this chapter has shown, there exist a number of defenses that often arise in cases of organized crime. Likewise, there are defenses applicable only in certain situations or for particular types of crimes. There are, of course, other available defenses, but the ones presented here come up most often in organized crime cases. An understanding of how these defenses apply in principle will enable one to anticipate their relevance in actual cases in the future. The issue of "mob-connected" lawyers appears to be small, but greater effort toward detection and disciplinary actions against violating attorneys appears necessary.

Using the legal principles discussed in this chapter, respond to the scenario below. Be sure to indicate how and why the principles you select are appropriate.

The Case of the Informant, Prostitute, and the Heroin Dealer

The FBI employed Helen as an informant to investigate Simpson, a suspected heroin dealer. Helen was a prostitute, heroin user, and a fugitive from Canada. She ultimately became sexually intimate with Simpson and obtained drugs through him, resulting in his arrest.

Questions:

1. Was Simpson entrapped, using the objective formulation of the entrapment defense?

2. Was Simpson entrapped, using the subjective formulation?

References to Chapter 10

[1]   Robert W. Greene, *The Sting Man: Inside Abscam* (New York: Ballantine, 1982).

[2]   *Sorrells v. United States*, 53 S. Ct. 210 (1932).

[3]   at 215.

[4]   *Sherman v. United States*, 78 S. Ct. 819 (1958).

[5]   at 827.

[6]   at 830.

[7]   *United States v. Russell*, 93 S. Ct. 1637 (1973).

[8]   at 1643.

[9]   at 1648.

[10] 18 U.S.C. Sec. 2552(a)(2)(A).

[11] *Jacobson v. United States*, 112 S. Ct. 1535 (1992).

[12] at 1541.

[13] *Paris Adult Theatre I v. Slaton*, 93 S. Ct. 2628 (1973).

14   *Jacobson v. United States*, at 1542.

15   at 1543.

16   *Sorrells v. United States*, at 212; *Sherman v. United States*, at 820.

17   Paul Marcus, "The Entrapment Defense," *Criminal Law Bulletin*, v. 22 (May-June, 1986), pp. 197-243.

18   *United States v. LaFleur*, 971 F.2d 200 (9th Cir. 1991) at 204.

19   at 206.

20   *United States v. Bailey*, 100 S. Ct. 624 (1980).

21   *United States v. Keung*, 761 F. Supp (S.D.N.Y. 1991).

22   *United States v. Jones*, 900 F.2d 512 (2d Cir. 1990) *cert. denied,* 111 S. Ct. 131.

23   *United States v. Keung*, at 255-256.

24   *United States v. Jones* at 519.

25   *United States v. Keung*, at 256.

26   *Reves v. Ernst and Young*, 113 S. Ct. 1163 (1993).

27   *Baumer v. Pachl*, 8 F.3d 1341 (9th Cir. 1993).

28   *Tose v. Greate Bay Hotel and Casino*, 819 F. Supp 1312 (D.N.J. 1993).

29   at 1318, 1320.

30   George E. Dix and M. Michael Sharlot, *Basic Criminal Law: Cases and Materials* Third edition (St. Paul, MN: West Publishing, 1987), p. 213.

31   President's Commission on Organized Crime, *The Impact: Organized Crime Today* (Washington, DC: U.S. Government Printing Office, 1987), p. 221.

32   President's Commission on Organized Crime, *Transcript of Proceedings: Testimony of Martin Light* (Washington, DC: U.S. Government Printing Office, 1986), pp. 74, 40.

33   *The Impact*, pp. 228-229.

34   Frank Ragano and Selwyn Raab, *Mob Lawyer* New York: Charles Scribner's Sons, 1994.

35   Ragano and Raab, *Mob Lawyer*, p. 357.

36   Ibid.

37   Ibid., p. 362.

38   Ibid.

39   *The Impact*, p. 249.

40   *The Impact*, p. 253.

41   Ibid., p. 269.

42   Ibid.

Chapter 11

Sentencing
Organized Crime
Offenders

If there were no bad peo-
ple, there would be no
good lawyers.
Charles Dickens (1840)

Some 20 years ago, an evaluation of the success of the federal effort in combatting organized crime was critical. There was "no agreement on what organized crime is," and, predictably, the government had "not developed a strategy" in fighting organized crime.[1] Similar conclusions were drawn in an evaluation of state and county "rackets bureaus." That report found "no consensus" about the type of criminal activity to be targeted. A "variety of limitations" were found with agency jurisdictions, and training of police and prosecutors was found to be "woefully inadequate."[2] An analysis of gambling prosecutions in 17 cities found "no system of accountability" to guide the prosecution effort.[3]

A follow-up investigation four years later found improvement but underutilization of the law. Only 50 RICO cases had been prosecuted since the earlier evaluation, and "no organized crime organizations" had been eliminated through prosecution.[4]

Since that time, things have changed. A series of significant prosecutions occurred beginning in the mid-1980s and continuing to the present (as outlined in Chapter 5). Existing laws, providing for extended penalties and asset forfeitures, were employed in most cases. This chapter will examine sentences imposed in racketeering and drug trafficking cases, as compared to other federal criminal sentences. The types of racketeering convictions achieved, and the background of those convicted, will be presented. Trends in assets forfeiture as a sentencing mechanism will be assessed.

Sentences Imposed in Racketeering and Drug Cases

The sentences imposed in recent organized crime cases can be evaluated by comparing them with past sentences, and the sentences imposed for other, non-organized crime-related federal offenses. Table 11.1 presents sentences of convicted federal offenders prosecuted by U.S. Attorneys' offices nationwide for cases ending in 1990. These are compared to similar cases closed a decade earlier.[5]

Table 11.1
Sentences Imposed on Convicted Offenders

U.S. Attorneys 1990 Cases	Probation	Prison	5 Years or Less	6 to 10 Years	11 years or More
Racketeering (RICO)	38%	73%	78%	12%	10%
Predicate Offenses	54	61	90	5	4
CCE	11	98	10	23	68
Other Drug Violations	18	91	59	23	17
All Other Offenses	50	45	89	6	5
Organized Crime Cases in 1980*	45 (non-jail)	55	87	13**	—

*These cases are taken from a sample of federal strike force cases terminated from 1977-1980.[6]
** Includes all sentences more than five years in length.

Compiled from: Kenneth Carlson and Peter Finn, *Prosecuting Criminal Enterprises* (Washington, DC: Bureau of Justice Statistics, 1993) and U.S. Comptroller General, *Stronger Federal Effort Needed in Fight Against Organized Crime* (Washington, DC: U.S. General Accounting Office, 1981).

Table 11.1 indicates that prison sentences are very common in all organized crime-related cases. In racketeering (RICO) cases and continuing criminal enterprise (CCE) drug conspiracies, 73 and 98 percent of convicted offenders are incarcerated, respectively. Other drug offenders (non CCE) are incarcerated at a rate of 91 percent. Drug offenses result in incarceration more than twice as often as do other, generic federal felonies. The last row of Table 11.1 compares federal organized crime Strike Force prosecutions from a decade earlier. Interestingly, probation sentences were significantly more common, and prison sentences less frequent than they are in contemporary organized crime cases. The length of sentences to prison has also increased in the last decade. Then, 13 percent of federal organized crime offenders sentenced to five or more years in prison. Now, 22 percent of racketeering offenders and 91 percent of CCE offenders are sentenced to more than five years in prison.

This difference in incarceration rates is due primarily to the extended penalties provided under the RICO and CCE laws. Although these laws were effective in 1970 and 1987, respectively, they were not immediately utilized, due to their complexity. They allow for prosecutions of *ongoing conspiracies*, as well as for individual crimes committed during the course of those conspiracies (i.e., predicate offenses) (see Chapter 9). RICO permits penalties up to 20 years in length, in addition to any sentences for the crimes underlying the racketeering conspiracy. The CCE law has a mandatory *minimum* sentence of 20 years with a maximum of life imprisonment. These statutory changes, together with increasing usage of these laws by prosecutors in more serious cases, has resulted in a significant increase in the incarceration of offenders in organized crime-related cases.

It should also be noted that the incarceration rates of organized crime offenders is higher than that for either "street" criminals or white-collar offenders. A study of white collar offenders found that 60 percent are incarcerated, while two-thirds of conventional criminals who commit crimes of violence or property crimes are incarcerated.[7] In comparison, Table 11.1 shows that 73 percent or more of RICO, CCE, and federal drug law offenders are incarcerated. In addition, 61 percent of those convicted of underlying predicate offenses in organized crime cases are incarcerated. The data also show that organized crime offenders serve longer sentences than any other type of offender, except for those convicted of violent crimes.

Types of Racketeering Convictions

The offenses that underlie a racketeering conspiracy provide an indication of the types of activities now being pursued by organized crime groups. A comparison of these predicate offenses to those of 15 years earlier illustrates how the nature of organized crime activity has changed, at least as it is reflected in criminal prosecutions.

Table 11.2 presents the predicate, or underlying, offenses committed by those convicted of racketeering during a three-year period. It is important to understand that a racketeer must engage in a particular type of illegal activity to support an ongoing criminal enterprise. An understanding of these activities provides clue as to which endeavors may be at "high-risk" of racketeer involvement.

Table 11.2
Predicate Offenses of Racketeering Offenders
(Percent of Convictions)

Predicate Offenses*	1990 Cases**	1975 Cases***
Drug Offenses	24%	9%
Extortion/Loansharking	22	3
Gambling	21	22
Fraud	10	2
Tax law violations	4	7
Embezzlement & Theft	3	3

*The most serious conviction offense, other than the racketeering charge.
**Racketeering offenders convicted 1987-1990 by U.S. Attorney's Offices nationwide.
***All convictions from six federal organized crime strike forces, 1972-1975.

Compiled from: Kenneth Carlson and Peter Finn, *Prosecuting Criminal Enterprises* (Washington, DC: U.S. Bureau of Justice Statistics, 1993) and U.S. Comptroller General, War on Organized Crime Faltering (Washington, DC: U.S. General Accounting Office, 1977).

It can be seen that in 1990, drug offenses, extortion/loansharking, and gambling comprised two-thirds of all racketeering convictions. These vices obviously attract a great deal of attention by organized crime groups and by the criminal justice system. Fraud, tax law violations, and embezzlement/theft cases were the next three most common predicate offenses, even though they accounted for only 17 percent of all racketeering convictions. These three offenses are more closely associated with the infiltration of legitimate business than with the provision of illicit goods and services, and may be more difficult cases to develop.

In contrast, the cases of 15 years earlier are less concentrated on these six offenses. Organized crime-related convictions from that period are scattered over nearly 60 different types of offenses.[8] Nevertheless, the six most common offenses in 1990 are the same as those from 15 years earlier, although in different order and accounting for a smaller proportion of all convictions. The most noticeable changes over this 15-year span is the increased attention to drug cases, and extortionate credit transactions commonly associated with loansharking. Also, an increased number of fraud convictions suggests a focus on the infiltration of business.

If one tallies the percentages presented in Table 11.2, it will be seen that these six offenses accounted for 84 percent of all racketeering convictions in 1990. On the other hand, these six offenses comprised only 39 percent of Organized Crime Strike Force cases 15 years earlier. Other crimes that account for less than three percent of organized crime-related convictions during both time periods include bribery, murder, prostitution, stolen property, among others. This comparison suggests that prosecutions against organized crime have become more focused on a smaller group of offenses in recent years, and that racketeering conspiracies are often developed around the provision of illicit goods and services (accounting for two-thirds of all racketeering convictions in 1990).

The figures presented here may reflect law enforcement and prosecution priorities in making cases, the difficulty in developing infiltration of business cases (given comparatively their lower numbers), or they may provide a true indication of current racketeering conspiracies in the United States. It is likely that each of these possibilities has a degree of merit, depending on the geographic location under consideration and the specific case(s) one highlights.

Backgrounds of Convicted Offenders

The background of those convicted of organized crime-related offenses is quite different from that of street criminals. Table 11.3 presents the backgrounds of offenders convicted in organized crime cases, and compares them to conventional criminal offenders.

Table 11.3
Backgrounds of Convicted Offenders

U.S. Attorneys 1990 Cases	Male	White	Hispanic	Age Under 21	Age 21-30	Age 31+	Incarcerated Before?
Racketeering (RICO)	89%	82%	6%	1%	18%	80%	76%
Predicate Offenses	87	77	5	2	24	74	78
CCE	97	76	19	0	18	82	76
Other Drug Violations	86	74	26	6	41	54	75
All Other Offenses	80	69	13	6	36	58	82
Offenders in State Prison*	95	35	17	12	43	56	61

*These are offenders serving state prison sentences during 1991. More than two-thirds of these offenders were serving time for state drug offenses, burglary, robbery, murder, and sexual assaults.[9]

Compiled from: Kenneth Carlson and Peter Finn, *Prosecuting Criminal Enterprises* (Washington, DC: Bureau of Justice Statistics, 1993) and Allen Beck et al., *Survey of State Prison Inmates* (Washington DC: Bureau of Justice Statistics, 1993).

As Table 11.3 indicates, offenders convicted in federal court of organized crime-related offenses are overwhelming male (90% on average), white (77%), and over 30 years old (72%). These numbers vary somewhat by type of offense, but the backgrounds of these offenders are remarkably consistent.

The only offenses for which there are a significant proportion of offenders in their 20s are federal drug offenders and those convicted of non-organized-crime related federal offenses. The advanced age of some of the organized crime offenders is high-lighted by the fact 53 percent of RICO offenders are over 40 years of age. Forty-two percent of both CCE and predicate offenders are over 40.

When compared to "street" criminals serving time in state prisons, the differences are dramatic. The proportion of male versus female offenders is still overwhelming, but only half as many are white (35 versus 72%). The proportion of offenders under age 21 is four times that in organized crime cases (12 versus an average of three percent in organized crime cases). The proportion of offenders in their 20s and 30s is somewhat higher, although offenders in RICO, predicate offenses, and CCE cases are significantly older than any other group.

Three-quarters of organized crime offenders have been incarcerated before, as compared to 61 percent of conventional criminals. This is probably due to the younger ages of the conventional criminals, who have not had as much elapsed time to break the law.

Another reason for the differences observed in Table 11.3 is that organized crimes often are carried out by career criminals with long-time relationships. Street criminals, on the other hand, most often commit crimes against property or crimes of violence that involve little planning or organization. Their apprehension for these street crimes may well be a function of their age and relative lack of sophistication, at least when it comes to law violation.

Trends in Asset Forfeiture

In addition to longer prison sentences, another trend in sentencing has been forfeiture. The large revenues generated from narcotics trafficking and other organized crime activity can adversely affect the legitimate banking system, as well as the economy in general, through untaxed profits and illicitly funded investments.

Congress enacted two laws that provided the government criminal forfeiture authority. The RICO provisions of the Organized Crime Control Act state that an offender forfeits all interests in an enterprise when convicted for racketeering involvement. The Comprehensive Drug Prevention and Control Act allows for forfeiture of profits derived from a Continuing Criminal Enterprise (CCE) that traffics in narcotics.

Civil forfeitures (i.e., those not requiring a criminal conviction) generally result from actions of the Drug Enforcement Administration (DEA) and U.S. Customs Service. Rather than attempting to seize the profits from illicit enterprises, civil forfeitures are usually directed against contraband (e.g., drugs or guns) and derivative contraband (e.g., vehicles, aircraft used to transport contraband).

Unfortunately, forfeiture laws were not employed very often until recently. Between 1970 and 1980, the RICO and CCE provisions were applied in only 98 drug cases. Assets forfeited amounted to only $2 million. This is a poor record when one considers that more than 5,000 Class I violators (the most serious group) were arrested by the DEA during this period. Furthermore, these statutes were designed to combat the infiltration of organized crime into legitimate business, but a General Accounting Office evaluation found "no forfeiture of significant derivative proceeds or business interests acquired with illicit funds."[10]

The Organized Crime Drug Enforcement Task Force Program (OCDETF) was established in 1983 by the federal government to "identify, investigate, and prosecute high-level members of drug trafficking enterprises and to destroy their operations." The program is comprised on 13 task forces around the country. A National Drug Policy Board, consisting of the directors of 10 federal agencies and department, provides national oversight for the program. The Board reviews national policy and interagency coordination required for OCDETF.

The federal agencies that participate in the task forces include the U.S. Attorney's Offices, DEA, FBI, U.S. Customs Service, ATF, IRS, U.S. Marshals Service, Immigration and Naturalization Service, and the U.S. Coast Guard. State and Local agencies also participate in the program. Nearly 1,800 positions were made available for enforcement personnel for the OCDETF. In its first two years of operation, the OCDETF development more cases than in the previous 20 years.[11]

The OCDETF program seized $52 million in assets in two years in cases involving 1,408 offenders.[12] Through 1990, federal law enforcement agencies had seized $1.4 billion in cash and property.[13] The GAO has concluded that "the traditional law enforcement remedy, incarceration of drug dealers, has not made much of an impact on drug trafficking." Despite years of new laws and enforcement efforts, the drug problem continues. The GAO admits that the potential effectiveness of forfeiture "in combatting the domestic drug problem cannot be projected with any degree of precision," because more experience in the application of the forfeiture laws is needed.[14] Nevertheless, greater use of forfeiture offers the opportunity to disrupt continuing illicit enterprises and to curtail the effect of large amounts of illicitly obtained cash on the economy.

During the last 10 years, there has been a growing body of case law and policy regarding the seizure and disposition of property in assets forfeiture cases. These concerns generally fall into one of three categories:

1.   The lawfulness of the assets seizure,

2.   Protecting the rights of third parties, and

3.   The management and disposition of seized assets.

Lawfulness of Asset Seizure

The legal principle behind forfeiture is that the government may take property without compensation to the owner, if the property is acquired or used illegally. There are two methods of accomplishing this: civil and criminal.

In a criminal forfeiture, property can only be seized once the owner has been convicted of certain crimes (such as RICO). The forfeiture action in these cases is part of the criminal trial. Civil forfeiture occurs independent of any criminal proceeding, and it is directed at the property itself, having been used or acquired illegally. The conviction of the property owner is not relevant in a civil forfeiture. In addition, there is a form of civil forfeiture called "administrative" forfeitures. In these cases, the seizing agency mails notices to all people known to have any ownership interest in the property, and a notice is also placed in the newspapers. If no one claims the property within 20 days, it is forfeited without court action.[15] This administrative procedure was designed to reduce the extent of processing and costs incurred if all seizures went through the courts. Civil forfeitures have been defended as an aid to law enforcement, because it takes illegal property from those who purchased or owned it unlawfully, it may serve as a deterrent to criminal behavior, and it compensates the government for the cost of enforcing the law.[16]

The procedure for a civil forfeiture is different from other civil actions in that many forfeiture laws require only that the government show *probable cause* that the property was implicated in criminal activity. The burden then shifts to the property owner, who must establish by a preponderance of the evidence that the law was not violated, probable cause does not exist, or he or she has an affirmative defense.[17] The determination of probable cause is made by considering the "totality of circumstances" involved.[18] Certain types of circumstantial evidence can be used in evaluating these circumstances: "close proximity" between the asset and drugs, concealment efforts, extensive cash expenditures, and net worth analysis, are examples.[19]

All "proceeds" of crime are subject to forfeiture, which has been interpreted to include interest, dividends, income, and real property. In North Carolina, for example, drug traffickers used their illicit profits to buy property in the state. Later, they sold the property and bought other property in Florida. The government was able to obtain the Florida property as "derivative proceeds." It was also able to keep any appreciation earned on the investment.[20]

Protecting the Rights of Third Parties

A problem arises concerning the rights of individuals not involved in criminal activity, but whose property was used, or derived from, the criminal activity of others. This might include lienholders, uninformed purchasers, joint tenants, or business partners.

A person who suspects his or her property is the target of a criminal or civil forfeiture investigation may sell the property, give ownership to family members, or otherwise dispose of it. The rule known as the "relation-back doctrine" holds that the forfeiture occurs at the time the illegal act was committed. Therefore, subsequent transfers to third parties is not dispositive in forfeiture proceedings.[21]

Third party claims on seized property are delayed in criminal forfeitures because the claim cannot be litigated until the end of the criminal trial. As a result, third party claims may not be heard until several years after the property is taken. The procedure is quicker in civil forfeitures, because the forfeiture hearing usually occurs very soon after the forfeiture, usually within days. In criminal forfeitures, it is more difficult to make a successful third party claim. A purchaser of an illegally used piece of property, for example, must have been "reasonably without knowledge" of any illegality. This has caused problems for defense attorneys whose fees may be subject to forfeiture, "since an attorney virtually always has reason to know that fees paid by an alleged narcotics dealer are proceeds of crime."[22] The U.S. Supreme Court has upheld pretrial freezing of a defendant's assets, even where the defendant seeks to use the assets to pay his or her attorney.[23] In subsequent cases, however, the Court has held the owner of property must be notified before the property is seized and given some chance to challenge the seizure before it takes place.[24]

In civil forfeitures, third parties are protected under the "innocent owner" exception *if* they can establish they lacked "knowledge, consent, or willful blindness" regarding the illegal usage of the property.[25] This is a difficult burden to meet, because the third party must prove a negative (the absence of guilty knowledge) by a preponderance of the evidence.[26]

After John Gotti's racketeering conviction, for example, the federal government filed a civil forfeiture suit aimed at seizing seven buildings and three businesses it contends were used to conduct illegal gambling and racketeering operations. A Hunt and Fish club, a bar, a restaurant, a garment manufacturer, the Ravenite Social Club, and other properties were targeted.[27] It is the task of the owners of these properties to demonstrate by a preponderance of the evidence that they lacked knowledge, consent, or willful blindness in how their property was used.

Disposition of Seized Assets

The most commonly seized assets are cash and cars, followed by boats, planes, jewelry, and weapons. These items comprise 95 percent of all seized assets, although less commonly confiscated residential and commercial property has a higher monetary value.[28] Once an asset is seized, it must be appraised. This appraisal determines the property's value, less any liens against it. The item must be stored and maintained while ownership and third party claims are heard in court. If the challenge to the seizure is not effective, the property is taken for government use or auctioned. Notices of these sales, and lists of forfeited property, are published in the newspaper *USA Today* each month.

Storage and maintenance can be both profitable and costly. Cash seizures are kept in interest-bearing accounts. An arrangement in Fort Lauderdale allows the bank to count and simultaneously photograph every bill before depositing it in the law enforcement agency's account.[29] Cars, boats, and planes must be stored so that they are preserved and do not suffer damage. Storage of these things can be costly, as can maintenance of real property, and disposal can be difficult to arrange.[30]

Due to the administrative issues posed by the management and disposition of seized property, the U.S. Marshal's Service has more than 200 full-time and part-time employees assigned to handling assets seized by federal agencies. The U.S. Customs Service has more than 100 full-time paralegals to handle seized property.[31] Occasionally, there is property that is difficult to dispose. In Broward County, Florida a load of maple wood had been surrounded by a load of hashish. They considered donating the wood, or giving it away, because they could not justify returning it to the owner. They eventually destroyed it.[32]

Summary

This chapter presents a review of the problems posed by unsuccessful organized crime prosecutions in the past. In recent years, a significant effort has been made through legislation, law enforcement, and prosecution initiatives, to target organized crime operations more successfully. This effort has produced profound results. Prison sentences in organized crime cases now occur more often, and are longer in duration, than for virtually any other kind of crime. In the long term, however, the use of assets forfeiture may do more to destroy ongoing criminal enterprises than will the incarceration of its current members.

Read the scenario below and answer the questions that follow, applying principles from this chapter.

The Case of a Close Family Friend

You decide to go away to college, but you don't know what to do with your 1995 Camaro. It won't fit in your family's garage, you are afraid to leave it parked on the street, and you can't bring yourself to sell it.

A close family friend, Elvis, offers a solution. He offers to care for the car and keep it in his garage, in exchange for you allowing him to drive it while you are away at college. When you come home for vacations and summers, the car will be yours. It sounds like the only possible solution, and you only hope your friend treats your car gently.

After you are away to school for a month, you receive notification that your Camaro has been seized by the U.S. government. Elvis has been charged with using your car to transport illegal narcotics.

Questions:

1. What is the standard by which the judge should make his decision?

2. What reason does the judge have to believe you innocently loaned your car to a close family friend?

3. How would this case be different if you were a car rental agency, and merely rented a car to Elvis from which he was caught transporting drugs?

References to Chapter 11

[1]   U.S. Comptroller General, *War on Organized Crime Faltering: Federal Strike Forces Not Getting the Job Done* (Washington, DC: U.S. General Accounting Office, 1977).

[2]   G. Robert Blakey, Ronald Goldstock, and Charles H. Rogovin, *Rackets Bureaus: Investigation and Prosecution of Organized Crime* (Washington, DC: U.S. Government Printing Office, 1978).

[3]   Floyd J. Fowler, Thomas W. Mangione, and Frederick E. Pratter, *Gambling Law Enforcement in Major American Cities* (Washington, DC: U.S. Government Printing Office, 1978).

4   U.S. Comptroller General, *Stronger Federal Effort Needed in Fight Against Organized Crime* (Washington, DC: U.S. General Accounting Office, 1981).

5   The old cases were a sample of 271 taken from four federal strike force offices (Chicago, Los Angeles, New York, Philadelphia) and include cases disposed of from 1977-1980.

6   U.S. Comptroller General, *Stronger Federal Effort Needed Against Organized Crime* (Washington, DC: U.S. General Accounting Office, 1981).

7   Don Manson, *Tracking Offenders: White-Collar Crime* (Washington, DC: Bureau of Justice Statistics, 1986).

8   *War on Organized Crime Faltering*, pp. 38-39.

9   Allen Beck et al., *Survey of State Prison Inmates, 1991* (Washington, DC: Bureau of Justice Statistics, 1993).

10   U.S. Comptroller General, *Assets Forfeiture—A Seldom Used Tool in Combatting Drug Trafficking* (Washington, DC: U.S. General Accounting Office, 1981), p. 11.

11   U.S. Comptroller General, *Drug Investigations: Organized Crime Drug Enforcement Task Force Program's Accomplishments* (Washington, DC: U.S. General Accounting Office, 1987).

12   Ibid., p. 9.

13   U.S. Comptroller General, *Asset Forfeiture: Need for Stronger Marshals Service Oversight of Commercial Real Property* (Washington, DC: U.S. General Accounting Office, 1991), p. 3.

14   Ibid., p. 15.

15   Executive Office for Asset Forfeiture, *Federal Forfeiture of the Instruments and Proceeds of Crime: The Program in a Nutshell* (Washington, DC: U.S. Department of Justice, 1990), p. 4.

16   *United States v. One Tintoretto Painting*, 692 F.2d 603 (2d Cir. 1982).

17   George N. Aylesworth, *Forfeiture of Real Property: An Overview* (Washington, DC: Bureau of Justice Assistance, 1991), p. 8; *United States v. $250,000 in Currency*, 808 F.2d 897 (1st Cir. 1987).

18   *United States v. Thomas*, 913 F.2d 1111 (4th Cir. 1990).

19   Michael Goldsmith, *Civil Forfeiture: Tracing the Proceeds of Narcotics Trafficking* (Washington, DC: Bureau of Justice Assistance, 1992), p. 20.

20   *United States v. One Parcel of Real Estate*, 675 F. Supp 645 (D.Fla. 1987).

21   Michael Goldsmith and William Lenck, *Protection of Third-Party Rights* (Washington, DC: Bureau of Justice Assistance, 1990), p. 8.

22   *Protection of Third-Party Rights*, p. 28.

23   *United States v. Monsanto*, 109 S. Ct. 2657 (1989).

24   Tony Mauro, "High Court Says Suspect Must Be Warned of Seizure," *USA Today*, (December 14, 1993), p. 1.

25   21 U.S.C. 881(a)(4)(C), effective 1988.

26   *United States v. A Single Family Residence*, 803 F.2d 628 (11th Cir. 1986).

27   Joseph P. Fried, "Government Sues to Seize Gotti's Ill-Gotten Assets," *The New York Times*, (January 15, 1993), p. B1.

28   G. Patrick Gallagher, *The Management and Disposition of Seized Assets* (Washington, DC: Bureau of Justice Assistance, 1988), p. 2.

29   Ibid., p. 4.

30   U.S. Comptroller General, *Asset Forfeiture: Need for Stronger Marshal's Service Oversight of Commercial Real Property* (Washington, DC: U.S. General Accounting Office, 1991); U.S. Comptroller General, *Asset Forfeiture: Noncash Property Should Be Consolidated under the Marshals Service* (Washington, DC: U.S. General Accounting Office, 1991); U.S. Comptroller General, *Asset Forfeiture: Customs Reports Over Sales of Forfeited Property* (Washington, DC: U.S. General Accounting Office, 1991).

31   Ibid., p. 6.

32   Ibid., p. 8.

Chapter 12

The Future of Organized Crime

> Crime is a logical exten-
> sion of the sort of behav-
> ior that is often considered
> perfectly respectable in
> legitimate business.
>
> Robert Rice (1956)

Organized crime is a fascinating form of criminal behavior in the way it is able to adapt to changes in public demand, legal regulation, prosecution success, and new criminal opportunities. Given the massive prosecution effort in recent years in the United States, Italy, and other countries, the question remains, "If organized crime won't go away, how can we combat its most serious manifestations with the criminal justice system, while also working toward prevention strategies for the long term?"

Ten Challenges

This chapter presents 10 challenges to the control and prevention of organized crime that we have either yet to face, or that we have yet to face successfully. These 10 challenges are of two types:

1. What can governments do better to *control* organized crime through a criminal justice response?, and

2. What longer-term *prevention* strategies can be developed outside the criminal justice system that will reduce the inci-dence of organized crime in the future?

Satisfactory responses to these 10 challenges lie at the foundation of a more successful and longer-term approach to the problem of organized crime.

The Criminal Justice Response

A response to organized crime that is both swift and certain occurs only when such investigations and prosecutions receive a high national priority and adequate resources for the task. This has been the case over the last decade, and the results have been impressive (as noted in Chapter 5). Organized crime is not a static phenomenon, however, and it will change in nature, form, and technique in response to the government's recent success, as it has in the past to other obstacles. Five challenges for the future are paramount: internationalization, the immigration problem, political corruption, law enforcement cooperation, and imagination in sentencing.

Internationalization

Drug trafficking in the late twentieth century will be remembered as the primary catalyst in the internationalization of organized crime. Worldwide demand for illicit drugs, combined with poor source countries looking for a new cash crop, enabling technology (e.g., widely available telecommunications capabilities and accessible air travel), and political changes around the world that made international travel possible almost everywhere, came together to create a profitable opportunity for organized crime interests.

In the past, traditional organized crime has had links with Italy, but these have been sporadic. Further, there has never been evidence to suggest that American "mafias" controlled what occurred in Sicily, or vice versa. The Pizza Connection trial, described in Chapter 5, demonstrated for the first time a true Sicilian-American linkage in the heroin market, a linkage that included South American and Asian nations as well.

Organized crime groups around the world have entered into these "marriages of convenience" because of the huge profits to be made, and the need to transport narcotics from source countries, refine it into consumable form, and then distribute it around the world. This is a task simply too large for a single group to handle by itself. Hence, organized crime groups in different parts of the world now communicate with each other, a significant departure from the problem of "local crime groups" which characterized virtually all organized crime not long ago.

Two scenarios are likely to emerge in the future: international agreements and policies will be necessary to combat international organized crime more effectively, and organized crime groups will take measures to reduce their dependence on foreign groups. International agreements have already begun to emerge. The FBI opened an office in Moscow in 1994 in an effort to pool intelligence about alleged Russian-American organized crime links.[1] A new police intelligence agency, called "Europol," was also established in 1994 to focus on drug trafficking and money laundering among western European nations.[2] The United Nations has worked with 14 nations on a draft of "U.N. Guidelines on Organized Crime Control."[3] These guidelines are designed to facilitate international cooperation and also to share technology, so that nations are on equal footing in law enforcement technology and legal tools to combat money laundering, drug trafficking, and other abuses of international concern.

Second, organized crime groups are likely to make changes in their operations to remain successful. As Mary McIntosh has pointed out, criminal organizations respond to "given opportunities for crime" and to "given techniques of crime prevention and law enforcement."[4] She argues that criminal groups must become increasingly sophisticated in order to maintain acceptable levels of success. This seems to be occurring in the case of contemporary organized crime. In response to the decline in the export of chemicals needed to manufacture illegal drugs, for example, domestic laboratories have been set up to produce the drugs within the United States. Laboratories can produce synthetic drugs, such as methamphetamine and PCP, as well as combine coca leaves with solvents to produce cocaine. According to one estimate, "Illegal domestic laboratories are now capable of producing enough illicit drugs to satisfy U.S. consumers' demand."[5] The Chemical Diversion and Trafficking Act established federal recordkeeping, reporting, and transaction requirements for essential chemicals, but only 18 states have enacted similar legislation to track chemicals, and they vary widely in the number and types of chemicals covered and in drug tracking requirements.[6] The same variation exists at the international level.[7] It is important that law enforcement officials are aware of trends like these, and that legislation and enforcement regarding the availability and tracking of the chemicals themselves are responsive to changes in the criminal marketplace.

The Immigration Problem

There are many legislative and policy controls on immigration to the United States, but the fact of the matter is that the United States is a geographically large nation, and it may be impossible to completely protect its borders from unwanted immigration, as has been the problem with drug importation and interdiction.[8] This does not mean, however, that significant improvements cannot be made in the current system.

Perhaps the most pernicious role that organized crime plays in the immigration problem is alien smuggling. Groups from Latin America and China appear to be the most involved in this effort (as described in Chapter 7). The Chinese are highly organized and police estimate there are more than two dozen smuggling rings in New York City alone.[9] Most often the aliens are smuggled by boat and must pay fees of up to $30,000 for their passage. Sometimes they are dropped off in Canada or Mexico and then smuggled across the borders by land. The exorbitant passage fee makes them slaves to their transporters, once they reach the United States. The aliens cannot work at any normal job, because they are illegal aliens. As a result, they are exploited by unscrupulous employers, or become active in prostitution, the drug trade, or other parts of the illegal economy.

Therefore, the problem lies not only with the criminal groups arranging these passages, but also in their passengers, many of whom end up as part of the crime problem in the United States, either as victims or offenders. Authorities concede they may interdict only five percent of the vessels carrying illegal immigrants.[10] Given the size of our borders, this is unlikely ever to become an effective enforcement strategy. What is needed is a better effort on the other end of the operation in China and Latin America. There must be a concerted effort to stop these smugglers *before* they set sail to the United States. This will entail pressure from the United States, as well as better cooperation between Chinese and U.S. law enforcement authorities. With the merging of Hong Kong and mainland China in 1997, a good opportunity to forge such cooperative ties has presented itself with a unified China.

In Colombia, legislation has been passed to increase the benefits to drug traffickers and other criminals who become informants for the government.[11] Periodic crackdowns on smuggling of contraband (mostly drugs) between Lebanon and Syria and also between Pakistan and Afghanistan must be advocated and offered international incentives to maintain.[12] Similar efforts in other countries, with strong encouragement and technical assistance of the United States and other nations, can make a substantial difference in international smuggling of people and contraband.

Political Corruption

Corruption of government officials is not as common in the United States as it once was, but it still exists. In many other countries, the problem is massive. According to the National Strategy Information Center, "We are confronted with a world with increasingly weak states and governments."[13]

In the United States, for example, it is uncommon for organized crime to physically attack or kill a police officer or other government official. In Italy, Colombia, and other nations with organized crime problems, such attacks are common. Why? It is because organized crime figures in the United States know that an attack on a government official will exact the wrath of a very powerful government that will not stop until it finds the perpetrator. In many other countries this is not the case. Governments are weak, corrupt, police forces are untrained and unprofessional, and retribution for strikes against the government are uncertain and often unsuccessful.

Keep in mind the lessons of history. During the "gangster" era in the United States, during the 1920s and 1930s, most law enforcement officials were untrained, unprofessional, and easily corrupted. The same was true for local government officials. Eliot Ness and the "Untouchables" were so named because they could not be corrupted, something that was unusual at that time. The situation has changed dramatically in the United States since then, corresponding with police training, education, good salaries, and a general professionalization of law enforcement. This has served to promote loyalty to the profession and reduced the extent of corruption.

Instances of political corruption, and the suggestions of the influence of organized crime, emerge less often, although they have not disappeared. A newspaper investigation, for example, found that New York State paid $184 million in state contracts to firms that have been linked to organized crime.[14]

Nevertheless, corruption continues to occur on a broad scale overseas. The role that the United States and western European nations can play is one of international pressure, enforcement role model, and technical assistance. As noted earlier, the U.S. has opened an FBI office in Moscow to help in the fight of international organized crime, but it has a second, longer-term, role to play. That is, technical assistance (in law enforcement methods) and role models (for professional investigators) show how law enforcement tasks can be carried out with proficiency. In a nation overrun with corruption and black market profiteering, the presence of the FBI should help Russian police remain diligent and dedicated to their task.

Such subtle pressure can work in the other direction as well. In 1994, for example, the United States stopped sharing evidence it had on Colombian drug dealers with Colombia because it believed the prosecutor general intended a "lenient prosecution of cartel members."[15] Colombian police responded in 1995 with the arrest of two leaders of the Cali cartel, brothers Miguel and Gilberto Rodriguez.

In Italy, it took the assassinations of two leading judges, Giovanni Falcone and Paolo Borsellino, to move the Italian Parliament to finally pass laws enabling police to use undercover "sting" operations and wiretaps. Even so, the politicians there made these investigative tools unavailable in cases involving political offenses of most kinds.[16] It remains to be seen whether Italy's law enforcement agencies can become more effective and obtain the respect of organized crime groups operating there.

Law Enforcement Cooperation

Virtually every evaluation of the organized crime control effort in the United States or abroad has cited the lack of interagency cooperation as a fundamental stumbling block to more effective enforcement. In addition, law enforcement must cooperate with the law itself, if confidence in their work is to be maintained.

There is much evidence to suggest that law enforcement agencies are cooperating better than ever before. The new Europol agency in western Europe, described above, is an example, as is the cooperation between Italian and American law enforcement agencies in drug trafficking cases in recent years.[17] Operation "Green Ice" ended with 201 arrests in five countries in an international cocaine ring operating between Italy and Colombia.[18] Operation "Dinero" resulted in the seizure of nine tons of cocaine in Canada and the United States, $52 million in cash, and the arrest of 88 people. The investigation involved British, Spanish, Italian, and American law enforcement agencies.[19] In another case, more than 800 pounds of heroin, valued at $1 billion was seized, and 17 people arrested in New York, Buffalo, Detroit, Canada, and Hong Kong. The group, allegedly led by Fok Leung Woo, apparently smuggled the heroin into the United States in hollow cart tires.[20] Nevertheless, the United States is a nation of small police departments, nearly 20,000 of them. More must be done in standardizing police training, salaries, and the establishment of lateral entry for better career mobility. Moves like these will further professionalize law enforcement and make interagency communication and cooperation more common.

On the other hand, issues of unprofessional and corrupt behavior continue to surface. Some police departments have used asset forfeiture, for example, to equip their departments with cars and equipment. The issue that arises is a conflict of interest when police directly benefit from their own decisions.[21] This provides temptation for self-serving behavior. As explained in Chapter 11, a showing of probable cause is all that is needed to seize property in civil forfeitures. Guidelines for these seizures are needed to remove the incidence or appearance of unprofessional behavior.

Corruption among police in organized crime cases is extremely serious because it feeds public fears regarding the potential misuse of investigation and prosecution tools. Scandals in Ohio, Connecticut, Missouri, and other locations, have found police using wiretaps illegally.[22] These invasions of privacy re-kindle controversy regarding the intrusive nature of electronic surveillance. They also serve to mobilize public opposition against these and future law enforcement tools designed for the public welfare. Leaks by police, or other government officials, to organized crime figures also do much to harm public confidence in the effort against organized crime. In San Jose, California, a judge was convicted of leaking wiretap information to an organized crime figure, and lying about it to the FBI. He was sentenced to six months in jail, and faces impeachment as a judge, and disbarment as an attorney.[23] A New York City Police detective was indicted for leaking secrets to John Gotti. It was alleged that Gotti learned the addresses of jurors in his trial from the detective.[24] In New Jersey, a police detective is believed to have blown an ongoing undercover operation of the Lucchese crime group by tipping off one of the suspects.[25] In a more pernicious manner, 11 current and former inspectors in the New York City Sanitation Department were indicted for extortion. They were charged with taking payoffs for "promising to overlook violations or threatening to harass shopkeepers and vendors with summonses for nonexistent infractions.[26] Cases like these make front-page news, damage the reputation of all law enforcement, reduce public confidence in the police, and work against citizen cooperation with police in the future.

Imagination in Sentencing

For too long, "fines, probation, and incarceration" were the only penalties considered in criminal cases, including those involving organized crime. More imagination in recent years has helped break this mold, and other innovations are limited only by an unwillingness to try new ideas.

The most innovative method to defeat organized crime groups in the last decade has been asset forfeiture. As career criminals have long held, incarceration is viewed as a cost of being in the profession of crime. Being locked up for a few years is seen as an undesirable, but necessary, part of the job.[27] Extending prison sentences under the racketeering and drug laws have raised the stakes, and certainly these changes have elicited the new breed of "underworld informant." Nevertheless, asset forfeiture makes it possible to seize the proceeds of crime, leaving the jailed offender with nothing to return to upon release. Forfeitures reduce the probability that a criminal enterprise can continue operating while a leader is in jail, and they also make it difficult to resume that enterprise after serving the sentence. For example, the *Kenmore Hotel* in New York City was the subject of a forfeiture in 1994, when the government established it had become a "supermarket" for drug users and dealers.[28] Similar to the problem of crackhouses, discussed in Chapter 2, asset forfeiture can cripple a criminal enterprise by confiscating its headquarters. Re-establishing such a base for criminal operations is an expensive proposition.

Other variations of asset forfeiture have occurred with mixed results. Forfeiture of foreign assets in the United States for violation of foreign drugs occurred for the first time in the 1990s, demonstrating America's willingness to support enforcement efforts within other nations.[29] The "zero-tolerance" program of the 1980s was dropped because it produced absurd results.[30] For example, the seizure of a marijuana cigarette on a boat was used as a rationale to seize the entire boat. This betrays common sense, and provoked a public outcry against the policy. It is important that penalties remain strongly linked to common sense notions of proportionality. Otherwise, public support in the effort against organized crime rapidly turns into opposition.

So-called "electronic bracelets" have been used on organized crime offenders not involved in violent crimes. This permits 24-hour monitoring of one's movements electronically without the expense of incarceration. Although there have been a few problems in managing these monitoring programs, so far only one offender has managed to shed his bracelet without detection.[31] This technology may be the middle ground between probation and prison that people have been looking for.

Perhaps the most interesting strategy to emerge in recent years has been direct government intervention in organized crime-controlled businesses. This has occurred most prominently in the case of the Teamster's Union and the Laborers International Union of North America. In these cases, the government obtained the authority to appoint trustees to run the unions, investigate and remove corrupt union officers, review union finances, and supervise union elections.[32] This authority resulted from a showing that these unions have been unable to operate within the bounds of the law. Criminal prosecutions against a series of Teamster presidents, including Jimmy Hoffa, resulted in the convictions of those leaders, but no change in how the union was run.[33] Court-approved agreements between the government and the unions establishing trustee control is an innovative way to deal with entrenched organized crime influence in a business. Its long-term effect remains to be seen, but it shows a willingness on the part of the government to recognize that past prosecutions have not accomplished their objective and that new methods are called for.

A similar effort is underway in New York City where management and inspection of the Fulton Fish Market, the largest wholesale seafood distrbution center in the nation, has been taken over by the City government. The City hired new managers and inspectors to rid the market of the influence of organized crime.[34] The problems at the market included vendor leases with the City that had not changed in amount for 12 years, evicting those who failed to pay rent, curbing the influence of the Genovese crime group which allegedly has "no-show" jobs at the market, and regulating the seafood "unloaders" who indirectly control market operations and priorities.[35] In still another case of this kind, 10 leaders of Local 2 of the Plumbers Union in New York were barred from participating in any union business while the judge considered a prosecution motion to appoint a trustee to oversee the union.[36] These direct interventions in organized crime-influenced businesses are a creative way to deal with the entrenched presence of organized crime in certain settings.

Long-Term Prevention

Having considered actions the criminal justice system can take to control organized crime more effectively, it is important to recognize initiatives that do not involve the criminal justice system, but that can contribute to the reduction in the incidence of organized crime over the long-term. These include: infiltration of legitimate business, why the vices won't go away, the problem of increasing violence, citizen intolerance, and the ethics of organized crime.

Infiltration of Legitimate Business

It can be argued that the infiltration of business is the most serious form of organized crime. It directly impacts the legitimate economy, it often involves extortion, and it usually involves an unwilling victim. These characteristics distinguish it from the probvision of illicit goods and services.

There are two ways that organized crime infiltrates business: skims and scams. The differences between the two methods are presented in Table 12.1.

Table 12.1
Typology of Infiltration of Legitimate Business

Type of Infiltration	Nature of Activity	Harm
Scam	Using a legitimate business primarily as a "front" for illegal activity (e.g., pizza parlors to launder drug money).	• To government in tax evasion. • To other businesses in non-competitive practices. • Use of coercion and/or co-optation.
Corruption (or "skim")	"Bleeding" a legitimate business of its profits through illegal means (e.g., no-show jobs, creative bookkeeping).	• Legitimate profits siphoned. • Business can be bankrupted. • Use of coercion and/or co-optation.

As Table 12.1 indicates, the infiltration of legitimate business generally occurs in one of two ways: (1) using a legitimate business as a "front" for primarily illegal activity (*a scam*), or (2) "Bleeding" a legitimate business of some of its profits through illegal means without the use of force and (hopefully) without causing it to fail (*corruption or skimming*).

A scam often involves a quiet change in ownership or management of a business, where a large bank deposit is used to establish a credit rating. Large orders are placed, goods are received and quickly liquidated, the management disappears, and the company is forced into bankruptcy by its competitors.[37]

In the "Pizza Connection" case, pizza parlors were used as a front for illegal activity. Morphine was smuggled from Turkey to Sicily, where it was processed into heroin. Then, the heroin was smuggled through U.S. airports and distributed through pizza parlors in the northeast and midwest. Finally, illegal profits in excess of $40 million were funneled back to Sicily in a money laundering scheme that involved banks in the Bahamas, Bermuda, New York, and Switzerland. This case illustrates how linkage is established between legitimate businesses (i.e., pizza parlors and banks) and their knowing misuse to engage in illegal acts (i.e., distribute heroin and accept and transfer large sums of cash in small denominations with no questions asked).[38]

In many cases of infiltration, the purpose is not to steal from the business until it is bankrupt. Instead, it makes more sense to misuse the business in way that it can provide a steady source of illegal income without endangering its survival, i.e., using the golden goose without killing it.

A massive investigation of corruption and racketeering in the New York City construction industry found that control of construction unions was the "base of power and influence in the industry" by organized crime, together with direct interests in contracting and construction supply companies. This hidden interest in construction companies was accomplished by using outsiders who "front" for the company on public records for purposes of certificates of incorporation, accounting, licensing, and permits.[39] The report found that Anthony Salerno, later convicted as "boss" of the Genovese crime family in New York City, controlled *Certified*, one of the two major concrete suppliers in Manhattan.[40] Paul Castellano, boss of the Gambino crime family until his murder in 1985, controlled Scara-Mix Concrete Company, which was owned by his son.[41]

In other cases, it was discovered that known organized crime figures were openly listed as owners, managers, or principals of construction companies. Salvatore Gravano, counselor to John Gotti, was president of JJS Construction Company. John Gotti, Jr. is President of Sampson Trucking Company, and John Gotti, convicted boss of the Gambino crime family (and for murder of Paul Castellano) held the position of salesman for ARC Plumbing Company.[42] Even though these individuals were sometimes found to have very little to do with the business that employed them, such an "on the books" profession "provides a legitimate position in the community and a reportable source of income."[43]

The ability of organized crime interests to infiltrate the construction industry in New York City was promoted by several factors. Unlike most industries, the employment of a construction worker lies in the hands of the union, rather than the employer. In the construction marketplace itself there are "a large number" of contractors and subcontractors, with many "small firms" among them, all locked in intense competition. This makes legitimate businesses "vulnerable to extortion." Racketeers can coerce payoffs by threatening loss of labor, loss of supplies, delays, or property damage.[44] Likewise, businesses can be easily corrupted when given competitive advantages by powerful racketeering elements, such as sweetheart contracts (to avoid some union requirements) and cartels that allocate contracts among favored firms.[45]

A case study of the garbage (solid waste) collection business in New York City and in an unnamed northeastern state found the market to be dominated by small partnerships or family corporations. The garbage collection business "has a longstanding reputation for anti-competitive practices and racketeer involvement."[46] The investigators discovered there are "mutual benefits derived by entrepreneurs and criminals in the operation of cartel arrangements" where independent businesses are organized into a "cartel" that prevents open and fair competition in the marketplace.[47] As a result, the role of the infiltrating racketeers centers around disputes about "customer allocation agreements" in dividing up the garbage collection market. Corruption characterizes the role of organized crime in this instance, more than does extortion. Indeed, "policies which assume that the racketeers are parasites on unwilling hosts, and that the legitimate entrepreneurs would welcome a clean-up of the industry, are doomed to failure."[48]

This combination of corruption, co-optation, and extortion can be used to develop a model of factors predictive of high-risk businesses for organized crime infiltration. If the conditions that give rise to the infiltration of organized crime into legitimate businesses could be predicted, law enforcement agencies could realize major benefits:

1. Resources would not be wasted on fruitless investigations,

2. Personnel could be allocated more rationally according to which industries are predicted to be especially vulnerable, and

3. Long-range interests of the community would be served through a concentration on serious manifestations of organized crime.

A prediction model for the infiltration of legitimate business has been proposed and subjected to a partial empirical test.[49] The six-factor model is presented in Table 12.2.

Table 12.2
Predicting Organized Crime Infiltration Into Legitimate Business

Predictors	**Low Risk**	**High Risk**
Supply	Few available small, financially weak businesses	Readily available small, financially weak businesses
Customers	Elastic demand for product	Inelastic demand for product
Regulators	Difficult to enter market	Easy to enter market
Competitors	Monopoly/oligopoly controlled market	Open market with many small firms
Patronage	Entrepreneurs are professional, educated managers	Entrepreneurs are non-professionals ill-equipped to deal with business problems
Prior record	No prior history of organized crime involvement in market	Prior history of organized crime infiltration in industry

The six factors are taken from prior studies of organized crime markets and criminological prediction studies. Application of this model to 167 organized crime cases found businesses not related to adult entertainment or labor union activity, and cases involving no violent crimes were the best predictors of infiltration, accounting for almost half the cases in the sample. Nevertheless, there were numerous limitations to the sample of cases used in this study.[50] Of the 22 independent variables examined, however, it is remarkable that *type of organized crime group* involved (Cosa Nostra, local syndicate, etc.) was *not* a significant predictor. This suggests that the focus on organized crime *groups* in the existing literature could be misplaced,[51] and might be replaced by an emphasis on the *activities* carried out for these appear to be much better predictors of organized crime.

How a model like this might be used in practice can be illustrated using an actual case study. In the investigation of the solid waste collection industry in the New York City area it was easy for individuals to enter the market (little regulation), the industry was populated by numerous "small, frequently family-based, enterprises," with little difference in service among vendors (open competition in a market of non-professional managers), there was inelastic demand for the service (customers always available), and many firms were identified with "minimal capital and no reserve equipment" (supply for illicit patrons). This illustrates how a local market can be analyzed in assessing its risk potential for infiltration.

An analog to this procedure has already been attempted in case screening techniques developed for use by police. The Rochester, N.Y. Police Department developed a system called "Early Case Closure" where information was gathered to assess the "solvability" of robberies and burglaries. By directing their resources toward crimes with the best chance of solution (and by spending *less* time on cases with little chance of solution), the department was able to significantly improve its clearance rates for those crimes.[52] A similar effort was undertaken by the Stanford Research Institute and Police Executive Research Forum. They developed a model for screening burglary cases, based on factors associated with the crime. Applying the system retrospectively, they were able to predict whether a burglary case would be solved 85 percent of the time.[53] In a similar way, law enforcement officials can reduce the amount of time spent on dead-end organized crime investigations, that invariably occur in proactive police work, with the use of a prediction model like the one proposed here. A law enforcement agency could use such a model as a screening device in its jurisdiction. Investigative resources could be focused on those markets identified as "high-risk" for infiltration, and perhaps less time would be wasted on investigations that do not lead to prosecution.

Why the Vices Won't Go Away

It has been suggested by some influential Americans that the decriminalization of certain consensual behaviors would seriously reduce organized crime activity, if it was properly designed. The consensual behaviors under discussion are gambling, prostitution, and drugs.

As many investigators have noted (see Chapter 4), there is often an arbitrary distinction between legal and illegal gambling. It is legal to play the state's numbers game (the lottery) or bet at the state's racetrack, but it is illegal to place a bet with your local bookmaker. As the director of the Chicago Crime Commission stated in 1932, "Just why . . . the law discriminates between betting at the race tracks and betting in places away from the race tracks is difficult to understand . . . It presents a situation entirely unreasonable and altogether hypocritical."[54] If state-sponsored gambling was designed to better compete with illegal games, would illicit gambling be eliminated?

The answer is no. Legal gambling will never compete effectively against illegal gambling for at least five reasons: illegal games have no minimum bet, the odds are better, credit is available, sporting contests and other popular events can be wagered, and winnings are not taxable. Legal gambling initiatives which have mushroomed in the 1990s are revenue-enhancing measures. Minimum bets, lower odds, no credit, and taxable winnings work against this goal. Professional sports strongly resist any attempt at legalized gambling, due to the fear of corruption of players. Gambling has taken place since the beginnings of recorded history, and while legal games may divert some money to the state that previously had gone to the bookie, the bookie is not about to be replaced.

Prostitution is legal in rural Nevada counties and appears to thrive there. Illegal prostitution exists in virtually every American city. It may be the second oldest vice. Why not legalize it, tax it, and raise revenue for the state? The reasons why such a proposal has never been taken seriously have remained unchanged for many years. First, the government does not want to be in the position of encouraging extramarital sex. How are they supposed to advertise legal prostitution? Second, legal prostitution activities can be seen as a government-sponsored attempt to enslave and objectify women (as men comprise the overwhelming majority of prostitute customers). Third, the fear of AIDS and other sexually transmitted diseases is a real concern, even given regular medical examinations of prostitutes.

Marijuana has been decriminalized in several states, and other states will likely follow suit, given the negligible impact in the states where implemented. Other drugs, such as heroin and cocaine, are unlikely to be decriminalized simply due to their addictive qualities. Similar to prostitution, the government does not want to be placed in the position of advocating something that is considered harmful or immoral. Now that gambling has come to be considered "recreation," the morality issue has all but vanished from discussions of legal gambling. The same cannot be said of prostitution and drug use.

The arguments for decriminalization of consensual offenses between adults can be summarized in four major points.

1. Illegal gambling, narcotics, and prostitution create a "black market" to which those who desire these services must turn. This market becomes the breeding ground for organized criminal enterprises to provide these services in a systematic and profitable manner.

2. Police resources are diverted from predatory street crimes, when so many arrests each year are for victimless crimes which produce no complainants.

3. The lack of involuntary victims (unlike the case in violent or property crimes) provides an incentive for police corruption as they attempt to enforce an elusive moral standard for consenting adults.

4. A "counter-culture" is created, wherein a significant segment of the adult population, which desires to engage in gambling, narcotics use, or prostitution is labelled "criminal." Support for law, police, and government is eroded when the behavior of a large portion of the society is considered "deviant" or criminal.

On the other side, decriminalization of consensual offenses can be considered harmful to the community.[55] Summarized into four propositions, the arguments against decriminalization include:

1. Order in the community is a more important concern than are possible problems faced in enforcing laws against the vices.

2. The fear of crime in a community results in large part from street encounters with addicts, drunks, gamblers, and prostitutes. This lack of order in the streets, even though non-serious in the individual case, coalesces to create community disorder and fear.

3. Police are expected to maintain order in the community. A large part of their job is not necessarily crime control but, rather, the enforcement of a certain standard of acceptable public behavior. This "order-maintenance" role of the police officer is as important (and is related to) his or her role in apprehending serious criminals.

4. Street crimes will flourish in areas where disorderly behavior goes unchecked. Street addicts, drunks, prostitutes, and gamblers, who are left unchallenged by the police, will eventually cause the neighborhood to deteriorate, as the community at large feels unsafe and more stable elements move elsewhere.

These two perspectives on decriminalization, pro and con, have existed for many years, and public opinion changes slowly. Gambling and marijuana are two "vices" about which public opinion has changed dramatically in the last two decades. Whether or not opinion continues to shift regarding other drugs and prostitution remains to be seen.

The Problem of Increasing Violence

Regardless of the debate over the impact of the organized crime prosecutions of the last decade or so, one outcome is certain: violence. First there was the killing of Gambino boss Paul Castellano, ordered by John Gotti.[56] Then, Bobby Boriello, John Gotti's driver was shot and killed while Gotti was in jail awaiting trial.[57] Several killings took place within the Colombo crime group in a struggle for power and loyalty to imprisoned boss Carmine Persico.[58] Another struggle for power resulted in a violent death in the Lucchese group.[59] The same occurred in the Philadelphia Cosa Nostra group.[60] Similar violence occurs within Chinese gangs,[61] a Harlem drug gang,[62] and Vietnamese street gangs.[63] This is only a sampling of the organized crime-related violence that has occurred since the mob trials began in the mid-1980s.

There is no doubt that many "turf," market, and gang leadership wars are being fought, but what will be the outcome? Why is so much violence tolerated by the public?

The answers to these questions are not straightforward. The outcome of the violence has already been seen in the emergence of nontraditional organized crime groups in many American cities (as shown in Chapter 7). There may also be a war for "non-leadership" of some of these crime groups. A significant error made by John Gotti is the same one made by Al Capone more than one-half century ago. He enjoyed publicity. A primary reason why Al Capone was made "public enemy number one" was his high profile and the manner in which he taunted law enforcement. In a similar way, John Gotti's high profile made him a sought after prosecution target. It should be remembered that Gotti's predecessor, Paul Castellano, kept a very low profile and ran his crime group for a long time. Gotti and Capone, on the other hand, had very short tenures as organized crime leaders. They simply attracted too much attention to themselves.

AP/WIDE WORLD PHOTOS

John Gotti, reputed mob leader of New York's Gambino crime family. Gotti has been implicated in widespread criminal activity, including gambling, loansharking, racketeering, hijacking, conspiracy, assault, and murder.

This is why it is unlikely that the level of violence within organized crime groups will diminish significantly in the future. Organized crime groups are run largely by uneducated, eogcentric people. Sometimes people are assaulted or killed just to "prove" that one should be feared. These feelings of superiority and hyper-masculinity are outgrown by most boys in their teenage years. In the case of organized crime, it is likely that the unenlightened leadership of organized crime groups, with few exceptions, ultimately leads to their prosecution or undoing within their own criminal group. This is not a new phenomenon. A study of organized crime in the Netherlands during the seventeenth and eighteenth centuries had a similar conclusion: "The most striking characteristic of the chronology of Dutch rural organized crime is its lack of unity."[64]

Despite the demise of many leaders of organized crime groups in recent years, the group persist, not because of a well-ordered structure in the organization, but because the criminal opportunities are multitudinous. If all it takes to obtain money is a bad reputation and occasional threats and violence, it's surprising there are not more people doing it. The reason why this level of violence and intimidation is tolerated by the public is a more serious question, and is the subject of the next section.

Citizen Intolerance

In Ebitsuka, Japan, citizens erected a small building across from a known Yakuza headquarters, and videotaped everyone who frequented it. The citizens sent 1,500 postcards to, and filed a lawsuit against, Tetysuya Aono, a Yakuza Leader. Yakuza members founght back violently, but the town's police force of eight officers was supplemented by 300 from surrounding coumunities, and extensive publicity ensued. Ultimately, half the Yakuza group were arrested, and Aono settled the lawsuit out of court, agreeing to abandon the building.[65] Why have actions like this not occurred in the United States? Is it fear, cynicism, collusion?

Many people care little about what goes on in organized crime "as long as they kill each other." It is true that most criminal groups do victimize their own members and neighborhoods, but occasionally this violence spills over into the community at large. The reckless "drive-by shootings" of drug gangs in recent years is the best example of this, and it is probably the one occurrence that helped mobilize public intolerance for drug trafficking more than anything else.

How is it possible to mobilize public opinion more effectively against organized crime, when many Americans are willing to buy "hot" property, gamble illegally, or engage in other illegal vices? Citizens commissions is one avenue discussed in Chapter 8. They provide a forum for public education and objective investigation of organized crime, although the demise of the Pennsyvlania Crime Commission in 1994, when it criticized the state attorney general, is not a hopeful sign of political will to support public opinion. Another method is the special grand jury provisions of the Organized Crime Control Act (see Chapter 9). It will be recalled that under this law, special grand juries are to be called *at least* every 18 months in large federal judicial districts. In addition, they have the authority to issue *public reports* on organized crime and corruption in their area. Since this law was passed in 1970, however, this provision has rarely been invoked. A significant way to educate the public and to mobilize public opinion in a community has been ignored. It is easy to forget that the effort against organized crime is made only in part by the prosecution of criminals. Without vocal public support, it's a lonely, and often futile, task.

> It is the dream of the visionary that some day an aroused public opinion will eliminate organized crime. The vision is Utopian. Organized crime will never be eliminated but it may be minimized and controlled whenever public sentiment is sufficiently aroused and stays aroused and wisely directed. To be directed properly there must be fact-finding and research. This is something the average citizen declines to support because it is neither spectacular or interesting. Merely stirring public opinion to white heat because of some existing abuse or disorder is not sufficient. To be successful there must be devised a comprehensive plan which will provide the public with information concerning the efficiency and integrity of its law enforcing agencies in connection with the activities of criminals.[66]

This was a statement by the director of the Chicago Crime Commission in 1932. It still holds true today. Greater attention to fact-finding in a way that actively involves the citizens of the community is a way to develop strong public support for organized crime control initiatives.

The Ethics of Organized Crime

Ethics and morality lie at the root of all discussions of crime and justice, although they are rarely mentioned explicitly. As Chapter 3 indicated, crime is a moral failure in decision-making. It is not the likelihood or apprehension and punishment that keeps you and I from breaking the law. If they were the only important factors, we would all be criminals, given the low odds of apprehension for most crimes. As a result, it is not apprehension fears or punishment that will ultimately curtail organized crime.

Too often, organized crime groups merely play on our weaknesses. Our weaknesses for gambling, drugs, prostitution, or our failure to stand up to extortion threats. Imagine a society where *everyone* refused to be victimized by drug traffickers or extortion threats. To whom would the organized crime groups turn? Our failure to stand up and be heard as a collective community is a victory for organized crime interests. As long as the public is divided, fearful, cynical, or unethical, there is no reason to expect organized crime to diminish. In one of the Gotti trials, for example, a juror was charged with *soliciting* a bribe from Gotti's friends to help bring an acquittal![67] The FBI arrested federal and state employees, mostly from Motor Vehicles Departments, for *selling* fraudulent driver's licenses, social security cards, "green" cards, and passports.[68] Such crimes, that also involve an abuse of one's citizenship, are at least as shocking as many of the activities of organized crime groups.

Ethics are developed from an early age. It is hoped that ethics will become part of the educational process, so that the accumulation of facts ceases to be equated with knowing what to do with them. Learning to live within the law because law violation fails to bring you *pleasure* is the essence of ethical behavior. Apprehension and punishment are important social reinforcements to your morality. But the law provides the *minimum* acceptable behavior required, not the optimum level. In a drug raid in New York, some residents, who were not targets of the raid, threw automatic weapons out the windows, when the police pulled up.[69] A better quality of life will be achieved when fewer people are living so close to the line that separates the good from the bad.

Summary

This chapter has presented 10 challenges for the future of organized crime; five challenges for the criminal justice system, and five challenges for long-term prevention, are addressed. There have been great strides made in recent years in the effort to control organized crime. Better coordination of multi-national efforts and in the conduct of law enforcement will be needed in the future. In addition, continued use of more imaginative sentencing options beyond fines, probation, and prison will be needed.

The infiltration of legitimate business by organized crime can be better anticipated with a combination of local business analyses and criminological prediction tools. The vices, violence, and citizen tolerance for organized crime activity are entrenched problems, but specific ideas for changes have been proposed, including a closer examination of the ethics behind organized crime and how these self-interested crime figures too often resemble a sizable segment of the general public.

References to Chapter 12

1   San Vincent Meddis, "'Legendary' FBI Director Sets up Shop in Moscow," *USA Today*, (July 5, 1994), p. 5.

2   Marlies Simons, "New European Police to Fight Regional Crime," *The New York Times*, (February 17, 1994).

3   "U.N. Guidelines on Organized Crime," *CJ International*, v. 8 (January-February, 1992), p. 3.

4   Mary McIntosh, *The Organisation of Crime* (London: Macmillan, 1975), p. 29.

5   Sherry Green, *Preventing Illegal Diversion of Chemicals: A Model Statute* (Washington, DC: National Institute of Justice, 1993), p. 1; James R. Sevick, *Precursor and Essential Chemicals in Illicit Drug Production: Approaches to Enforcement* (Washington, DC: National Institute of Justice, 1993).

6   Ibid., pp. 3-5.

7   U.S. Comptroller General, *Illicit Narcotics: Recent Efforts to Control Chemical Diversion and Money Laundering* (Washington, DC: U.S. General Accounting Office, 1993).

8   U.S. Comptroller General, *Drug Control: Interdiction Efforts in Central America Have Had Little Impact on the Flow of Drugs* (Washington, DC: U.S. General Accounting Office, 1994); U.S. Comptroller General, *Drug Control: Heavy Investment in Military Surveillance Not Paying Off* (Washington, DC: U.S. Genral Accounting Office, 1993).

9   Alien Smuggling is the Dangerous New China Trade, " *Organized Crime Digest*, v. 14 (June 9, 1993), p. 10.

10 Ibid; U.S. Comptroller General, *Immigration Enforcement: Problems in Controlling the Flow of Illegal Aliens* (Washington, DC: U.S. General Accounting Office, 1993).

11 "Colombia Offers Carrot to Cartel," *The New York Times*, (November 3, 1993), p. 9.

12 Jeff Builta, "Current Middle East Narcotics Activity," *Criminal Organizations*, v. 9 (Summer, 1994), pp. 7-8.

13 Betty B. Bosarge, "International Organized Crime Poses New Threat to U.S. That Can't Be Met by Law Enforcement Alone," *Organized Crime Digest*, v. 14 (August 25, 1993), p. 1.

14 Harvey Lipman, "State Contracts Linked to Mob," *The Buffalo News*, (November 11, 1993), p. 17.

15 Jose de Cordoba, "Washington, Irked by Colombian Official, Ends Evidence Sharing on Drug Cartels," *Wall Street Journal*, (March 8, 1994), p. 10.

[16] "Italy Passes Broad Anti-Mafia Package," *The Buffalo News*, (September 1, 1992), p. 3.

[17] Robert J. Kelly, "Cooperation Between Italian And American Law Enforcement Agencies: The Fight Against Organized Crime," *Italian Journal*, (1990), pp. 16-22.

[18] Sam Vincent Meddis, "Cocaine Bust Links Mafia, Cali Cartel," *USA Today*, (September 29, 1992), p. 1.

[19] Charles Abbott, "Two Year Probe Links Mafia, Colombian Drug Cartel," *The Buffalo News*, (December 20, 1994), p. 1.

[20] "Record Drug Seizure," *USA Today*, (February 22, 1989), p. 3.

[21] Richard N. Holden, "Police and the Profit-Motive: A New Look at Asset Forfeiture," *ACJS Today*, v. 12 (September-October, 1993), p. 1.

[22] "Police Wiretaps," *USA Today*, (October 23, 1991), p.3; David Wells, "Wiretap Case has Cincinnati Buzzing," *USA Today*, (February 14, 1989), p. 1; Gregory Katz, "Police Bugs Could Taps City for Millions," *USA Today*, (April 29, 1983), p. 3.

[23] "Judge Sentenced," *USA Today*, (November 2, 1990), p. 3.

[24] Selwyn Raab, "Jury Indictes a Detective in Gotti Leaks," *The New York Times*, (December 12, 1991), p. B1.

[25] Clifford J. Levy, "Drive on Mob Sabotaged in New Jersey," *The New York Times*, (August 12, 1994), p. 8.

[26] Selwyn Raab, "Inspectors are Accused of Extortion," *The New York Times*, (October 14, 1993), p. B1.

[27] See Nicholas Pileggi, *Wiseguy* (New York: Simon And Schuster, 1986).

[28] Bruce Frankel, "Checkout Time for NYC Drug Dealers, *USA Today*, (June 10, 1994), p. 2.

[29] "Property Seized," *USA Today*, (October 7, 1992), p. 3.

[30] "Little Tolerance," *USA Today*, (October 12, 1989), p. 3.

[31] Junda Woo and Wade Lambert, "Lawbreaker Outsmarts Electronic Anklet," *Wall Street Journal*, (April 9, 1992), p. B10.

[32] Dan Herbeck and Michael Beebe, "Local 210 Told to Purge Mob Ties," *The Buffalo News*, (February 16, 1995), p. 1.

[33] U.S. Comptroller General, *Labor Law: Criminal Investigations of Mr. Jackie Presser and Other Teamsters Officials* (Washington, DC: U.S. General Accounting Office, 1986).

[34] "NYC Mayor Finally Decides to Go After Smelly 'Action' at Fulton Fish Market," *Organized Crime Digest*, v. 13 (May 13, 1992), p. 1.

[35] Selwyn Raab, "Fish Market's Problems Revert to New York City," *The New York Times*, (March 27, 1994), p. 1.

[36] Selwyn Raab, "Judge Bars 10 from Plumbers Union Activity," *The New York Times*, (October 27, 1993), p. B4.

[37] Edward J. De Franco, *Anatomy of a Scam: A Case Study of a Planned Bankruptcy by Organized Crime* (Washington, DC: U.S. Government Printing Office, 1973).

38 For interesting summaries of the Pizza Connection case, see Ralph Blumenthal, *Last Days of the Sicilians: The FBI Assault on the Pizza Connection* (New York: Times Books, 1988); Shana Alexander, *The Pizza Connection: Lawyers, Money, Drugs, Mafia* (New York: Weidenfeld and Nicolson, 1988); Donald Baer and Brian Duffy, "Inside America's Biggest Drug Bust," *U.S. News and World Report*, 104 (April 11, 1988), pp. 18-29.

39 New York State Organized Crime Task Force, *Corruption and Racketeering in the New York City Construction Industry* (New York: New York University Press, 1990).

40 Ibid., p. 84.

41 Ibid.

42 Ibid., pp. 84-5.

43 Ibid., p. 85.

44 Ibid., p. 57-8.

45 Ibid.

46 Peter Reuter, Jonathan Rubinstein, and Simon Wynn, *Racketeering in Legitimate Industries: Two Case Studies* (Washington, DC: National Institute of Justice, 1983), p. 10-12.

47 Ibid., p. 13.

48 Ibid.

49 Jay Albanese, "Where Organized and White Collar Crime Meet: Predicting the Infiltration of Legitimate Business," in J. Albanese, ed. *Contemporary Issues in Organized Crime* (Monsey, NY: Willow Tree Press, 1995), pp. 35-60.

50 Ibid.

51 see, for example, President's Commission on Organized Crime, *The Impact: Organized Crime Today* (Washington, DC: U.S. Government Printing Office, 1987).

52 Peter B. Bloch and James Bell, *Managing Investigations: The Rochester System* (Washington, DC: The Police Foundation, 1976).

53 David Greenberg, *Felony Investigation Decision Model: An Analysis of Investigative Elements of Information* (Menlo Park, CA: Stanford Research Institute, 1975).

54 Henry Barrett Chamberlin, "Some Observations Concerning Organized Crime," *Journal of Criminal Law and Criminology*, vol. 22, no. 5 (January, 1932), p. 654.

55 James Q. Wilson, *Thinking About Crime* Revised edition (New York: Basic Books, 1983).

56 Arnold H. Lubasch, "Shot by Shot, An Ex-Aide to Gotti Describes the Killing of Castellano," *The New York Times*, (March 4, 1992), p. 1.

57 "Gotti Driver Killed," *USA Today*, (April 15, 1991), p. 3.

58 George James, "Man Tied to Crime Family is Shot to death in Queens," *The New York Times*, (October 22, 1993), p. B6.

59 Selwyn Raab, "Ex-Unionist Shot to Death in 'Mob Hit'," *The New York Times*, (May 18, 1990), p. B1.

60 Michael deCourcy Hinds, "FBI Arrests Reputed Leader of Philadelphia Mob and 20 Others," *The New York Times*, (March 18, 1994), p. 16.

[61]   "Prosecutors Say El Rukn Leadership is Smashed," *Organized Crime Digest*, (June 10, 1992), p. 9.

[62]   Richard Perez-Pena, "The Killings of Witnesses Cause Alarm," *The New York Times*, (November 22, 1993), p. B1.

[63]   "Vietnamese Street Gangs Make Mark Nationwide," *Organized Crime Digest*, v. 13 (December 23, 1992), p. 1.

[64]   Florike Egmond, *Underworlds: Organized Crime in the Netherlands, 1650-1800* (Cambridge, MA: Polity Press, 1993), p. 179.

[65]   Howard G. Chua-Eoan, "Thugs Beware: Citizens Rout the Yakuza," *The*, (March 14, 1988), p. 42.

[66]   Henry Barrett Chamberlin, "Some Observations Concerning Organized Crime," *Journal of Criminal and Criminology* vol. 22, no. 5 (January, 1932), p. 670.

[67]   "Gotti Juror Charged with Soliciting Bribe," *USA Today*, (February 25, 1992), p. 3.

[68]   "37 Arested in the Selling of Documents," *The New York Times*, (November 4, 1993), p. B15.

[69]   "Record Drug Seizure," *USA Today*, (February 22, 1989), p. 3.

Index